DATE DUE

NOV 0 4 1997	JUL 2 4 2001	
OCT 2 1 REC'D		
JUN 0 9 1998	JUL 0 9 2001	
JUN 2 2 REC'D	AUG 0 3 2001	
JUL 2 9 1998	AUG 1 8 2001	
AUG 2 4 REC'D		
OCT 2 1 1998		
OCT 19 '98		
JUL 1 5 1999		
JUN 2 5 1999		
JUN 0 8 2000		
JUL 1 8 2000		
DEC 1 6 2000		
DEC 1 4 2000		
MAR 1 4 2001		
APR 1 8 2001		
GAYLORD		PRINTED IN U.S.A

DEC 1 4

Inside

the

Mouse

POST-

CONTEMPORARY

INTERVENTIONS

Series Editors:

Stanley Fish

and

Fredric Jameson

Inside
the
Mouse

work and play
at disney
world

• • •

The Project on
Disney

DUKE UNIVERSITY PRESS

Durham and London 1995

CONTENTS

. . .

acknowl-
edgments

. . .

Inside the Mouse is the exclusive product of the Project on Disney and has no connection with or support from Walt Disney World or the Walt Disney Company. The members of the Project on Disney are Karen Klugman, Jane Kuenz, Shelton Waldrep, and Susan Willis.

We would like to thank all the people whose direct and indirect help made this book possible: earlier writers on Walt Disney World, Disneyland, and the Walt Disney Company whose work guided and inspired our own; employees of and visitors to Walt Disney World in Orlando, Florida, who took the time to discuss their experiences with us; and our families and friends who provided lodging, child care, tour guides, and other amenities while we wiled away our days in Disney World.

All photographs are by Karen Klugman.

Inside

the

Mouse

THE
problem
with
pleasure
. . .

"**W**hy are you so critical? Wasn't anything fun?" This was how one listener greeted our panel on Disney World. We, the coauthors of this book, were in New Orleans at a post–Mardi Gras American Studies conference. Together, we had assembled what Karen Klugman refers to as an "alternative ride" through Disney and we wanted to test our ideas on an audience as a way of gauging our book's reception. Many in the audience seemed to agree with our critical observations. Some academics said Disney just didn't appeal to them and they had no intention of ever visiting the park. One man said he was bored during his entire Disney stay; another said his trip was pleasant, but "everything was so contrived." Consensus was broken by one obviously upset woman who resented everything we had to say. Her question—put in a rather hostile manner—has preoccupied me* ever since. As a group, we have offered a number of panels at scholarly conferences and it seems there has always been someone in the audience who has raised the question of pleasure— either pointedly as did our inquisitor in New Orleans, or with consternation—as if the questioner felt she might have been duped into some sort of false enjoyment. During all our trial runs, I don't think any of us adequately answered this question. In canvassing adults as to why they go to Disney World, I tend to get positive, but uninteresting assessments: "It's fun," "It's safe," "It's easy," "It's clean." I suspect these responses betray

*Susan Willis

a comfortable acceptance of Disney ideologies, which in turn reside in the pleasure of *not* having to confront the flip sides of Disney's patriotism, hygiene, and gender codes. To get a better handle on what's enjoyable about Disney World, I polled my children who, like most kids, know exactly what they like about the park and responded emphatically: "The rides," "Staying in a motel," "The characters," "No school."

The problem of whether or not Disney World is pleasurable begs the question of the larger cultural context. My own meditations on whether there is any pleasure in mass culture predate the Disney Project. They began one afternoon on a street corner in Claremont, California. I was jogging, but had gotten stuck at a four-way signal light where one traffic-clogged boulevard intersected with another. To my left was a grove of stunted, water-starved lemon trees soon to be bulldozed for yet another development, to my right was a strip mall, and in front of me loomed condo-city. I peered into the cars, saw drivers drumming their fingernails on the steering wheels, punching the radio scan button, fluffing their hair, or just sitting like zombies, and I asked out loud (although no one could hear) "What are you all doing here—where's the pleasure?" Surely it's not reducible to Southern California's commodity glut: the private health spas, the hair and nail salons, the frozen yogurt and doughnuts.

The problem of pleasure comes up and is dealt with throughout our book. It haunts Shelton Waldrep's concern with storytelling; it teasingly emerges from Karen Klugman's photos; it shapes Jane Kuenz's stories of people who use the park alternatively; and it hangs suspended in my accounts of peoples' vacations. My aim here is to interrogate pleasure more directly. As always I approach culture as a consumer, so my inquiry is guided by the perspective of a visitor to the park. Taking my cue from John Kasson's book on Coney Island, I'm most interested in the sorts of pleasure that users/consumers make. In *Amusing the Millions*, Kasson argues that the rides at Coney Island enabled visitors to subvert the structures and mechanisms of early twentieth century industry.[1] Technology could be experienced as fun. Moreover, visitors to Coney Island could reap the pleasures of challenging social hierarchies. As Kasson puts it, this was the only place in the city where Anglo shop girls could rub shoulders and more with Italian immigrants. On both counts, Disney World is the antithesis of Coney Island. Its relatively homogenous population makes both risk and risqué social encounters unlikely. The fact that Disney World deploys some of the same technologies that facilitated the Gulf War is nowhere imprinted in the amusements as were the wheels, gears, and conveyors of industry rendered visible at Coney Island. Hence the subversive pleasure of bending arms into ploughshares, turning militarized technologies into fun, is not available at Disney World. The specifics of Kasson's observations can't be translated into Disney World; however, the notion of consumer participation in the production of pleasure is inseparable from amusement and can be the basis for deciphering what's affirming—possibly utopian—about a trip to Disney World.

"This ain't Disney World." This is how our cab driver introduced us to New Orleans at Mardi Gras. We had arrived a few days before our conference in order to take in the sights before getting down to business. Truer words were never spoken. The reek of urine nearly knocked me off my feet. And I had yet to discover the brisk trade in tits for beer and beads. My teenage daughter, who has no qualms about marching through a moshing pit, was so taken aback that she and her girlfriend spent most of Mardi Gras in the hotel bathroom dying their hair various shades of punk. My daughter's reaction enabled me to see how thoroughly our culture condemns carnival: the bawdy and rude revel of the appetites and its consequent waste and dissipation. In my experience the only thing that comes close to Mardi Gras is the North Carolina State Fair (and I suspect other state fairs do as well), although sexuality is less a feature than the carnival delights of greasy fried foods. Otherwise, ours is a proscribed and prescribed society that monitors consumption: no salt, no fat, no cholesterol, no calories, no sugar; and heaven forbid drugs, alcohol, and cigarettes. Fiber is clearly all that's left. No wonder many of my neighbors in the South flaunt their cholesterol and tobacco intake in the face of what they perceive as bourgeois or yuppie ideas about health and taste. Being in "bad taste" can be, as Pierre Bourdieu points out, an act of resistance.[2] Bourdieu based this conclusion on his observations of the French working class and peasantry. I don't know if cassoulet represents the same level of defiance as fried pork rind, but I would argue that southern obesity (both black and white) can be partly attributed to the oppressive victimization of a society that makes junk food fun, sexy, and plentiful and partly to the individual's active resistance to a perceived bourgeois norm. What's clear in our culture is that the fast food industry intercedes where more carnivalesque indulgences might be invented, and makes available to the lower and underclass a ready supply of foods for defiance.

Over the years, Disney World has cleaned up its food act. During my first research trip some four years ago, I remember overdosing on french fries. Now many healthy choices, such as yogurt and fresh fruit, are available at restaurants singled out by a tiny apple in the guide brochure. While french fries may be scarce, references to the sexual dimensions of carnival are nonexistent at Disney. There are certainly no devils with hugely packed crotches, like the ones Derek Walcott recalls from the carnivals of his West Indian childhood. In the "Overture" to his play *Dream on Monkey Mountain,* Walcott describes being kept on a balcony above the tumultuous crowd by his middle-class parents who didn't want their child mixing with the bawdy street elements.[3] In New Orleans I saw many middle-class families with children along the parade routes, some up in trees for a better view or a better chance for some beads, others in chairs mounted atop makeshift ladders. I wondered if children from New Orleans pester their parents for trips to Disney World or if any of the folks who drove great distances to get to Mardi Gras would also drive great distances to get to Disney World. Clearly, the drunkenly reeling and lewdly gesturing crowd in the French Quarter was as antithetical to the folks at Disney World as aliens to Earthlings. The bastion of family values long before the Bush campaign made much of the slogan, Disney World is systematically elaborated to eliminate carnival. To be sure there are parades—probably a dozen a day—each one a highly orchestrated spectacle played to an audience that docilely accepts crowd control. "No climbing in trees." "Cross the street only where indicated." "People in front must be seated." It goes without saying that no one is expected to get swept up with the marchers as kids might have done in some bygone era of small town circus parades. Disney World may well represent the culmination of the centuries' long campaign of suppression waged against carnival, which aimed first to marginalize it and later to exterminate it or render it harmlessly touristic. Peter Stallybrass and Allon White date the suppression of carnival with the nineteenth-century rise of the bourgeois class.[4]

It is in this context that I find the Disney characters remarkable. In the midst of Disney's rational and controlled environment, the characters are patently grotesque. Mickey and his crew may not have packed crotches, but they certainly have big heads. Something more is going on here than the propensity for the infantile that Stephen Jay Gould remarked in his account of Mickey's backward development from the skinny ratlike adult figure of the thirties to his present balloonlike baby face.[5] Many parents with young children have told me that they feel they have to put off their first trip to Disney World until they think their kids can handle the big heads. I'm sure I'm not the only visitor to Disney World who has seen young children running away from the characters, tearful and screaming. Other children stand in awe, unwilling to approach even for the sake of the photo that Dad or Mom is urging or for the possibility of an autographed trophy. Then, too, there are children so taken by the characters that they mob them, fling themselves smack into Donald's tummy and topple him over, duck feet and all.

Youngsters aren't the only ones who recognize the power of the grotesque. My fifteen-year-old daughter, who otherwise impresses me with her cultural judgment, is not at all embarrassed to admit that what she most likes about Disney World are the characters: "And there should be more of them. I didn't see nearly enough the last time I was there." I always take my informants' testimony seriously, but until I read Stallybrass and White I didn't understand the attraction of the grotesque. Besides charting the historical suppression of carnival, Stallybrass and White read Freud's account of his hysterical patients and develop the thesis that during the course of suppressing the carnivalesque, the bourgeois subject fell victim to the reemergence of carnival in the ritualized symptoms of the hysteric. As they put it,

> The demonization and the exclusion of the carnivalesque has to be related to the victorious emergence of specifically bourgeois practices and languages which reinflected and incorporated this material [as] negative. In one way or another Freud's patients can be seen as enacting desperate ritual fragments salvaged from a festive tradition, the self-exclusion from which had been one of the identifying features of their social class. The language of bourgeois neurosis both disavows and appropriates the domain of calendrical festive practices.[6]

Disney World, the quintessential enactment of the hysterical bourgeois subject, programatically prescribes prudery as a disavowal of anything having to do with carnival, all the while appropriating its excluded "other" in the grotesquery of a carnivalesque Mickey. I assume that where repression is the most enforced, the eruption of carnival must solicit the greatest fascination. Recently I've been curious about the way children, roughly six to ten years old, painstakingly teach themselves to belch on demand. It's a great trick for the school cafeteria and even more audacious when employed in the classroom. It may be that children, whose socialization means learning to control the body in repressive ways, are more attuned than adults to eruptions of carnival, and can thus better spot it when it happens (even when it wears a big head).

Stallybrass and White also give a clue for interpreting the significance of Orlando when they mention that the seaside was suited to the development of the carnivalesque because it "combined the . . . medicinal virtues of the spa resorts with tourism and the fairground."[7] Like its precursor, Anaheim, Orlando is not a seaside town; but more so than its sister park, Disney World capitalizes on the aura of a resort environment. Where Disneyland is girdled with tacky motels and fast food restaurants, Disney World, as Shelton Waldrep points out, has successfully separated itself from Orlando—and its feeder interstate—and has developed an internal network of "resort" hotels, each themed to represent the sorts of places most promoted by the tourist industry: generally southern and particularly Caribbean. There are no Nordic resorts nor any accommodations that would remind the visitor of winter. Moreover, the landscape is set to bloom year round, a strategy not wasted on me. There's nothing like seeing bougainvillea and hibiscus in December.

The importance of sunshine should not be overlooked in determining the sources of Disney pleasure. As Carey McWilliams observed in describing the economic development of Los Angeles, sunshine facilitates certain types of economies, which in turn give a region a particular spatial organization.[8] In Los Angeles, it's the infrastructure of sprawl occasioned by the largely outdoor origins of both the aircraft and movie industries. Orlando, the amusement capital of the world, inherits this tradition. Regions defined by open-air industries also give rise to an ambience of openness, whether or not it has any grounds in political reality. What's most peculiar about both Southern California and North Central Florida is the populist conservatism that predominates and seems at odds with the utopian fantasies attached to both places. Bill Pomerance, who organized the cartoonists who struck Disney, put it in a nutshell when he commented to me, "Well, you know what they used to say about L.A.: 'Everything blooms in the sun.'" He was referring to the curious array of political and social tendencies that have found fertile ground in L.A., but his remark captures the utopian connotations associated with a land where the sun holds sway and seasonal variation is minimal.

Disney World, where "the fun always shines," makes an advertising campaign out of a real utopian longing. But, in doing so, it doesn't cancel the longing. Drawn by the promise of a sun-filled vacation, great numbers of visitors to the park yearn to experience the sort of plenitude that the sun represents. Many Marxist critics have argued for the existence of repressed utopian content in the objects of mass culture.[9] What's compelling about mass culture is its figuration (oftentimes unconsciously apprehended by the audience) of capitalism's antithesis: that is, a society governed by reciprocity and structured on communal relationships. The utopian fantasy that haunts both sunshine states is as fundamentally social as it is meteorological. Indeed it connects with the primal world of the carnival calendar and gives expression to the renewal of hope and energy that the return of the sun meant to agrarian economies. Disney World will surely never mount a springtime fertility rite, but its attraction taps a deep-seeded, perhaps unconscious, longing for the possibility of renewal that an older world celebrated with carnival. Of course, the power of carnival derives from the yin and yang fluctuation between a time of fasting and a time of indulgence, winter and spring. The horrifying threat of perpetual carnival is something only Disney's workers experience. Luckily, the time constraints of the visitor's vacation enable him or her a more manageable dose of plenitude. Safe within the bounds of a five-day vacation, many children are tempted to imagine how they might prolong their Disney experience. I've talked with a number who know exactly where to hide so as to stay in the park after closing. This fantasy has a number of liberating and subversive meanings sewn into it, not the least of which is the desire to stretch time, to live in Never-Never Land.

My son's ambitions are more modest. When I asked him what he likes about Disney World, he responded: "Staying in a motel." And then, more emphatically: "No school." Simple pleasures whose utopian content also resides in the social. Cade may not be aware of Disney's regard for decorative detail in the creation of the themed resorts, but he certainly appreciates the resort environment and the use of the motel room. Children like motels because they're not home. If anything, the motel signifies a restructuring of the relationships that define the child's life at home. All the family's repressed libidinal concerns that need never be confronted in homes where family members sleep in separate bedrooms come tantalizingly (or disturbingly) to the surface as Mom, Dad, and the kids discuss who's sleeping with whom in the motel's two double beds. Some families resort to a democratic rotation system that has family members changing their sleeping assignments every night of their vacation so that none of the overdetermined sexual arrangements between siblings or parents and children ever takes precedence.

Staying in a motel often means that some of the restrictions placed on children in their homes will be lifted. Jumping on the bed, staying up late, exploring the lobby, weight room, or pool—these may be trivial pursuits but they connote independence. Disney resorts are more than motels; they are huge complexes and plentifully equipped. There are arcades, shops, restaurants, beaches, and paddleboats. If home is a place that requires certain labors for its upkeep—where kids might be threatened with a "grounding" unless they clean their rooms, the motel/resort gives the impression of unlimited, self-replenishing use. Because young children don't fully grasp the realities of money and credit cards (particularly middle-class kids whose parents, even while grumbling about costs, tend to satisfy most of their children's desires), the motel/resort seems to offer itself as freely provided as the "free" soap and shampoo in the bath. The single-family dwelling that many Disney families lock up and leave behind when they take their vacations is a form of private property that can be apprehended as such. It burdens people with its upkeep and mortgage. By comparison, the motel as corporate property presents itself for public use. In a capitalist society where housing is controlled by market forces, the motel is the answer to utopian socialism's call for free universal housing. The resort with its food court, laundry, and leisure facilities offers a consumerist version of a society that provides for its people. By reason of their status as economically dependent, children are in a position to better appreciate the benefits of unrestricted housing in a pleasurable and caring environment. "Staying in a motel" may be fun, but the source of its pleasure resides in an unconscious social yearning for security and community.

"No school," the other half of Cade's reason for liking Disney World, expresses more obvious utopian dimensions. The regime of school, even more than the curriculum, is an enforced indoctrination into the rigors of the work week. Now that fewer and fewer children are needed to meet the seasonal demands of agrarian production, the long summer "vacation" has become obsolete and many school districts are instituting year-round schools whose temporal structure better meshes with the employee's year-round calender. Getting up early, rushing through breakfast and into clothes, "don't miss the bus": the morning routine is a lesson in the individual's lack of control over the most basic features of his or her life. It's a dehumanizing ritual that middle-class families accept for the sake of their children's future. Besides, it's a burden that's democratically shared by two-income parents who enforce their own routine with alarm clocks and coffee. Once at school there's the pressure to conform to a host of institutional regulations—rules for how to walk and when to pee. "No school" voices the desire to have the day on one's own terms.

All vacations capture the liberating energy inherent in a day off from school or work. It's a pleasure I know I'll never have. This was my other insight that day on the street corner in Claremont. As someone who works on culture, I realized I could never be outside of work. Everything that other people do for leisure or to escape is what I do for work: observing, reflecting on my responses, always one step critically removed from the culture I'm participating in. I suspect the same holds true for the coauthors in general, and this may be why we've been accused of missing Disney's pleasures. Indeed, Karen Klugman commented that she can never naively participate in any social gathering or cultural event without perceiving it through her photographer's eye—selecting images, framing them, apprehending aesthetics and meanings. It would be wrong, however, to posit a simple polarization between the people we perceive as happy consumers of culture and ourselves as unhappy critics. In fact, all consumers are critical, especially children who have a high degree of cultural literacy. They debate the media with their friends; many have a good understanding of media technologies and their effects. If anything, I was more naive as a child than kids are today. I certainly didn't come into this world as a critic. Disney was very much a part of my childhood. I saw Disney cartoons at the drive-in theater, my brother and I tucked into the back seat and expected to fall asleep while my parents watched the feature. I grew up in Southern California, close enough to Disneyland to expect a trip there every couple of years. As Disney moved into television, I was there, a regular fan of the *Mickey Mouse Club* and the *Wonderful World of Disney*. My experience growing up with Disney is different from that of Shelton Waldrep, who missed the fifties and was instead shaped by the Disney culture of the seventies. Nevertheless, we both have Disney in our childhoods. Because Disney tends to redefine and remarket itself every five or ten years, we can all visit Disney World and discover some nostalgic connection to our childhoods. Disney World might be thought of as an immense nostalgia machine whose staging and specific attractions are generationally coded to strike a chord with the various age categories of its guests. My youngest daughter entered commercial culture during the reign of Ariel, Belle, and Jasmine; my eldest son became a consumer with Disney's version of Winnie-the-Pooh. I suspect I'm more fixated on Cinderella's Castle.

Besides the capacity for childhood nostalgia, visitors bring the desire for a good time. To a large extent, Disney World works because its visitors make it work. The park would be nothing without the color and energy of its guests. This is why their smiling faces are so much a part of the Disney publicity. A depopulated Disney World would be an empty stage set. This is how I imagine EuroDisney: an elaborate setting whose sparse crowds give it the appearance of a party that's been cancelled before all the guests could be notified. Many have commented that Disney World is spectacle on a grand scale. I think of the bemused crowds, each face sporting sunglasses, and I recollect the cover photo of Guy Debord's book: a 3-D movie audience, all wearing their paper spectacles.[10] But people milling about in the Disney spectacle aren't passive zombies like those in the 3-D movie audience. Most adults who say they like Disney World report the fun they have "people watching." This is probably the most important and yet most understudied phenomena of mass culture. People watching is an active means for coping with the boredom, fatigue, stress, and duress associated with mass culture. Besides, people watching has its rewards. You're bound to spot some family with kids more unruly than your own, or someone whose feet look like they hurt worse than yours, or someone whose waistline shows he really shouldn't be eating that ice cream. But people watching isn't only one-upmanship. Friends report the joys of discovering communality with others, seeing aspects of ourselves in another's body or family. Watching in public can also titillate sexuality. It can be flirtatious or give rise to romantic fantasy. Women are people watchers as are men. It's a form of looking that turns the tables on other definitions of looking where domination is at stake, such as the Sartrean "look," the "male gaze," and the Foucauldian "panopticon." When engaged in people watching, we become fascinated with another's clothes or body, speech or gestures. We catch ourselves trying to imagine the other person's life. People watching breaks down the anonymity of spectacle and exercises the wish fulfillment for community. We marvel at the others we watch and feel a sort of affinity with them even though the whole point of watching has to do with their being somehow different from us. People watching originates in a utopian impulse different from the subversive intent of the carnivalesque. Rather than taking apart the dominant order so as to give expression to suppressed pleasures, people watching creates a sense of community in the midst of mass society.

As coauthors, we have worked in the utopian spirit of collective enterprise for over three years. My own desire for collectivity is born of the peculiarities of my coming of age in the university of the seventies, a time when strikes and demonstrations gave rise to the collectivized practice of teach-ins. This is a history we don't all share. Indeed, I suspect that for Jane Kuenz and Shelton Waldrep this collective project has provided a means for surviving the fragmentation, anonymity, and isolation that currently prevails in the academy. Of course, the model for collective work in culture is the Centre for Contemporary Cultural Studies, whose heyday saw the publication of such works as *Women Take Issue* and *Resistance through Ritual*. Never widely circulated and long out of print, I recall these books as amazing documents of the tremendous effort required to achieve a unified and theoretically articulated position through which the collective spoke. While we never strove to emulate the Birmingham scholars, we recognized early on that a critical account of Disney World requires multiple engagement. Besides ourselves, there are all the people who vacation and work at Disney World, whose experiences are embedded in our reflections.

We visited Disney World both separately and together. We had formal working sessions and innumerable casual conversations. We learned how to read each other, how to let go of our ideas so that they might become the object of the group's concern, and how to give and take criticism. We brought four different sets of desires and perspectives into the project. Over the course of the research and writing, the trips to Disney and the discussions, we began to see that particular concerns—or particular Disney phenomena—were emerging as things we all wanted to address. These will crop up throughout the book, treated somewhat differently by each of us. Our aim was never to achieve a unified perspective, but to appreciate the value of our different talents and insights. Perhaps this book will serve as a model for people who wish to reactivate the spirit of collectivity while giving expression to diversity.

REALITY

REVISITED

· · ·

There's apparently no market for greeting cards from mothers who leave their families on major holidays, so I* settled for one with the words "To a Wonderful Mother" inscribed over a rose, crossed out the word "To" and replaced it with "From." I realized how sentimental I was feeling only when I nearly started to cry because I thought the Sachem Card and Party Shop had sold the last of its accordian stand-up turkeys. By then it was obvious to the sales clerk that I was a desperate case, so she searched the back room and found one left over from last year. At five o'clock the next morning, when I placed the surprise present and card on the dining room table, I felt that they perfectly expressed my mixed emotions about going to work without my family at a place where I would be surrounded by families at play.

On the plane, but still ambivalent about my mission, I chatted with my seatmates who, like just about everybody else on the plane, were flying to Orlando to spend Thanksgiving with relatives and planning to go to Disney World as a side trip. (And, as an aside, I'll just mention that I actually ran into them at the Disney-MGM Studios Theme Park and took a picture of them having lunch.) When I explained that I had just left three children and a husband at home in order to spend five days "working" in Disney World, they kept saying how much they admired me. And I kept thinking that at any moment the plane could crash and deprive my loved

*Karen Klugman

ones of me for the rest of their lives—all because of my wanting to do this Mickey Mouse job.

I have to admit that I *did* feel professional. After all, everybody else was on holiday and just goofing off, whereas I felt this obligation to make my family's sacrifices worthwhile. Thus I began photographing the moment I stepped off the plane. I was all eyes and was surprised to find that the world around me was already all ears, for Delta, the "official airline of Disney World," had passed out Mickey hats on the plane. In the airport lobby, a monolithic rectangle decorated with Delta logos and mouse ears, and topped with a model of Cinderella's Castle, cast its shadow across the floor. A crown of skylights in the ceiling added to the magical effect by creating spokes of sunlight around the base of the centerpiece. Here was serious architecture (by that I mean a structure that either supports my weight or is over my head) collaborating with what could be described as a gigantic trophy; it certainly wasn't necessary to read the inscription "Twenty Years" to infer a long-standing partnership between Disney and Delta.

At this time of year, the architectural wonder was adorned with a mixture of Christmas and Disney symbols so that, for a few moments, I confused these two institutions. Surrounded by wrapped presents and topped with the castle spire, the monument suggested a Christmas tree. But the larger-than-life tin soldier that flanked the left and a Frosty the Snowman on the right—were they members of Disney's gang? Images from the *Nutcracker Suite* and Little Golden Books flashed before my eyes, as I tried to untangle my character references, Mickey and Minnie stood before this backdrop in place of Santa, it seemed, to greet passengers and, of course, to pose for photographs.

Much as I had imagined how I might photograph people posing with the characters in the park, I was unprepared for this preview performance. I felt shy around them. Also, I was nervous, afraid that they would identify me as an intruder or a spy, doing something illegal by taking pictures of someone else's relatives. But let me tell you it is impossible to read anything other than goodwill into those happy faces. The characters *do* demonstrate body language, which I'll explain later. But it was absurd to imagine Mickey making an accusatory gesture wearing that constant grin. It's infectious, too. Annoyed at myself for lapsing into being a participant rather than an observer, I kept trying to keep my mouth from doing what it has instinctively done since I was about six weeks old— mimic that silly smile.

With amazing speed and efficiency, Mickey and Minnie processed the passersby. They would size up their subjects, quickly locate the recording device, and strike up a pose. Because I was quicker with a camera than most of the relatives, the characters would often direct the posing group to face me. I would take the picture and the poor relatives, still trying to focus, would lose out. Fortunately, Minnie and Mickey never seemed to mind posing again for the "other relatives." But they mistook me for the next-of-kin so many times that I assumed the characters were either operating on automatic or that, in those bulky costumes, they were essentially two blind mice.

Minnie, though, can certainly see at close range. As a person approaches her, she instantly selects the appropriate response from a set of choreographed moves and gestures, according to the person's age and gender. For the children, depending on how shy they are, she beckons to them, maybe dances a little, then stoops to hug them. Always with an intent to record a pleasant moment on film, she faces upstage to locate someone with a camera. The coy, flirtatious poses for the men provoke a slight embarrassment about having to react in front of the photographer-wife to a sexual provocation—even if it is coming from a mouse. Minnie tilts her head, covers her mouth with a big white-gloved hand as if to suppress a giggle, snuggles up to the photographic subject, and bends one leg for the camera. This gesture, which I learned from old movies and also from my parents' generation of engaged women who would kiss and bend a leg when they posed for pictures with their fiancé, always embarrasses me. What is the connection between the kiss and bent leg, anyhow? It seems to imply an uncontrollable reaction happening somewhere between the lips and foot. In this case of Minnie, however, it is doubly ridiculous because of the presentation of that oversized high heel. Nonetheless, the men leave with their chests expanded, obviously taking the advances as flattery, not as sexual harassment.

Mickey, on the other hand, could never get away with such obvious provocations. Not, at least, since the Clarence Thomas hearings. And besides, Mickey's lack of differential treatment of the sexes, his small stature, and his high-pitched voice have always called into question his underlying gender and sexual preference. And, although I didn't get to see any "decapitated" Mickeys on the Behind-the-Scenes tour, I wouldn't have been surprised to find that, inside, Mickey was really a girl.

During a quiet interlude in the passenger traffic, a shocking thing happened. A Delta pilot came by and, at first, Minnie flirted with him according to her older man routine, only without the intent of being photographed. Then she spoon-fed him from his dish of frozen yogurt. And he loved it. Obviously they had a familiar relationship—Minnie Mouse and the man who was possibly *my* pilot. There I was—a character witness, having two childhood myths challenged at once. Minnie was actually having another relationship, be it with a man or a mouse. And the pilot, one of the rare examples of an authority figure in whom I place my trust, was displaying down-to-earth human sexual reactions. In both cases, I wondered whether the person inside the mask was considering the other one only as a costumed official or as some other underlying character. All that I could think of was what a friend of mine had said before I left: "You realize, don't you, that Delta and Disney are in bed together?"

With that thought I left the scene at the airport to take a shuttle to my hotel. I was determined that the minute I arrived, I would go with only my camera bag to the Magic Kingdom to begin photographing. The first thing that happened when I stepped out of the bus at the hotel was that I was told that the procedure was to give my bags to the baggage manager, who would move them to the van that moves between the cottages at the Caribbean Beach Resort. I had packed minimally so that I could manage my own luggage and save time. To make a long story short, I followed the procedure instead of my instincts, which cost me a half hour. Although it should have been a pleasant half hour, sitting on a bench, caressed by a warm breeze, surrounded by decor and plantings meant to suggest that I was on a southern island, I was annoyed at myself for giving in to the system against my better judgment, and so I spent my time trying to find something to be critical of. Was my entire trip going to be like this— trying to criticize a chance to simply sit back and enjoy life?

Later, when I found myself politely listening to the porter explain how to operate the TV, which I had no intention of watching, though together we watched on the Disney Channel a preview of what I would later experience in "real life," I realized that I was already at my destination. I was taking my first ride. I was in a controlled queue where it was impossible to cut ahead in line. Where the people who were dealing with me were "cast members"—the term Disney uses to describe any of its World employees. Where even the soap smiled back.

On the bus ride to the Magic Kingdom, I tried to follow along on the map. But when it comes to queuing theory, Disney is a master of finding the longest distance between two points. Not only do these circuitous routes, known as "infinity roads," confound one's sense of direction, but they also discourage any impulse to get there faster, when that is obviously not the point. The point is that you are no longer in control, so you might as well just sit back and enjoy the ride. So I sat back and enjoyed my ride by thinking of how frustrating this relaxing ride would be to my husband's well-developed "cranium command," and how good it might be for him to commute to work everyday via the scenic route. I was deeply involved in a memory of his showing me a shortcut on I-95— taking the exit ramp near Toys-R-Us then immediately getting back on the highway a quarter mile down the road, which he had discovered saved a minute or two in heavy traffic—when Fantasyland appeared before me in picture-postcard style.

Not one to easily give up trying to control my life, either, I remembered the most quoted passage from Steve Birnbaum's *Walt Disney World*—that when there are two lines leading to an attraction, most people head for the one on the right.[1] This tip has served me well at the bank, the supermarket, and numerous other overpopulated queues, but here at the entrance gate to the Magic Kingdom, there were an awful lot of people toting copies of the "Official Guide" and too many of them were heading left. While I waited in line, I thought about how life is full of these negative feedback systems. And how the speed with which they operate increases with population growth and information retrieval so that to-day's shortcut becomes tomorrow's traffic jam.

Once through the turnstile, I felt as if I had walked into the Disney Channel, except that the bright sun bouncing off the sidewalks and the pastel Victorian houses was too glary and everybody seemed to be wearing white. I wished that I could adjust the contrast control. And now that I had, at last, the opportunity to photograph, all I could think of was food. I didn't want to spend either the time or money to eat at a sit-down place, so I sat on the sidewalk devouring a hot dog, popcorn, and Coke probably at the same time that my family was eating their Thanksgiving dinner.

Every so often, I noticed someone aiming a camera up the street and I amused myself by playing a game similar to Where's Waldo—trying to find the subject of the photograph. Sometimes as far as forty feet from the camera, the smiling family would be huddled together, leaning toward their joint center of gravity. Did they actually think that they wouldn't fit in the frame? It looked to me as if the photographer was including just about everybody on Main Street in the lens. It is no wonder that in so many Disney brochures, photo tips encourage photographers to fill the frame with the subject. "Especially when shooting people, remember that the larger the subject appears in the picture, the more interesting it will be."[2] But people alone are rarely the main subject of photography in Disney World. Rather, the photographs are meant to be proof that the vacation really happened. And in the shots that I was observing on Main Street, U.S.A., the authenticating background was provided by Cinder-ella's Castle. But back home, it was going to require a blow-up job for anyone to identify the "distant" relatives in these snapshots.

On the subject of image problems, consider the marriage between Disney and Kodak. Together they produce thousands of offspring every day—little $3\frac{1}{2} \times 5$ glossies or 4×6 jumbo prints. In spite of brochures that say that a variety of film is available, in fact only Kodak film is sold and only a limited selection of their color emulsions at that. Someone who wants to use black and white film, as I did, must bring a sufficient supply from home and forget about having it processed within Disney World. Across Main Street, the Kodak Camera Center (there's one in every park) handles cameras from a variety of manufacturers, including Canon, Minolta, Nikon, and Pentax. But choice of equipment poses no threat to Kodak reproductions of Disney World, which depend on large numbers for the survival of the species. Let's face it—it simply doesn't matter which type of diaphragm is used, there is no effective birth control for this prolific couple.

When I finally did start to take my own pictures, nothing else went as planned. First of all, every time I put my camera to my eye, I stopped traffic. Like many other anachronistic practices that now occur only at Disney World, such as picking up your own garbage or turning in lost wallets, it's an unspoken etiquette that anybody taking a picture has the right-of-way. And, whereas I once witnessed a teenage boy drop a straw wrapper and pause long enough to exchange eye contact with his father before stooping to pick it up, I never saw anybody display the slightest reluctance to halt for the making of a picture.

Although I'm sure the park managers didn't intend it to be this way, this polite custom interacts with the signs that say Kodak "Picture Spot" in a way that can severely impact traffic patterns. Those little markers are strategically placed throughout the parks to denote photogenic scenes, but people are confused about how to interpret them. Some people situate their relatives next to the sign, including the sign itself in the picture, and some people stand near the sign, trying to figure out which direction is supposed to be the scenic view. At World Showcase at EPCOT, where walkways encircle a central lake and provide the only access from one country's pavilion to the next, photographers standing at picture signs on the lake side create invisible blockades by pointing their cameras at posing relatives on the pavilion side of the walkway.

Another problem that I had early on was that, whenever I tried to photograph people, they assume that I was interested in the scenic view behind them (it's true, by the way, that behind every person at Disney World is a scenic view) and would move out of the way. If I asked people if I might photograph them, they seemed to think that I wanted them to fill in as surrogate relatives and assumed the standard, smiling pose.

Before this trip, I had anticipated that park guests might be stiff and self-conscious around a photographer interested in something other than the ritualistic snapshots. But I had failed to take into account the unsurprising fact that almost everybody at Disney World would have a camera. This simple discovery temporarily laid to rest my biggest worry, but, at the same time, it introduced a new problem. On the one hand, I wasn't going to stand out in a crowd as "a photographer," but on the other hand, most of my pictures of people would have optical recording devices

in them. In fact, I discovered that some pictures would include more cameras than humans.

At MGM Studios, it was not unusual to see a family of five managing three pieces of equipment: a 35mm programmable model with zoom, a heavy-weight video camcorder, and a compact point-and-shoot. The father might be recording a street performance by the Muppets, while carrying a toddler on his shoulders, the child's feet riding just above the lens of the second camera. The mother would be carrying a baby, the other camera, and at least two drinks, while assuring a third child that it would soon be his turn to get a good view.

At first, I regarded these omnipresent cameras as obstructions. I chose angles and shots that would minimize them. Not only did the dangling straps and various shapes of black metal interfere with the gestures that I love to record, but the presence of cameras in the photographs made the whole process seem self-conscious. Even if the people seemed unaware of my camera, the cameras in my viewfinder seemed to be looking back. How could I take seemingly candid pictures that called attention to the ritual of taking pictures?

I gradually gave in to the inevitable. Things finally started to click when I began to regard the cameras themselves as rightful subjects. After all, they go to the bathroom and on the rides along with the people. Like

babies, they rest on diaper changing tables and ride in strollers. Instead of regarding the cameras as intrusions, I started seeing them as cultural adornment—necklaces, belts, or shoulder pads. Or, when pressed to someone's face, they seemed to be a part of the body itself. It was only after I accepted their rightful existence that I was able to look eyeball to eyeball and lens to lens at all of the grotesque cyclopic faces like my own.

But, alas, this new and unorthodox style of seeing resurrected my concern about being identified as a photographer. I would ask to take still-life pictures of the family's fast-food lunch, a bizarre enough request in itself, but when they tried to remove the video camera that served as the centerpiece, and I asked that it stay, the truth about me was clear. I might as well have been wearing a press badge or been hunched under a black cloth with a view camera set on a tripod for all the attention I was causing. But even the people whose lunch I had interrupted seemed to appreciate the visual joke. Instead of wanting me to leave, they would cooperate by pointing out other funny combinations of life and recording devices.

While I was aware that I was making waves by calling attention to myself as a photographer, I also noticed that in my wake I had stirred up conversations among strangers. Sometimes this happened because

people overheard the small talk between me and my models and found that they had something in common, such as living in Iowa or possessing Disney merchandise that was not available in the parks. (It turns out that lots of people bring in Disney contraband to dole out daily to their un-suspecting children. But I didn't think of this in advance, so I bought my kids genuine full-priced souvenir T-shirts.) Other than being queue-mates or greeting one's "cousins" at the 50's Prime Time Cafe, guests usually interact very little with one another. But after a couple of days of serving as a conversation piece, I couldn't walk down Main Street without greeting several familiar faces or people I recognized by their photo-graphic paraphernalia.

　The other picture-takers at Disney World, though, wanted their photo-graphic remembrances to preserve the magic—the notion that what is represented in their pictures is reality itself and not some fiction framed by technology. Holding to this belief as surely as they would have their children believe that Mickey's Surprise Celebration Parade extravaganza is an annual affair that they were lucky enough to catch, they avoid the presence of cameras in the snapshots that will gradually become memory itself. When posing for a picture, they sling them behind their backs or hand them over to the photographer. Unlike old cars or animals that have passed away, the family cameras will not be fondly preserved in photo albums.

Far from being immune to this romance and nostalgia, I thought long-ingly of the requisite pictures that I would be taking if my own family were with me—Goofy teasing Leah, Mickey hugging Seth, and Pluto licking Zoë. That's why, when I noticed family members taking turns operating the camera so that each person would be represented in pictures, I offered to help. I would use one of their cameras to photograph the whole group and then, invariably, they would ask if I would mind doing it again with each relative's camera. Many times, families thanked me profusely, saying it was the only time that they had all been together in a picture. In one touching case, it was the last shot on the roll before they left for home. I finally had to stop myself from offering my services, for I was feeling more like a cast member, "the roving photographic assistant," than the observer of life at Disney World that I wanted to be.

When I did restrain myself from participating in other people's photographic dreams, I began to see the process of picture-taking as a play about human relationships. The most entertaining performance was given by a group of teenagers posing in front of a swan topiary. In over a dozen permutations, members of their group took turns standing before the sculpted bush. First, larger groups were photographed, followed by couples, and finally some individuals, though some were more reluctant to pose than others. After a while, it became clear that, although they felt impatient with the ritual, they were trapped by social convention and

were looking for a graceful way out. As is probably the case in most
teenage interactions, change occurred when the most dominant member
of the group simply got up and left. He was followed by the others in what
I supposed was the pecking order, leaving the swan behind to mind the
nest.

Recently, video cameras have expanded the ritual of take-home experience to include the attractions themselves. On rides where motion makes
still photography impossible, videos rise to the challenge and give Dad
something absorbing to do while riding in the teacups or on "Dumbo."
And, since they are capable of recording in low lighting, video cameras
are used in the attractions where the phrase "No Flash Photography
Permitted" gets repeated so many times that some announcers ask the
audience to say it in unison, like the Pledge of Allegiance.

Another recent trend in photo-socio phenomenon is the peripatetic
videotaper. Following the scenic routes suggested in the guidebooks,
people (most often men) record while walking, softly narrating a voice-
over into the soundtrack. This activity seems to be especially popular in
World Showcase, where, like tracing the source of ants on some primal
mission, you can follow in the tracks of men talking to their cameras.
"Here we are at the Moroccan Pavilion," they say. "In the distance, you can
see Japan."

I saw one happy Disney guest strolling along near the Mexican Pavilion, watching not the surroundings visible through his eyes, but instead gazing at a screen that rode on a bar attached to him at waist level. This apparatus enabled him to see the world as a two-dimensional rectangle within an out-of-focus area that was his peripheral vision of the immediate environment. The man had discovered a way to create a personalized Disney Channel, broadcast *live* from his own viewpoint. Like Sunday football games, this bulky machinery drew the attention of other men—equipment buffs, who gathered to "participate" in this cultural sport by watching the screen together and sharing statistics. Why, I wondered, were they so interested in a gadget that replaced the experience of actual sight with a distorted version of reality?

First, I had to consider that the "reality" in question was a view of "Canada" from "Mexico" across a man-made "ocean." The scene also included a moon, but I have to tell you, my sense of reality had been so shaken by dioramas of plastic flora that look more real than the sculpted gardens and by audio-animatronic characters that display more fluid movements than some of the tour guides that I began to question the moon. I don't mean that I was asking questions of the man in the moon (I hadn't totally flipped out), but as I strolled alongside the lagoon at EPCOT, I questioned whether the moon was real or some kind of Disney moon—a holographic projection, perhaps. I then questioned what difference it should make whether that thing that formed the impression of a bright circular disc upon my eye was a Disney version or the other moon. Although I desperately wanted it to be the same moon that my family might be seeing from our living room back in Connecticut, I concluded that I couldn't be sure. And if the moon could not be proven in the presence of the warm, sensuous breeze, then what difference should it make whether it was a real moon or some lunar simulacrum that was projected onto the man's waist-level monitor?

Perhaps, because "reality" at Disney World is already a construct, transforming it further into a two-dimensional screen is a way to actively participate in the magic. The guest who was experiencing the instant replay of the present moment did not delude himself that he was in Mexico; he knew that, in terms of EPCOT's definition of a technological utopia, he was in Heaven. Just like me, he was playing a game with technology, aware that the goal is not an objective copy of the original, but a fictional version based on the original. And, when the original is

Disney World, then you might say that the resulting image is not a cousin to reality, but a first cousin once removed.

At MGM, where the attractions themselves reveal how films are constructed, I met an even more distant relation of good old-fashioned tangible reality, for not only did I see someone filming films about the making of films, but I photographed him doing so. While most people were enjoying the rides, I joined the ranks of those who get their thrills by coasting on a metalevel, thinking about the layering of images.

The first time that I saw somebody videotaping a computer monitor screen, I immediately looked around for an undercover copyright police force. While any of the hundreds of people at the Wonders of Life pavilion wearing shorts, character shirts, and sneakers could have been Disney spies posing as guests, nobody stepped forth to arrest the man, so I turned my attention back to the optical illusion that was being recorded—a hypnotic rotating spiral. Drawn into the center of the spiral, I contemplated the meaning of videotaping a monitor screen and why I had instinctively thought that the act violated some ownership law. Then it dawned on me. If the video camera were recording only the monitor screen, it was possible that the original and the copy would be identical. A guest could take home not just the memory of a Disney experience, but the experience itself—hook, line, and sinker. The world is falling deeper and deeper into a vortex of simulacra, I mused. Worse than being trapped in Plato's cave, we are now stuck in Pluto's doghouse.

"If lost, please return to Mickey Mouse," says Pluto's oversized ID tag. Poor Pluto. Imagine being a dog with multiple, identical masters—Mickey Mouse appearing simultaneously in ice shows in Toronto and New York, signing autographs in the Magic Kingdom in Disney World, EuroDisney, Tokyo Disney, and boarding the bus at EPCOT after his special appearance with the other characters. With his owner's image reproduced on clothing, watches, dishes, books, posters, telephones, and just about every other object you can think of; his form reshaped into furry stuffed animals, miniature plastic figurines, and 14-kt. gold-plated, signed, limited-edition knickknacks; his silhouette so familiar that his entire identity can be evoked by the shape of mouse ears on hats or incorporated into monumental architecture: how can poor Pluto recognize his true master, the ideal Plutonic form of Mickey? After only a few days in Disney World, I got stuck in the mousetrap of recurring images and began to hallucinate mouse ears. One time I had to explain to an

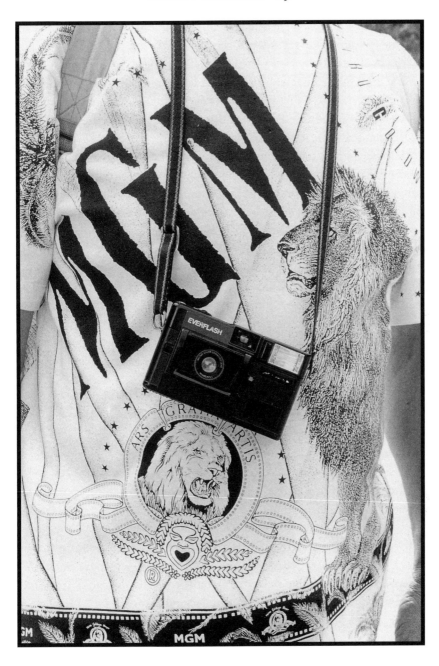

elderly man why I was staring at his flipped-up sunshades. Another time, I found myself following a woman in a black halter top, which formed arches over her breasts, wondering if Disney designers had gone that far.

In spite of his universally recognized form, Mickey is not common property. I remember that shortly after the child-care center at my health club engaged someone to decorate the walls with authentic-looking Disney characters, I heard on the news that Disney sued a day-care center with Disney characters painted on its front entrance. Sometime after that suit, I read about another lawsuit involving a sculptor whose work featured Disney characters that (in the newspaper photograph, at least) did not look all that "realistic." I was not sure about the naiveté of the sculptor, but I was certain that character ownership came as a surprise to the day-care staff who must have seen hundreds of crude drawings of the characters by preschoolers, some of whom will draw counterfeit-quality Mickeys, Donalds, and Goofys by the time they enter middle school. Acknowledging public sentiment regarding the power if not the right of Disney to use legal force, a CBS radio broadcaster began: "You always hear about Disney suing the little guy. Well, here's a case of the little guy suing the Disney Corporation. A restaurant owner in Florida claims that Disney stole his idea."

Questioning the originality and the ownership of images, postmodern photography had, until my epiphany around the spiral, seemed like the work of an elite few. But, at Disney World, where everything from babies to roasted turkey thighs are wrapped in copyrighted symbols, the T-shirts alone—imprinted with Mickeys and Minnies, of course, but also Elvis, Einstein, Bruce Springsteen, Malcolm X—turn even amateur snapshooters into postmodern photographers, claiming existing images for their own. A naive entrepreneur could contribute to the endless spiral of degraded images by sending off his or her negatives to be emblazoned on new T-shirts and then selling them on the street. Or a less naive photographer like Sherrie Levine, who rephotographed photographs by the old DWM (dead, white, male) masters and declared her images to be original works, might sell the T-shirts at the Mary Boone Gallery for a lot more money.

Original moments at Disney World are as rare as original material. Photographers seeking to capture decisive moments in the more traditional style of Cartier-Bresson's street photography will think twice (once when they take the lucky shot and the same time the next day when they

see it happen again). If you miss a shot one day—such as a child riding on a man's shoulders, pouting while the enormous Minnie balloon in the Surprise Celebration Parade passes in front of Cinderella's Castle—your chances are pretty good that, given the large number of people and the fact that the parade starts at 3 o'clock every day, you can recreate the scenario. In addition to diurnal regularity, there is the more frequent repetition of the attractions, which from the point of view of someone photographing people, causes recurrent traffic patterns, groupings, and postures. It is rare indeed for an individual or an individual behavior to stand out (although I did see an entire family dressed in form-fitting black leather outfits and a twelve-year-old boy on a bridge in EPCOT who was timing how long it took his spit to fall into the lagoon). Mostly, people in Disney World appear to be acting out ritual behaviors, affirming the postmodern claim that there is nothing new left to photograph.

I began to see Disney World, with its mass reproductions and controlled, repetitive behavior, as a concentrated form of global homogenation. I had to admit that it was an interesting place to visit, but I knew I didn't want to live there and it bothered me to think of the entire world becoming infused with molecules of Disney fat. I wanted to be able to go home to something else. But references to Disney are proliferating with increasing frequency and showing up in unpredictable places: on towels at the beach where I photograph, on greeting cards from New Orleans, and on Easter egg coloring kits in the supermarket back home, which on first glance seemed blasphemous because of the new neon dyes, then I realized that Mickey Mouse was on the package instead of the Easter Bunny. In the same way, it struck me as downright un-American that Disney appropriated New Year's Eve and turned it into a nightly happening at Pleasure Island. I guess the Founding Fathers forgot to copyright the national holidays. There are few limits to the Disney Corporation usurping tradition and repackaging it for self-promotion. (Though, admittedly, it is hard to imagine Mickey endorsing products approved kosher for Passover. Mickey Matzo?)

I realized that, to my knowledge, Disney has not yet capitalized on Thanksgiving (I would knock on wood if I could be sure it was authentic). I thought longingly of home and of joining my family around the paper turkey and gave thanks that we could still imagine Pilgrims and Indians gathering around a Horn of Plenty, for someday we may all be celebrating a Disney version of a Thanksgiving around the Spiral of Simulacra.

THE family VACATION

. . .

NARRATIVE SNAPSHOT I: THE LUCKY BREAK

I[*] know I'm a gullible consumer when I catch myself clipping coupons. But I'm not so gullible as to enter contests or believe that those grinning, ordinary faces in the ads for the Publisher's Clearing House Sweepstakes are real people, actual lucky winners. So it was against my better judgment, egged on by my kids, that I responded to a postcard promising four nights in a Disney hotel. I had only to dial the 800 number indicated. Lo and behold. The serial number on my postcard matched one of the preselected winning numbers. So, why is the voice on the phone asking for my credit card number? This is clearly a gimmick. My kids are staring at me; they're about to pop; they want the "prize" vacation and they're sure we've won. When they were younger they believed in Santa Claus; now they believe in contests. And just as I was complicitous in maintaining the Santa Claus myth, so did I find myself facilitating the myth of the lucky break. As I read my credit card information into the phone, I wondered if my kids would grasp the subterfuge. But they were too excited. Four nights at Disney World, transportation not included. At least we get a packet of coupons "worth seven hundred and fifty dollars on area attractions," none of them Disney. What can they be? I start to imagine alligator farms and other tourist traps—a real alternative trip. But no, the kids want Disney.

Organizing a family vacation to Disney World demands managerial

*Susan Willis

and economic decision-making skills equal to those required by big business. Browse the newspaper, TV ads, and travel agencies and you will find
a perplexing array of package deals with prices so numerous and variable
as to require familiarity with spreadsheet analysis. There are airline tie-
ins to hotels and rental cars, deals that hinge on departure date or duration of stay, packages that offer reduced rates for kids and others that
offer breaks for seniors. Families generally weigh the relatively expensive
convenience of a package that includes air travel, accommodations at a
Disney resort hotel, admission to all the Disney attractions, and a number
of fringe enticements against the more modest price of accommodations
in Orlando, the inconvenience of transport to and from the Park, and the
price of admission tickets purchased at the gate. Factoring in Orlando
with the possibility of side trips to Sea World and Universal Studios is apt
to be mind-boggling by comparison to the already daunting task of sorting through Disney's in-house options. These are so complex as to warrant a sixty-three page booklet put out by the Walt Disney Travel Co. and
available at travel agencies, where the features of Disney's "all-inclusive
packages" are charted against those of the "classic packages," and where
the difference between a "Resort Magic" vacation is detailed against one
that promises "Resort Romance."

   Planning a Disney Vacation is more apt to be a frustrating ordeal than a flight of fantasy. Disney World presents itself as a Never-Never Land of unlimited vacation possibilities, but most families have to negotiate real time and real money constraints. Parents often go round in circles, weighing the different travel options. Is saving money worth losing time on awkward, piecemeal arrangements? Or, will the family get the most out of its vacation by spending more so as to have the maximum in park time? The time versus money equation is a fact of daily life. It underpins family economics and has as much to do with leisure time as labor time. Because more women than men work in two spheres—the home and the workplace—women are especially familiar with and often voice dismay over the impossibility of ever coming out ahead on either time or money. Mothers who work outside the home are always performing a time versus money balancing act. Frequently this boils down to the mathematics of money paid for child care computed against income. The question working mothers often face is whether the labor time facilitated by more child care hours really adds up to more income once the increased fee for child care is factored into the equation. Where's the point of breaking even, much less that of profit? And what about all the personal and emotional factors left out of the arithmetic? Daily life in a capitalist system means that nothing is free and that the market turns us all into accountants who try to balance economic equations against emotional variables. This is particularly true when families decide on a Disney vacation. Planning the family's trip foregrounds an arithmetic whose abstract simplicity belies a wealth of desires inherent in each family member's expectation of a "perfect" Disney holiday.

In planning my own family's trip to Disney World, I found myself wanting something sort of open-ended, but pressured into having to organize all the details. The desire I harbored for a more spontaneous vacation did not jibe with the corporate image of Disney that permeates the advertising and suggests the necessity of advance reservations. Actually, it's hard to imagine a spontaneous vacation anywhere. Even camping can require a call to an 800 number and the use of a credit card to ensure a campsite. A call to Disney's number opens the door to the Kingdom and immediately confronts the caller with a set of choices. Do I want the Caribbean Beach with its jogging trail, lagoon, and pastel architecture; or do I want Dixie Landings with its taste for the South. Of course, there's always the Contemporary, which features direct monorail service and a gym; or the Fairway Villas for a vacation that includes golf; not to mention the Swan and Dolphin for a more postmodern experience. The question of which themed environment and collection of amenities might best satisfy a family's notion of the perfect vacation is weighed against cost and commute time. While costs are spelled out, the latter is unfathomable. Everything at Disney World is dispersed. The only thing connecting the accommodations to the attractions is a meandering system of "infinity" roads. When I asked how new workers find their way to their job sites, I was told they are given a map. Somehow, I didn't think that would suffice. My first commute from the Caribbean Beach to the Magic Kingdom included a full circle tour of the Swan and Dolphin hotels, both to and fro. Even the most practical tourist is apt to choose accommodations purely on the basis of thematic decor.

In my own quest for a bargain, I was dismayed to discover that my projected stay of five nights and four days precluded my purchase of what looked like the best deal on admission tickets. I found myself trying to figure out how I might beat the odds. Maybe I should drive all night so as to arrive in the daytime and thus have the prerequisite stay of four nights and five days. No, I'd be exhausted. Whatever money I gained in admission to the attractions, I'd lose in time spent groggy and miserable. Like traders on Wall Street, tourists who hope to maximize their Disney deals have to research the options. No choice is gratuitous. Every decision activates a specific set of programmed options, which in turn activate and exclude others. As I ran the gamut of the Disney options, I felt I was inside a Nintendo game—a tiny tourist heroine scurrying about from option to option, reacting to choices but never achieving mastery of the game or even a sense of how the entire interlocking system works.

Families who enter the Disney system without the aid of friendly advice from a previous Disney vacationer or the definitive assistance of Steve Birnbaum's Guide are apt to wish they had indeed fallen into Nintendo's rational circuitry, instead of what more closely resembles Jorge Luis Borges's "Lottery in Babel." Implicit to Disney's infinite permutations of packaged possibilities is the overriding atmosphere of chance. The family might be lucky: make all the right choices; put together the optimal combination of vacation ingredients—like digits on a lotto ticket—and come out a winner. After all, isn't this the Magic Kingdom? All that promised magic ought to bestow a lucky break on someone.

Anyone who harbors fantasies of breaking the bank had best be prepared for the grim reality of the smiling in-house customer services host or hostess, who, with scratch pad and pen, will demonstrate the dollars spent or saved depending on the inclusion or exclusion of additional attractions such as Typhoon Lagoon, Pleasure Island, and River Country. What about a breakfast with the characters? I admit to coming away feeling slightly cheated. Clearly, there was no way to beat Disney at its system of endlessly recombinant possibilities with their various price tags. No matter how my hostess calculated the figures, I failed to hit the jackpot. My choice of a four-day pass would not include Typhoon Lagoon unless I paid an additional fee and I'd have to decide on the spot if I wanted it as an option during all the days of my stay or if I'd take it at the single-day price. Of course, I might shoot the works—go for the four-day pass with everything. But what if it rains? My hostess informed me that unused admissions would be valid for subsequent visits. However, admission to Typhoon Lagoon could not be carried over, unless it rains— but only if the rain commences at a certain point in the attraction's operating hours, particularly if there's a threat of lightning. Do I really care to come again? The second time around I might be a better player— or more lucky. The impression that the Disney vacation options might fall into lucky alignment like the fruits and stars in a slot machine bespeaks a system where the tourist's illusion of possibly coming out ahead is balanced against the house, which holds all the cards.

The comparison between games of chance and living in capitalist culture originates with Charles Baudelaire, whose poem "Le Jeu" designates the gambler as one of the emblematic figures of the modern era. Where Baudelaire's poem is dark, hellish, and satanic, Walter Benjamin's commentary on the poem written some eighty years later, when the industrial hell only glimpsed by Baudelaire had come to fruition, underscores fundamental connections between games of chance and a capitalism that dehumanizes its players by bending them to instrumentalized purpose. Benjamin saw in Baudelaire's poem something more profound than the simple recognition that life is risk. For the gambler, experience is reduced to the instant: the roll of the dice or the luck of the draw. So, too, for the worker under capitalism. Durational time is eliminated, replaced by the fragmented moments of assembly line work where each repetition presents itself as another turn in a game that can't be won. "Starting all over again is the regulative idea of the game, as it is of work for wages."[1] Bringing Benjamin's analysis up to the present, we realize that daily life as well as labor is structured on the temporality of chance. As one advertising campaign recently phrased it, "Tomorrow is the first day of the rest of your life." The notion of a possible lucky renewal belies a reality of many days that are not filled with Disney options, but all the repetitious and routinized labors that constitute daily life: getting the kids off to school, getting to work, picking the kids up, shopping at the supermarket, managing after school activities and carpools. It's hectic and humdrum at the same time. Embedded in the notion that tomorrow initiates a new beginning is a utopian desire for radical change. This is at the same time denied by the endless repetition of tomorrows whose lucky breaks are all mundane, like a day off from carpooling or a double (sometimes triple) coupon offer at the supermarket. Nevertheless, the aura of a lucky break permeates the culture. Does Borges chuckle in his grave to know that many states in the United States fund their roads, schools, and basic social services with revenues from government-run lotteries? This is not his fantastic Babel, but a wholly rationalized system whose citizens invent their own irrational responses by betting the numerical equivalent of their birthdates and those of their children against jackpots that occasionally exceed a million dollars. Meanwhile, appallingly meager funds trickle into schools and social services, thus creating a population whose impoverished real life options make the lottery appear to be the only viable chance for a future.

Narrative Snapshot 2: The Whole World in a Shopping Bag

A friend who lived for a number of years in Freeport, Maine once told me that a favorite pastime of the locals is to hang out at the huge L. L. Bean warehouse store to watch the tourists. "Families arrive at all hours. They shop the entire store; buy enough stuff for an expedition. Then they back their minivans up to the door and fill them to the top." My friend's description of consumer tourism captures something of the third world looking at the first. Indeed, there is a hint of magical realism in the notion of scruffy locals spying on the state-of-the-art tourists. In this turnaround view, the abundance of high-tech gear deemed necessary by the suburbanite is recast as surfeit and encumbrance by the locals. Both perspectives are charged with a fascination for the "other": the desire to imagine what it might be like to be in the other's place—if only for a moment. The fancy commodities are the point of mediation between tourists and locals. They offer the tourist a means to fantasize—maybe achieve—the locals' experience of backwoods; and they focus the locals' love/hate desire for the more developed world where consumer gratification is thought to be as regular as breathing.

I chuckled over the tourists because I saw them through my friend's eyes—gleefully setting off on their vacations all but buried in their new gear, getting away from it all with more stuff than they probably needed to get through a day at home. As a critic of consumer culture, I don't find shopping pleasurable. I try to avoid it until necessity forces me into a mall or supermarket where I mechanically and determinedly get the things I "need."

Imagine my surprise—resolute antishopper that I am—when I found myself hypnotically drawn into Disney World's gigantic shopping mecca. Armed with notepad and pen, I had set out to research the tourists: follow them, watch them, record their conversations. But here I was handling the merchandise. And in so doing, I was actively participating in the construction of one of Disney's themed environments. I might have shopped all day had I not run into my companion in research. We had separated earlier: she to take photos and me to take notes, only to find ourselves staring at each other across a rack of Colombian textiles.

We were in Adventureland, where a series of open-air shops gives onto a plaza reminiscent of towns in the American Southwest. I was surrounded by Venezuelan curios, leather sandals, Native American pottery, papier-mâché masks, piñatas, and embroidered blouses. Every item of merchandise is equally and simultaneously a stage prop whose combined effect is the creation of a themed environment more total than anything one finds in a Banana Republic shop but equally vague in its references to real places and cultures. I sensed I was somewhere in the Hispanic Southwest, while to my right the merchandise conjured up the jungles of Africa. Both localizations depend on the baggage of ideological assumptions the visitor brings into the park and finds activated in Disney's display of merchandise.

Moving through the merchandise, the shopper journeys from one culturally coded geography to another. Shopping is a ride not unlike the other amusements. Both are narratives. If you read the signs right (and it's easy to do because they are all stereotypical) your perusal of the merchandise is a touristic excursion from subtropical to tropical locales. Recovering my research mode, I stepped back from the merchandise and into the plaza. From this vantage point, I could better apprehend the transition

from the conglomerate of goods meant to suggest the Southwest, to the pith helmets and khaki meant to summon up the deserts of North Africa, then to the green Aussie ranger hats and brightly colored wooden toucans meant to suggest a more jungly environment. I was impressed; the transitions between environments were so subtle. I beheld the incredibly seemless merger of vastly different regions. A world comprised of distinct cultures and histories melted into an exotic—but homogenized—totality.

By comparison to Adventureland's shopping plaza, EPCOT's World Showcase appears retrograde for its insistence on a world defined by discrete nation states, each marketing its national products: trolls for "Norway," croissants for "France," huaraches for "Mexico." This bygone mode of capitalist production was already out of date when EPCOT opened. The rest of Disney World is actually more future-oriented in its globalized presentation of production and consumption. For the most part, a network of shopping areas spreads out over the entire park like a single continuous mall. This world without boundaries envisions capitalism as a global market place. It is a world where goods flow freely and are freely exchanged. It's a world where democracy comes to mean the compatible arrangement of vastly dissimilar goods offered up for sale. Curiously, this is a world without people. Aside from the sales clerks whose costumes make them indistinguishable from the merchandise, this world is peopled by commodities. If, as Jane Kuenz argues, EPCOT's corporatist view of the future envisions a world where people are replaced by the light bleeps that conclude each ride, Disney's shopping plazas suggest a world where commodity fetishism erases the workforce. Shoppers need never deal with the producers of all that culturally rich merchandise. Instead, they can sample and handle all the varied stylistic details of the merchandise without recognizing in them the disembodied traces of the producers long since erased from their purchases.

While Disney's one world consumerist mall depicts a globe depeopled of producers, it sports an abundant population of first world shoppers, who, like myself among the Southwestern merchandise, find ourselves free to trade in the signs of multiculturalism. Once tuned into shopping as a viable vacation activity, I began to observe a number of vacationers who had come to the park without their children. Some were in fact celebrating their wedding anniversaries. They toured the park's restaurants, golf course, and shopping venues. They'd take in the shows, maybe a parade. In the late afternoon, I'd see them on a Disney bus, returning to their resort accommodations, their plastic Disney shopping bags stuffed to the brim. In the mornings, I'd overhear their breakfast conversations as they plotted their shopping day and exchanged information on the best shops. Because I had come with children, I found it hard to conceptualize a five-day trip to Disney World devoted entirely to shopping. But these visitors were intent on harvesting the world's handcraft production. Reaching into their bags, they'd pull out exquisite jewelry, porcelain, silk, woolens, and a fair supply of Disney products.

These shoppers fully participate in the ideology of global capitalism, for which the duties of citizenship are equated with the practice of shopping. Such a world offers each and every shopper the experience of companionship with the rest of the global community through purchases. I didn't realize how conveniently the one world philosophy currently in vogue dovetails with consumerism until I returned home from my Disney vacation to discover this ad for a T-shirt in a New Age, multicultural mail-order catalog: "Remind everyone you meet—friends and strangers alike—that as living beings sharing the same earth and sky, we're all related in some way—one family." The T-shirt was emblazoned with Native American motifs and a fair number of endangered species. New Age multiculturalism and Disney's global marketplace both inject the shopper with a heavy dose of what Renato Rosaldo calls "imperialist nostalgia." That is, once global capitalism exterminates a significant number of the world's population and annexes the remainder as the workforce for overseas enterprise zones and production platforms, then the middle classes of the advanced capitalist nations find themselves harking back with nostalgia for those decimated peoples and their cultures. Similarly, we sadly reminisce extinct or endangered species. But consumerism offers a means to assuage our guilt—both for the animals and the people— with the purchase of a T-shirt, whose emblem or slogan celebrating the ideology of one world need not be taken ironically.

Narrative Snapshot III: The Simulated Trip

A friend was preparing for his dream vacation: a month-long family camping trip through the West. He invited me to inspect his new GMC truck bought for the occasion. In opening the doors, he explained how the gear would be stowed, where the kids would sit, and how he and his wife would alternate driving. As he spoke, the dream of the vacation began to fill his words and he described at length all the things he wanted to see and do. Finally, he said, "I want my kids to know distance. Everything we do is so fast. Our long trips have been by plane. I want my kids to see how big this country really is, and feel a little of what it was like for people long ago to journey over great distance." As I peered into the truck, imagining the gear stowed behind and between the seats where the safety-belted children would ride, I asked him how he thought the kids would manage the trip—how they would pass the time while covering the distance. "Well, they have their Game Boys."

As a nature enthusiast, I recoiled. I was dismayed to think of the kids absorbed into their individual mini vid-screens while hundreds of miles of unseen landscape passed them by. Transfixed by their video games' endless variations and repetitions, the kids would be oblivious to all the things their father wanted them to learn. Technology's flattened temporality would replace the boring time on the road. The numbing experience of driving over great distances would collapse into a handheld microcosm. I failed to recall the horrible tedium of my own trips: the endless cornfields—or worse yet, interstates. It didn't occur to me that the pioneers probably invented alot of pastimes to ameliorate the experience of distance. Days later, in rethinking my friend's story and my reaction to it, I realized that he and I share a longing for experiences deemed "authentic"; and as parents, we both harbor pedagogical designs born of a generational dislocation between our experience of the world and our children's technologically enhanced (or degraded) experience. Like my friend, I tend to regret that for too many of us today "real" experiences are apt to be less rewarding than simulated ones. But unlike my friend, I have learned to be intellectually skeptical of the real.

If a family camping trip that transects southern Illinois constitutes an experiential dichotomy between parents who live through the duration of cornfields and kids who lose themselves in the time and space of Tetris, what about a family trip to Disney World where the distinction between what's real and what's simulated is compressed into a man-made environment where everything is spectacular?

Dean MacCannell begins his book on tourism with this definition of tourist: "sightseers, mainly middle class, who are at this moment deployed throughout the entire world in search of experience." There's something sad in this: the quest for experience. I imagined avid antlike tourists scurrying about in desperate attempts to have experiences deemed more meaningful than the sort that happen everyday. Published in 1976, MacCannell's *The Tourist* is a landmark text—one of the first U.S. studies to take everyday life seriously and demonstrate the efficacy of what was then "French" semiotics and structuralism.[2] Reading the book today, I was struck by the fact that much of MacCannell's fieldwork documents a pre-postmodern experience of the world—a time when many tourists included the desire for authentic experiences in their travel plans. I doubt this is the case today. We take vacations, but are we tourists in MacCannell's sense of the term? Rather than sightseeing or mingling with the natives, most Americans I know are more apt to fill the weekend with amusements and plan vacations to hygienically packaged leisure resorts. I have a hunch that if MacCannell conducted his research today, he wouldn't frequent San Francisco's North Beach or bistros in Paris. Instead, he'd book passage on a five-island Caribbean cruise, visit a Club Med, or spend a week at Disney World.

MacCannell clarifies his definition of authenticity in his description of a restaurant where the kitchen—formerly separate and hidden from view—was architecturally re-staged to be a part of the dining area. Sightseers on the street could press their noses to the glass to watch diners and chefs. Those who ventured inside had to negotiate the cooks and the cooking in their quest for a seat. Once the kitchen becomes a part of the tourist's dining experience, all the tourists become actors in a larger performance staged for passersby, and the work of food preparation is recast as performance. Although MacCannell doesn't go so far, I sense that all the chopping, stirring, frying, all the aromas, all the noise, is rendered inauthentic by the very fact of their staging.

At the time MacCannell researched *The Tourist,* Disney World was just under construction. Today, its hundreds of acres of invented environment make MacCannell's descriptions almost quaint: "backstages" rendered visible and "staged authenticity" seem like clumsy dress rehearsals for Disney's full-fledged postmodern flattening of both stage and reality. Main Street's turn-of-the-century storefronts give way to an interior stage no different from a shopping mall. All the classic Hollywood movie topographies, from the Amazon to the Painted Desert, have been restaged as props for the tourist's amusement. Even nature is staged, from Discovery Island where pesky native species are trapped and relocated (or exterminated) to the precise marigolds that render every garden perfunctory.

At Disney World, all work is costumed and scripted. Indeed, the 50's Prime Time Cafe makes MacCannell's restaurant seem an amateurish production. I don't remember Formica and Fiesta Ware in my own childhood; but I certainly felt myself interpolated by the staged environment of the normative fifties household and family. Guests dine in mini-kitchenettes; black and white TV consoles feature *Leave it to Beaver, Lucy,* and *Lassie;* the waiter, cast as your uncle (or aunt), informs you that your "cousins," who share your table, have already washed their hands and if you've done likewise then you're ready for Mom's meatloaf. I couldn't wait for the S'more, promised upon cleaning my plate.

The decor features authentic fifties furnishings; while the social stereotyping—the clichéd sex roles and "balanced meals"—comes straight out of the TV monitor. This is "authenticity" as it was presented in the early sitcoms. Critics generally agree that Disney World is built on a cinematic principle whereby amusements are analogous to riding a tracking shot. At the 50's Prime Time Cafe, guests step out of the movies and enter the comfy domesticity of TV. They become patrons who trade themselves in for scripted players. So there I was, a forty-five-year-old woman positioned as a child and condescendingly spoken down to by my "uncle," the waiter. Why didn't I rebel? Was it because, as Jane Kuenz argues, I know I will derive pleasure only to the extent that I insert myself in the dominant ideology? Maybe I really wanted the S'more. Besides, there were all my

"cousins" whose possible good time depended on my playing my part. In any case, any punning snappishness from me was quickly met by "uncle's" more practiced verbal retorts.

Simulation is fast becoming a cultural commonplace. While much has been written to describe simulation as a manifestation of postmodernism, few critics take the argument further to demonstrate the connection between simulation and capitalism. Jean Baudrillard is one such critic, whose entire career can be charted as an ongoing effort to understand the various manifestations of simulation as the aesthetic equivalents of capitalist production. In an early book, Baudrillard argued that production is itself a mirror image, a reflection of the way capitalism structures all our ways of knowing, including language. From mirrors, he moved on to tromp l'oeil in whose visual trickery Baudrillard saw the sublime simultaneity of reality and its transcendence. Preoccupied with objects and their relationship to commodities, Baudrillard argued that the invention of the mass-produced series object (which makes the original Barbie indistinguishable from her one-millionth replicant) parallels the erasure of referentiality from conceptual thought. His most recent writing takes simulation to its apogee: the fractal arrangement of Michael Jackson's face and the staged massacre at Timisoara, which Baudrillard sees as emblematic of capitalism's global production of information.

Curiously, Baudrillard's interest in simulation has never provoked a long essay on Disney. Perhaps Disney is just too mundane, lacking the fascination of Michael Jackson's transformations and the uproar of Timisoara. Nevertheless, Disney World is this planet's most elaborate and sustained simulation, whose most interesting feature is finally not the perfected authenticity of its props, but the way visitors coincide in actively producing the simulation. Timisoara succeeded because the media bestowed the aura of authenticity on its staged drama. As Baudrillard puts it, televisual images "are virtual, and the virtual is what puts an end to all negativity, hence to all reference either real or anecdotal. Thus, a contagion of images, that generate themselves without reference to anything real or imaginary, is itself virtually without limits."[3] Disney World is Timisoara on a grand scale, whose most stunning achievement is the production of simulation as a collective practice. To John Berger's observation that women in our society learn to comport themselves with respect to a socially constructed dominant male gaze, I would add, following Baudrillard, that everyone at Disney World—men, women, and children—learn to comport themselves for the unseen eye of a socially constructed video camera. All are players, monitoring their behavior and producing in gesture, language, and dress the never-ending, unchanging virtual reality of a sitcom, which, if broken down into episodes, might air on the Disney Channel.

NARRATIVE SNAPSHOT IV: THE HAPPY FAMILY

I was getting my hair cut and trying to avoid the topic of sports, so I asked my barber if he had ever taken a family vacation. "Once," he said. "It was great. I'm still paying for it. We went to the Bahamas. Cost seven thousand dollars." He went on to describe how the vacation produced the feeling of family for himself, his wife, and their two children. "I talked to my kids. I mean I even talked to my daughter. She lives in another state now. My son's still around so I see him. But it was the last time we would all be together. We had a great time. We were relaxed. We all got along. I enjoyed every minute." He paused, then reiterated, "It was great. I'm still paying for it."

Listening to my barber, I noticed that the place, the Bahamas, never entered into his remembrance or description. Except for the hotel and the food, which were both "great," the family might have had the same feeling of togetherness on any suitably exotic island or resort cruise. For my barber, the vacation had not been the occasion to explore new places, new sights, new cultures, but to concretize the experience of family. By comparison to all the events that go unremarked but nevertheless constitute twenty years of marriage and childrearing, this one event truly signified family. My barber was brimming with patriarchal pride for the tremendous expenditure he had made for the sake of his family. Though his kids are now grown and primarily out of the house, the fact that he is still paying for their trip preserves his fatherly role. In a commodity-conscious society, paying for a vacation—something frivolous and pleasurable—comes to be more a testimony to family than paying for something that better approximates needs, such as braces or glasses or college tuition.

I have heard my barber's story retold with minor variations by a great many friends and acquaintances. Among these, the vast majority, particularly those with younger children, choose Disney World as the site for confirming family. Some, like my barber, betray an unconscious intentionality in the way they stage their vacations so as to reap the rewards of family. Others know right from the start that the experience of family is what they are really after. Whether it happens as if by accident or by design, the strong feeling of togetherness is what most often emerges when parents talk about their family vacations. I have heard testimonies to family from people I never suspected of harboring such desires, much less the urge to activate them at Disney World. Indeed, I was amazed when a woman in one of my adult education courses, someone who had made strong feminist observations throughout the term, explained that she annually sends her teenage children to Disney World with their grandmother during her kids' February school holidays. "The first time my children went to Disney World with their grandmother they really became close." She explained that her mother, now in her seventies, had grown up in Germany. "My mother was able to tell my children about her life in Germany—about the War—things she never talked about at home. Now, when I ask my children what they want to do for the February vacation, they say they want to go back to Disney World with their grandmother. They aren't crazy about the place the way young children are. And my mother doesn't go on the rides. They just like to be there together."

My research on Disney comprises volumes on family: ten years of informal interviews with visitors to the park and almost every one of them gives testimony to family. Even visitors who go as singles or in nonfamily groups, such as high school marching bands and sports teams, comment on the "familiness" of the place. As a Marxist and a feminist, I confess to a great deal of ambivalence toward family (even though I have one and have taken my family to Disney World). My resistance to family gives my research a particular slant. I've tended to push all this family business to the margins of my thinking. Seeing it as the boring and predictable norm, I've sought out the more unconventional park visitors: the teen groups, old folks, foreigners, singles, and subcultural groupies. So it is with a great deal of foot-dragging that I turn my thoughts to family. Not wanting to mire my comments in all the ways Disney enforces the patriarchal aspects of family in the service of profit-making, I'll focus, instead, on the utopian aspects of family. These are everywhere embedded in my informants' testimony, inextricably bound up with the patriarchal, but there, nevertheless, as dialectical antitheses to the nuclear.

The experience of family offers a sense of collectivity: albeit a degraded collectivity, constrained by the rampant individualism and patriarchal authority that defines our society as a whole. However, for many Americans being a family member is the only available means for getting in touch with a notion of social life that is larger than the self. The family can provide a nexus for imagining what more fully developed collectivities might be like. Children, especially, imagine extended social relationships on the basis of their families. They talk about creating their own collectivities by incorporating best friends into their families and inviting favorite teachers to birthday parties. I have a hunch that the suburban practice of keeping a combination of diverse pets—gerbils, goldfish, parakeets, cats, and dogs—expresses a desire to break down the nuclear homogeneity of the family. This impulse finds its way into mass culture, where a variety of "othered" characters from E.T. to Edward Scissorhands stretch the meaning of family; by their inclusion into the suburban household, these others raise the possibility of more diverse living arrangements. Science fiction isn't the only realm for mass culture's utopian reconstruction of family. Indeed, Fredric Jameson has pointed out that much of the appeal of the *Godfather* films was rooted in the way the mafia as "family" spoke to the viewers' unconscious yearnings for collectivity.[4]

The family enshrined by Disney and built into the park by his "imagineers" is not in itself utopian. But a family's desire for togetherness can have utopian dimensions when it concretizes a response to the absence of available collectivity in society at large. This utopian aspect is, however, compromised by the fact that the notion of togetherness is imbricated with leisure time consumption. You have to pay—and pay a lot—in order to achieve the experience of collectivity. In making the family the primary unit of consumption at Disney World, Disney expands the individualist orientation that more generally defines consumer culture, but in so doing, activates a purely consumerist model for collectivity. The oft-repeated delight that families express in recognizing and experiencing togetherness is wholly contained by the way the pleasure of a collective experience is produced by consumption and reinforces consumerism. The longer you stay and the more you participate by buying, the more you activate the feeling of togetherness and reap the returns of collectivity. This is the case outside the park as well. The consumerist model as collectivity permeates the entire culture and manifests itself in a variety of mini-family leisure time venues where togetherness can be recovered for an hour or two at a time. In talking to people, I have the impression that many families are actually together physically only when they all choose to do some leisure time activity "as a family." Otherwise, everyone keeps separate hours, separate friends, separate pleasures. This is not a plea for family, but an observation that our sense of family grounds our social vision. My barber's story offers a strikingly different perception of family from the one I recall in my grandmother's accounts of the Depression. She saw the family as a productive unit and togetherness as the experiential glue that ensured economic survival. This perception has been largely replaced by a notion of family as a collection of leisure time consumers. The distinction is important, since the definition of collectivity that each entails gives rise to very different social visions. A sense of collectivity rooted in production is inherently socialist. It's a vision that expands out of the originary unit to embrace all of society by way of grasping the interrelatedness of peoples' productive labors and circumstances. On the other hand, when collectivity is articulated with consumption it redounds in free market capitalism. It may be haunted by the utopian desire for fully developed and vital community, but it is shackled to its anti-utopian antithesis, the "me first" thinking associated with the quick commodity fix.

The happy family is part of the Disney dreamscape. But for some vacationers, the experience is a nightmare. "I've seen four couples break up at Disney World. I'd never go there with my boyfriend." The undergraduate who interjected this dramatically negative note in a discussion that had previously highlighted all the pleasures of Disney World was not referring to families, but to her unmarried age-mates who had chosen Disney World for a fun-filled, romantic holiday. There was a moment of stunned silence followed by a wave of testimony to less than pleasurable experiences at the park. Students who had begun by offering their fondest memories said that the park could be quite stressful. Other recalled moments of boredom. The consensus was that no one's real vacation could ever live up to the hype. What capped our discussion just as class was about to end was a story of a Disney kidnapping. The image of a utopian playland that the students had originally constructed suddenly took on the shape of a dystopian reality: "My mother's friend was at Disney World. She was getting off a train or a tram. It was really crowded and she got separated from her little boy. She thought he was right behind her, but when she looked around on the platform she didn't see him anywhere. I guess she looked pretty frantic because a security guard came right up to her. He immediately asked if she had lost a child. When she said she had, he quickly led her to what must have been 'security central'—a room full of monitors showing the various exit points. They told her to look for her son on the screens. She saw him being carried out of the park slumped over a man's shoulder. He had been drugged, his hair was cut, and he was wearing a different shirt."

I couldn't believe it. I let my kids go all over the park alone with no more precaution than an agreed upon meeting place and time. The students were speechless. Then one piped up: "I think it happens a lot. Last summer I did an internship with *America's Most Wanted*. I was doing research for a show on kidnappings that occur in public places like malls. They had a file on Disney World. I didn't get to look at it, but there was clearly stuff in it."

My first reaction to these stories was to dwell on the illusion of safety that we tend to associate with private commercial places and the reality of extensive in-house security systems and personnel required to maintain the illusion. I don't know if I'm in the minority, but when I'm at Disney World I notice all those clean-cut, predominantly white, young male security people. Is it my countercultural training or their obvious communication devices that make them wear their plain clothes like New Age FBI agents? This line of reasoning is, however, dissatisfying. It goes no further than to underscore the inherent contradiction of policing utopia.

What on second thought I find more interesting about the nightmare stories is the way their existence demonstrates that Disney World is as much a construction of the imagination as it is a built and programmed environment. It can be both utopia or dystopia: "the happiest place on earth" or the site of broken romance and kidnapping. The truth of the stories is not at stake in the production of meaning as the cultural imaginary. The nightmare tales can as readily express community as the happy tales. In fact, all my narrative snapshots are haunted images, mass cultural renditions of the portrait of Dorian Gray. The ghostly subtext they reveal is the repressed desire for collectivity. It emanates out of all the constructions of family—whether this be the nuclear unit of the 50's Prime Time Cafe or the global family of the worldwide marketplace. Family includes the wish for collectivity as surely as it can never fully be its realization.

iT'S A

smAll

woRld

AFTER All

. . .

In my family,* the story goes that my sister's engagement was orchestrated by Disney. One autumn night, she and her partner placed themselves in Bistro de Paris, located somewhere in the middle of "France," one of eleven mini-countries of World Showcase circling the lagoon at Walt Disney World's EPCOT Center. Amidst its mirrored rooms and under the approving glances of both personnel and other customers, he proposed, she accepted—both foregone conclusions–as they toasted themselves on their mutual good taste. Just as they stepped out of the restaurant and onto the brick streets of "Paris," they were greeted by the music of the *1812 Overture* and the dancing lights of EPCOT's laser show, "IllumiNations." Walt Disney World had begun its nightly celebration above their heads and seemingly in their honor.

They remember this story fondly; we repeat it with affection. We don't, by the way, always do so with a straight face, though even the story's translation into farce retains something of its original intent. What we might regard as its hokeyness—especially the opportune beginning of the music and lights—becomes something else again in light of the fact that my sister and her husband, self-consciously or not, staged the scene of their engagement. His proposal was no surprise or secret. Though they had forgotten at the time that the laser show and music would begin, they certainly knew that it did so every night at that hour, and its beginning

*Jane Kuenz

then was only more delightful for their having forgotten it in the heat of the moment. They did not wait around for Tchaikovsky's canons and didn't need to in order to enjoy the effect; they had been there before, already knew the whole show, and could relish its resonance for them on this particular night without having actually experienced it. In effect, they chose EPCOT as the locale precisely because they knew it would structure their evening and provide for them its meaning: they had been in a "French restaurant"—in "France" no less: signs par excellence of heterosexual romance, while around them raged the lights and music reminiscent of *Love American Style.*

This vignette nicely illustrates the way people establish and affirm an identity by locating themselves within already existing social structures and the power relations they express. Disney is pretty good at providing such structures, less so at removing them. Here, the pleasure of their engagement—which, whatever else it may be, is fundamentally a pleasure of identifying oneself as heterosexual and presumably reproductive in a culture virulently approving of both—is integral to the pleasure of seeing themselves as part of the big show: music, lights, atmosphere, and the normative sexuality those elements combine to signify. It's too easy to call their experience fake; even designating it as clichéd misses the point. It wasn't false to them. My sister, for example, remains confident that hers is a sexual identity existing prior to Disney, rather than one produced there as another of its effects, and it is through that confidence—the allocation to a prior, interior, or essential self the traits of the social—that she knows herself as real. This fact, perhaps paradoxically, confirms the validity of her sense of identity rather than compromises it. In other words, my sister's gender and sexual identities are as real to her as any she can know; that they are in large measure defined and structured in relation to the representational, political, and economic needs of social formations already out there is an insight perhaps less apparent.

I'm overstating the case, of course; Disney isn't quite the sole magnanimous purveyor of social definition it would like to be, though it does repeat and magnify the dominant social formations it finds elsewhere. Indeed, this appears to be one of its main functions. My sister's experience in EPCOT was primarily one of recognition: recognizing the experience and its meaning constructed there as versions of the same she might find and probably has found throughout her life. In this context, each retelling of her story by my family—ritualized and formative as family

stories tend to be—becomes its own end, not just a reaffirmation of their commitment, nor just a reenactment of it. Every time we repeat it we participate again in a process of recognizing and confirming that ideological formation, the logic of its structures, and the pleasure that comes from locating oneself within them. Like it or not, we also recognize and affirm the penalties that come from refusing to.

What interests me about Disney is the way it functions in this process of recognition and identification and how out of that identification or—sometimes, though perhaps only rarely and even then unconsciously—against it, Disney produces a feeling we find pleasurable. This has required some work and a stretch of the imagination for me; I've never found Walt Disney World all that enjoyable, though living in Orlando and visiting the park has made it abundantly clear that others do. Indeed, about 13 million others do every year, visit the park, that is, and, if press releases are to be believed, enjoy that visit as well. It's worth asking, then, what we find there or, better, what we look for and how, in turn, what's found confirms for us an identity, the individuality of which is felt and made meaningful through its ties to the social and economic formations replicated in the park.

Besides the excruciatingly normative heterosexuality suggested in the above example and the strict gender roles attendant to it, Disney incites a kind of unexamined nationalism and a system of social relations based on consumption. These combine with lesser capitalist virtues conducive to "progress" to encourage the reproduction of subjects for life in what we are continually told is our future. It's important to insist that this is not a top-down process. No one is compelled at Disney to become anything, nor necessarily and definitively inscribed in one identity or another. While most of the pleasures to be had there require these identifications from us, the pleasure itself is something we produce in ourselves as we learn or recognize the nature of these roles and how to perform them adequately. This amounts to making the best of limited options, of course, because it is only through taking on these identities that we are allowed to participate at all in what Disney designates as our culture; refusing or failing to do so means being completely left out of the park's totalizing picture of "America" or the "future." The very process of acquiring these identities—consumer, national subject, heterosexual "family member"—reproduces power relations, specifically those of the dominant capitalist ideology that shaped them and made them interdependent in the first place.

In order, then, for Disney World, and especially EPCOT, to be successful—that is, for a trip there to be fun—the park's visitors must perform complex ideological maneuvers that allow them to see themselves in the representations of American life offered there, and to find those representations entertaining or, in Disney's words, instructive. As this is not a simple top-down process, neither is it necessarily a sure one. It's easy to spot those who come to Disney World just to make a point of their alienation from it. There aren't many, but they are there. What's harder to uncover is whether visitors refigure the requirements of these subject positions to fit the specifics of their own lives or evade them altogether without at the same time seeing themselves as fundamentally disqualified from the life shown in the park. I'm interested in both of these maneuvers: how the pleasure we feel at Walt Disney World is negotiated through an ongoing process of identification with and—at least in part, one hopes—evasion of the ideal subject constructed by Disney's tireless "Imagineers."

According to Guy Debord, one function of the spectacle is to make a culture forget itself—forget its own history, the questions it asks of itself in order to get from here to there, even its notions of what here and there

are and why we want or need to move between them.[1] Certainly Walt
Disney World participates in this process: free floating between a nostalgic past and an endless future of "progress"—though never quite touching
base in the present—Walt Disney World confronts its visitors with a
narrative of itself and invites us to see ourselves and our history in the
workings of its own. At EPCOT, this story is epical, an ongoing tale of
social advancement in which technology and its corporate sponsors are
both the agent and the product of the history it writes. The rest of us are
encouraged to look on, consume it visually, and take it home as such:
technological power as manifest destiny whose telos radically excludes
our direct participation, creativity, and control.

In this environment, whatever fantasy or desires one brings to the
park get co-opted and structured immediately by what's already there.
Throughout Disney World and especially at EPCOT, the various attractions showcasing what is supposed to be technology for the future tend to
advertise their wares in dramatic homilies to that which is. The only
potential objects for desire and fantasy in this arrangement are technology and a culture devoted to it. Each of the major attractions at Future
World documents variously the same unfolding story of steady and inevitable progress from some prehistory, a.k.a. "the dawn of time," toward "a
future of amazing technological creativity . . . of adventure and discovery . . . of awareness and understanding." The nominal form is not
accidental; one continually hears of this future of "creativity" and "understanding" without ever hearing who will create what or what will be
understood by whom. History is repeatedly read as the evolution of machines and, when unavoidable, the people whose lives are attached to
them and inevitably benefited thereby. The whole experience is rather
like watching the Gulf War at home, where our investment as citizens
with events taking place was consistently characterized by both the military and media in terms of the performance of our weapons. As one
survey conducted in the midst of the war indicated, more Americans
could identify Patriot and Scud missiles than they could Sadaam Hussein.
In EPCOT, it is this conversation, the sound of commodities talking to
each other, that the rest of us are invited to overhear.

And so in "The Land" we learn that "the land is our partner" and we
need to "listen to what it can teach us," the primary example of which is
computerized irrigation in the service of agribusiness, Kraft specifically,
whose "partnership" with various unpopulated and unspecified locales—

the rain forest, "the desert," even the moon, here made equal in kind—presumably teaches it how to get along and prosper. No relationship to the land other than commercial use by business is posited as possible or even desirable. In General Motor's "World of Motion," history follows a direct line of descent from "transportation" via empire to "freedom," assuring us that "[w]hen it comes to transportation, it's always fun to be free" and concluding, in case anyone missed the point, in an actual GM showroom with (live) sales representatives ready to show you how to buy freedom. It's too easy to pull out similar examples in other attractions: Exxon's "Universe of Energy" takes you through a prehistoric romp with the dinosaurs to some vague generality about a future void of oil spills and energy shortages somehow made possible without the use of solar power, while AT&T's "Spaceship Earth" traces the history of the world as the history of communication devices.

The conclusions to these tales of progress are always curiously left unspecified, perhaps as a sop to the "imagination" glorified throughout the park and the ostensible goal of its creation. Inevitably, though, people drop out of the picture and are replaced entirely by some technological wonder or simply the mystical speculation of it. The typical "ride"—one hesitates about what to call these—ends in some variation of total darkness, dazzling though equally blinding light, or the ubiquitous grid, all three presumably representative of a future of endless choices and possibilities in the "cityscapes" we are soon to inhabit. These are worlds where people literally cannot be represented, which is perhaps just as well since, given the direction the attractions take to that point, the sight could not be pretty: in the future everything will be done for us by technology and its purveyors, and we will dwell, no doubt, in "awareness" and "understanding" of that fact.

What we know now is that regardless of what new horizon these rides take us to, it will necessarily be "more complex" than what we have had and, consequently, "more exciting" in large part because it will provide "more choices." This, at least, is the explicit message of the Magic Kingdom's "Carousel of Progress" and the implicit message of most everything else in the park. Not only will all social relations be mediated by stuff—in "Carousel of Progress," a history of exploiting and then "freeing" women's labor is traced in the development of electrical appliances—but all of the problems facing this country and begging for its attention are seemingly solved solely by the range of goods that will be available to and for us.

Because the world according to Disney is so alienating and because in its historical narratives and predictions for the future we are so thoroughly secondary, any identification with these scenes necessarily takes place on the axis of consumption and use of the technological devices we do not appear to have any say in developing. In a world where everyone is identified as consumers, fantasy is either attached to commodities (the well-being of which supposedly defines our own) or supplanted altogether by "imagination" or—its correlative in the park—technical expertise, which is not our own either.

The fantasy of the Magic Kingdom is largely not of our making but that of the robots (both Disney's famed Audio-Animatronics and the equally uncanny human guides) who perform stories already scripted or accompany us down "lost" paths toward already discovered "hidden" surprises and sights. There's no better example of this than the Magic Kingdom's "Jungle Cruise," where lions and restless natives appear on cue and just as conveniently disappear. As Louis Marin points out, Disney "reduces the dynamic organization of places" to a "univocal scheme allowing only the same redundant behavior."[2] This is the case even on "Tom Sawyer's Island," where the winding, wooded trails and relative seclusion suggest more potential for freedom and discovery than it can actually provide: eventually all paths return you to Aunt Polly's Landing and her $1.50 glass of lemonade.

In the "hands-on" attractions of Future World's Communicore East and West, the pleasure of using new devices is offset by the fact that "use" consists mainly of momentary contact with machines created and otherwise run by someone else. The only really fun games at EPCOT are in "Journey into Imagination," and these are less "educational" or "adult" and more "for children": coloring on the wall with light, making music by stepping on different squares programmed to produce various sounds, looking through a giant kaleidoscope, conducting a computerized orchestra. Elsewhere, the computer games reproduce on a smaller scale the lessons of all the larger attractions. Though touted as educational and fun, most of them are a monumental bore: civics lessons or spiffier versions of the Home Shopping Network.[3] At the "Fountain of Information" we're told that "the next best thing to being there is shopping there" and subsequently presented with the technology to participate in an auction by satellite. "Home Smart Home" illustrates technological devices for the home of the future, presuming, I guess, that we'll all have one. One game tests your skill in planning flight paths and schedules for a major airline. Another asks you to deal with the complexities of manufacturing by assembling a United States flag from parts moving rapidly across a screen as the machine reminds you that "getting the right parts in the right places, that's manufacturing." Since it's difficult to successfully complete either of these tasks, the effect of both games is to impress us with the skill and wherewithal of the computers normally performing them. Beyond that, the point of the computer games is apparently to dazzle us with their access to information and powers of recall. You can "Dial an Expert" for generic answers to questions you haven't asked. You can type in your birthday and receive useless information based on specious assumptions: how many hours you've slept in your life, the number of meals you've eaten, how many tons of food. A game purporting to demonstrate research technology instead provides tourist promos for all fifty U.S. states and selected individual cities, Puerto Rico, and Guam.

Many of these games suffer from the same problem: they operate from a limited menu of options from which to choose and consequently grow tiresome once you realize you can't use them as a real research tool or helpful device. For example, in the game offering information on each state, it's impossible to get anything from certain areas: cities and coasts are OK; but if it's the upper Midwest you want to know about, forget it. In another, we're invited to make a music video, but rather than actually letting us do that, the screen requests choices for lead singer (white man, white woman, or black man), type of music, etc., and then constructs the finished video for us, usually to comic effect.

This is a far cry from Coney Island, where one could pay a few pennies to smash fake china and crystal in a mock-up of a typical high bourgeois Victorian parlor.[4] The games at Coney depended in part on the thrill of doing something you otherwise couldn't but may have wanted to: express openly an alienated and hostile relationship to commodities and the frustrations associated with a life in which you maybe had fewer of them. The barker proclaimed, "If you can't break up your own home, break up ours," perhaps missing the point that at least part of the desire was for the opportunity to break up other people's homes. The games at Disney, however, are much different: rather than providing opportunities to violate social proprieties, everything in the park is designed to confirm them and make doing so fun. This is done partly by turning what is now for many people a piece of technology associated not with creativity and personal use, but with the drudgery of wage-labor—the computer terminal—into an item of fun without at the same time significantly altering their actual relationship to it: as with data entry, one simply selects from a predetermined list of options and fills in the blanks accordingly. This attempt to convert everyday items and activities into "themed" fun is made throughout Disney World, often to the point of banality. What, for example, is the "fun" or "fantasy" of GM's showroom? Elsewhere the exciting new information we're given about our world or its future is either hopelessly outdated or already available from traditional sources. As we left the introductory film at "The Living Seas" and prepared to enter "Sea Base Alpha," a prototype of an undersea research facility, one man remarked to me only half in jest, "I could have stayed home with my *National Geographic.*" Either the technology we're shown is not new at all or exposure to it does not allow anyone to take information or experience from it to their own lives and see the transformative effects therein.

Perhaps the most significant difference between Disney World and earlier amusement parks is in opportunities for direct participation in the "events" and construction of their meaning. One of the chief motivations for visiting Coney and the primary focus of attacks against it was that the place was a relatively unregulated social setting. The rides encouraged, indeed required, close physical contact, frequently between strangers, and made the spectacle of their interaction the object of entertainment for other visitors waiting to board. Part of the fun of Coney was to watch people embarrass themselves, usually in some physical way—falling onto or being jostled against each other, clothes flying up, etc.—before becoming yourself the embarrassed object of their fun. The heightened sense of sexual opportunity inherent in this situation was augmented by the feeling throughout the park and confirmed by its visitors that it was always open season for dating, casual encounters, or sexual fantasy. If fantasy is one of several "lands" in Disney World, it was the norm at Coney Island. John Kasson documents examples of young women visiting Coney Island in the guise of bourgeois ladies rather than the mundane office or factory workers they were and, once there, either pursuing relationships befitting their new station or working a bit of class privilege on the men and women with whom they would otherwise be associated.[5]

At Walt Disney World, such contact with other people is only minimally available and not at all desirable. Most of the rides are intentionally designed to disallow seeing anyone—much less touching or talking to them—other than who you're sitting immediately next to and probably came with. (Those who visit the park alone, as I have, are typically kept separate and alone.) As Margaret King has noted, the vehicles turn on cue, focusing attention away from other people and toward whatever new screen or display is next in line. It is often impossible to see anything other than what the car's perspective affords, and the theater-like darkness reinforces the feeling that one is essentially watching a movie alone.[6] Consistent with the park's often noted goal of using architecture and layout to control and ultimately inhibit movement, all the attractions force visitors to watch the programmed movements of Audio-Animatronic robots while remaining themselves immobilized.

This is given a new twist at the new Disney-MGM Studios, where video screens punctuate every turn in the lines and direct the attention of waiting visitors away from each other (and any possible exchanges or flirting they might engage in) and toward one "adformational" piece or another. If you're waiting in line for twenty-five minutes, you might see the same chatty narration four or five times. The people in lines at MGM resemble those in photographs of theater audiences decked in 3-D glasses. The common perspective created by the glasses and screen produces in the audience the same posture and tilt of the head: up, away, slightly out of kilter. The effect is both to limit the movement of many people and to regularize it, to take a basically stationary experience and make it even more so—everyone manages to look, perhaps paradoxically, both mass-produced and bovine. At least some people are aware of this; as we plowed our way forward in the line for "The Great Movie Ride," eyes upturned to the trusty video screen, one young man intoned in a mock-serious voice, "No mooing please, no mooing."

Where active audience participation is incorporated into the show, it's minor, kept out of focus, and finally beside the point. A family is selected to be Honorary Grand Marshals of one of the Magic Kingdom's parades—they wave absently from their seat at the front of a float, effectively kept from seeing the parade, which is unfortunate for them since the parades at Disney are among the best events there. In Tomorrowland Theater, members of the audience are pulled on stage, dressed in Disney shirts and Roger Rabbit ears, and then virtually ignored. The awful big dance numbers continue around them as they try to follow the steps. This would be similar to the use of other people's embarrassment as part of the ride at Coney except that nothing is really made of them by the cast; there is no

fun either with them or at their expense. From the audience's perspective, it's too easy just to ignore them because they aren't integrated into the show and because it's more fun to watch Mickey, Minnie, Roger, and the rest than to watch any of the dancers, professional or otherwise. In MGM Studios, this happens again when kids from the audience are selected for a reshooting of a scene from *Honey, I Shrunk the Kids:* the actual antics of them pretending to fly on a giant bug are ignored, and everyone watches instead the omnipresent screen where their flight has been rendered realistically. What we're supposed to be watching and enjoying is not our children having fun, but the technology of film production.

This lack of genuine participation at Disney in any capacity other than viewer mirrors our lack of participation both in the future we're told is always just around the corner and in the computer games, the mechanics of which prepare us for life in it. Moreover, any erotic potential inherent in an amusement park environment is channeled at EPCOT into consumption as well, either of these images of the future and the technology required to produce it or of the merchandise actually sold in the park. If we find these attractions and games pleasurable—at least in terms of the pleasure they are courting—then we are assuming the world they present as given, which in turn requires identifying ourselves in it in the only role available: technology's beneficiary, its grateful consumer. Because failing or resisting identification as consumers results in absenting ourselves from the "future," what we're buying is time in it. Refusal to do so reveals the true horror of that future and leaves us no recourse to illusions; we either identify as consumers, or we're just left out. Any other investments we may have in ourselves, individually or collectively, have to be ignored or forgotten.

The horror and dreariness of this future is reconciled for many of the park's visitors by the only thing that seems to counter it: a past, a place in the community life it narrates, and the opportunity to identify with variously inflected values such as those personified along the walls of "American Adventure"—individualism, innovation, freedom, independence, pioneering. This compensation is built into the structure of EPCOT Center, where Future World and the nostalgic past of World Showcase face each other across the lagoon of time.[7] Elsewhere in Disney, one is compensated by embracing a past that is relentlessly American, by which Disney means the United States. Some attractions are devoted entirely to making U.S. citizens feel good about themselves and their history in order to offset what has to be ambivalence about their future and quite possibly their present. In the Magic Kingdom these include "American Journeys," "Hall of Presidents," and all of Frontierland; in EPCOT, the "American Adventure"—the only "country" allowed to have an actual government—sits in the center of World Showcase, making itself the organizing principle of the whole "world."

In a period of intense cynicism about the possibility of change or improvement in the lives of United States citizens and doubts that the present political system could effect change even if it wanted to—a period, that is, like the current one—the attractions of Disney's brand of American history are not hard to miss. Visitors are allowed to identify with and imagine themselves as participants in a form of government with whose processes they still have direct contact and in whose decisions they still have some stake. The reenactment of the Lincoln and Douglas debates in the "Hall of Presidents," complete with heckling and serious questions to the candidates from the assembled crowd, is a stark contrast to current elections in which democratic participation exists primarily in the form of opinion polls. Beyond this, the historical attractions at Disney allow us to identify with a time of past achievement, when there was still a frontier to conquer and Indians to fight. In the modern period we have to settle for symbolic victories: the last image in the film at "American Adventures" is the winning goal in the 1980 Olympic hockey match when the U.S. finally gets to beat Russia. The rest of the 1980s do not appear in any form anywhere in Disney World. The only suggestion of our latest "victory" is EPCOT's new daytime outdoor show, "Surprise in the Skies" which, with its numerous kites flying in formation and aerial fireworks with their accompanying blasts and smoke, can't help but resemble the screen version of the bombing of Baghdad. Perhaps more than anything, these shows stress the importance of national "unity," how we got it, how to keep it. We are encouraged to identify with claims of national unity in a period in which the lack of it can no longer be covered over except ideologically.

In "American Journeys," the tour of the country beginning in New York and continuing to the Rockies attempts to capture the diversity of American life and culture only in the end to negate them by reducing us all to a common "love of the land" and respect for NASA. Our various stories, even that of the Native American voice recounting the migration of his people over Alaska, are subordinated to the grand narrative of American life told in words and images. As the solemn narrator explains that "Americans have always known how to have a good time together, and they know how to work together too," the images on the 360° screen shift from small children building sand castles to bigger people building bombers, what looks like a navy carrier, and finally the space shuttle. Lest anyone still has doubts, at Walt Disney World the space shuttle is clearly an extension of the military and its weapons. All the different kinds of play and work in the first part of the film—musicians at a bluegrass festival and Preservation Hall, sports activities in the West, children swimming, farmers—are subsumed to these later images of our common work.

The importance of securing "unity" is made explicit in the "Hall of Presidents," where the history of the presidency is told as a history of quelling domestic rebellion in the interest of solidifying federal authority. But while Washington is discussed with reference to the Whiskey Rebellion and Jackson and Lincoln in terms of the threat of secession and the actual war, more recent presidents escape this scrutiny: Johnson and Nixon are passed over without notice, and the Vietnam War—at home and abroad—is represented here as elsewhere by the white crosses of Arlington. Other popular movements to secure genuine unity—the Civil Rights movement, for example—are emptied of their subversive potential and ranked in the same category as the Wright brothers, Thomas Edison, and other figures crucial in the period of "amazing achievement" which, though it followed the Civil War, was somehow unconnected to Reconstruction. Apparently, the possibility of domestic disharmony existed only in the past, where it was effectively laid to rest. This show also ends with NASA, here made to represent our freedom "to explore new dimensions of our universe," and a reminder about internal divisiveness: danger, says Lincoln, "cannot come from abroad; it must spring up among us."[8] One assumes this is a warning, not advice.

Unlike these attractions, the more recent "American Adventure" pavilion in EPCOT actually tries to highlight some of the struggles in U.S. history that had racial, sexual, and ethnic difference at their core. Chief Joseph, Susan B. Anthony, and Frederick Douglass all have their say, and, while this is sometimes in the actual words each had used in speech or print, abstracting their words from the context in which they were made effectively neutralizes the acknowledgment of difference intended by their inclusion. Douglass, for example, extols the virtues of Harriet Beecher Stowe's *Uncle Tom's Cabin*. This is something he might have done in public for highly strategic reasons, but the truth is Douglass was ambivalent, to say the least, about Stowe's book and wrote his own "The Heroic Slave" in large part to counter her portrayal of black heroism. The irony of his inclusion in this way is that the very terms of his debate with her are ignored as he becomes representative of her model for political action. This problem is minor, though, compared to the more general one of a historical narrative loosely constructed out of isolated events and figures. Franklin and Twain narrate a story of American history whose plot charts our progress in learning how "to speak with one voice." In spite of its nod to difference, "American Adventure" implicitly and sometimes explicitly equates multiplicity and ethnic diversity with political chaos; hence our "adventure" has been to overcome our differences and become the same. "We built America," Franklin says, "and the process made us Americans, a new breed. In time we became more alike than we were different."

This would be fine, perhaps even a good thing, if, as with all the talk about our freedom ("free to speak, to worship as we please, to enjoy the fruits of our labor") it did not have what Theodor Adorno called "the embarrassing quality of impotent reassurance."[9] One doesn't have to be in Disney World too long before beginning to wonder why it is that we have to be always reminded of how free we are. The reminders are so frequent and vociferous that they approach the status of injunction: You are free, the robots exhort, get to it. But when faced with the prospect of deciding what we should be getting to now that we're free, suggestions are not forthcoming, and we're left with the suspicion that, in the park and quite possibly everywhere else, freedom can be manifested "only ideologically, as talk about freedom."[10] Much the same can be said about our vaunted unity. We do not speak with one voice now and never have, and while it is a truism to say that even the most diverse Americans are more alike than different, what unites us as far as this culture is concerned is our status as consumers. The point, finally, is not that differences no longer exist, but that under global capitalism they no longer *matter*. What's important is the unity and equality we've ostensibly achieved in the marketplace, which, as we've learned in EPCOT, is synonymous with history itself. What, then, does unity look like? It looks like EPCOT Center, like NASA, like the future.

It also looks like the nuclear family. If consumption and unity are Disney's favorite models for inclusion, a compulsive heterosexuality in the service of reproduction is its chief fetish. This is particularly true of EPCOT, where one continually rounds the corner to discover another remarkably similar grouping of mom, dad, and miscellaneous kids living under water, in space, in the desert—all versions of a domestic world that does not exist for many U.S. citizens, yet appears as though it continues unchanged by the otherwise drastic alterations in living conditions made possible by technological "growth." No one asks, by the way, why we would want or, more likely, have to live under water: at EPCOT, the future is simply presented; the social mechanisms producing it and the social consequences thereof are not. And if this aspect of the future resembles its current manifestation, then we can only assume that maintaining monogamous reproductive heterosexuality as "normal" serves some interest other than our own. While it is certainly no secret that capitalism depends in part on regulating sexual identity, fantasy, and desire, what needs to be understood is how it does so and how that process is re-enacted in the park.

I opened this essay with the thesis that the main source of pleasure at Disney World is a process of recognizing dominant ideological structures and identifying with the role we've been assigned in them. The park allows us space only as consumers and offers a revamped history intended to offset any qualms about that situation by tracing its lineage in various stories of our past and thus showing its obvious and inevitable correctness. As Susan Willis notes, it is the family—both as a single unit and as a collection of individually differentiated tastes or styles—that is the focus of this consumption and of all the park's efforts to induce it. The differences inherent in any of the above scenes of family life on new but parallel "horizons" dissolve into the same image of maximized consumption suited up for different environments.

As the most important unit of consumption, the family *as family* is recognized throughout the park and, indeed, other social groupings are literally not acknowledged and certainly not condoned. Human adults do not exist in Disney World except as parents. In "Tomorrowland Theater" the chorus tells us that "Disney World is a wonderland for girls and boys and moms and dads." This is in fact an accurate observation about Disney; as with the prescribed role of consumer, you either identify with the designation as child or parent, or the wonderland is not for you. This is implicit in all the attractions in EPCOT and is sometimes reinforced, as in "Horizons," by a husband and wife team of narrators whose banter is recognizable from situation comedies. Even the American Civil War is represented in "American Adventure" in terms of split families, literally a torn photograph—one son sent north, the other gone south. In the pre-show for Michael Jackson's "Captain EO," Kodak sponsors an extended advertisement for itself in which a miscellany of cute baby photographs gives way to a heterosexual plot of courting, marriage, and eventually more baby shots. Human reproduction is concurrent with the reproduction of capitalist subjects.

If, as Judith Butler says, gender is a "ritual social drama" that produces heterosexuality as a prediscursive or natural category, then one can see and take part in this theater throughout Disney.[11] The relentless parade of happy couples and families in the park's attractions is the necessary product of the equally relentless gendering of everything in them. Although Disney has taken pains to avoid obvious stereotyping by putting women in astronaut suits and at least one man in an apron, there can be no mistaking who is really supposed to be wearing what. Sometimes the effect is patently ludicrous: in the "Kitchen Kabaret," one "Bonnie Appetite," a Loni Anderson look-alike and the only feminine Audio-Animatronic allowed to narrate an entire show, confronts the audience in apron and fishnets and proceeds to preach the benefits of the four food groups. Other times, the result is just predictable: of the various civic virtues personified along the walls of "American Adventure," "compassion" is represented by a woman and "tomorrow" by a woman holding a baby. In the "Jungle Cruise," part of the scripted adventure is to watch the male guide single out young women on the boat and play the protector to their presumed need for it. This is done as entertainment for the rest of the boat's passengers and presumably the women themselves. When I complained in a letter to Disney about the latter, the written response was simply that the ride had always been popular.

And popular they all are. As in the story of my sister's engagement, at least part of this popularity has to come from witnessing the repeated validation of choices already made. It's not necessary that everyone see themselves completely in the kind of June and Ward Cleaver domesticity privileged at Disney, only that they recognize the standard and orient themselves around it. What we call "individuality" is that which is produced in this process of orientation: a combination of conformity to and deviation from a standard we otherwise treat as given and, to the extent that it functions as such, virtually is. Because one effect of this process is the gendering of people, which, by definition, is the means of their inclusion in the order of the sexual, acquiring proper gender is roughly synonymous with socialization itself.[12] This is probably particularly true for women whose bodies are already the site of multiple discourses, most of which claim that the individualization of women is virtually indistinguishable from their construction as sexed beings. If gender and sexuality can never be extrahistorical, then neither can the pleasures or desires we feel from them, which isn't to say that they are false, only that they exist and develop in relation to social formations and the discourses around them.

The integrity and coherence of this system of gendering and sexualizing people are maintained in part by having always present, but clearly peripheral or masked, the differences excluded to secure it, and it is often in these differences that you find the closest thing to eroticism or real sexuality in the park. Otherwise, it's just not there. The parade of happy families in EPCOT is constant, but one can't help but wonder whence they all came since, while heterosexual relationships certainly exist, sexuality itself does not. Walt Disney was ruthless in his attempts to purge his parks and films of any vestiges of actual sex, even to the point of discontinuing an early line of Mickey and Minnie watches because the face illustrated the two in an embrace. In spite of the sexlessness of most of the park—the absolutely unerotic character of its shows and attractions—or perhaps because of it, Walt Disney World is now the number one honeymoon destination in this country and may soon be also the number one site for marriages: Disney plans to open an on-site "wedding pavilion" where, for anywhere from $17,000 to $100,000, couples can say their vows in the shadows of Cinderella's Castle.[13]

Actual instances of eroticism tend to pop up as differences or exceptions, usually projected onto a variety of others who qualify as such by virtue of race, species, or, in the case of Michael Jackson, galaxy. The Magic Kingdom is much less subject to EPCOT's strictures primarily because of its closer ties to the earlier Disney cartoons in which gender and sexuality were transposed onto animal characters where they were, if not completely transformed, at least complicated somewhat beyond the usual models. One can see the Auntie Mame factor operating in a lot of them: miscellaneous characters of different ages and different species, distantly related, if at all, living together in roughly drawn communal units with not a mom or dad in sight. People have reminisced fondly to

me about childhood visits to the park and experiencing there a near-constant feeling of excitement, delighting not just in the park's vibrant primary colors and sense of constant activity (which to me felt, frankly, like disorientation), but also in the thrill of seeing, touching, and talking to the life-sized Disney cartoon characters. One boy's reaction to the recent *Beauty and the Beast* may illustrate what these characters represent for children: he liked the movie, he said, but was sorry it had such a sad ending. When asked why this conclusion—the quintessential happy ending—was sad, he said because "everybody turns back into real people."[14]

It is not clear to me yet the extent to which Disney World's conglomeration of exoticized, but also colonized, locales functions in a similar way in the psyches of the park's visitors. I can only assume that at some level it must. The history of colonialism has made abundantly clear the uses to which the colonized body can be put beyond mere exploitative labor: as a projection, for example, of the unorthodox or unacknowledged desires of the colonizers, which may be complicated by the position of the colonizer relative to his or her own culture. In EPCOT one can visit "Morocco" and "Mexico"; the Magic Kingdom offers the convenience of Adventureland where all exotic others are gathered under one tent: the tropics, a safari, the Caribbean, the "Dark Continent." Plans are already in the works for a new pavilion at EPCOT for equatorial Africa.

Since Africa now exists at Disney only in the barest of signifiers—a totem pole surrounded by the music of drums marks the future site of the pavilion—its eventual full-fledged appearance may make manifest what the others now only hint at: the use and enjoyment of other cultures, particularly of those whose representation in the park is primarily colonial, as the site for sexual fantasies and desire otherwise unavailable or unrepresented.

Unavailable, that is, with the possible exception of Michael Jackson's "Captain EO" in Kodak's "Journey into Imagination." With its cyborgian transformations, whipping scene, and Jackson himself, "Captain EO" is the most prominent example of gender bending and alternative sexuality allowed in the park, though, as is typical with Jackson, the motives and message of that inclusion are conflicted. Accompanied by his crew of ungendered companions, Captain EO must bring a gift (music or imagination, it's hard to tell) to the supreme leader of another planet. This leader is part woman, part machine, part Medusa; she is vaguely spiderlike, composed of wires from the waist down, and has a nasty temper. His "gift" effectively transforms her into a "normal" woman—Angelica Houston, in fact, a "movie star"—in a slinky dress who promptly comes on to him as the planet around her turns into what looks like an old *Star Trek* set: Greek columns in the middle of natural abundance attended by well-built men and women of uncertain tastes. What's odd about this is that, while she reenacts the Sleeping Beauty plot—transformed at first kiss—Jackson himself gets to remain as weird as ever; apparently he has the continuing mission to restore normative gender and sexual roles wherever he goes while remaining himself unaffected by them.

While a number of things might account for the show's popularity—Coppola's direction, for one thing, and an alternative version of the future, recognizable from recent science fiction films, as mechanical and ugly—it is finally our fascination with Michael Jackson that draws us to it. Although it's difficult to call him subversive, Jackson does stick out in Disney World, to say the least, as the locus of gender and sexual difference that hasn't yet been completely co-opted in the way certain gay cultural practices have been. (In the Magic Kingdom's Surprise Celebration Parade, for example, dancers in modified Mardi Gras costumes vogue at the feet of a forty-foot Donald Duck.) But Jackson is on display not to demonstrate imagination, but to be it. All other representations of imagination elsewhere in the park—dandelions and clouds—pale beside him. It is he and the pastiche of sexual and gender definitions he represents that are the attraction, the wonder, the piece of exotica we're invited to peruse. That such is not just allowed but actually showcased— "Captain EO" is one of the more popular attractions in EPCOT and promoted accordingly—is the result of Jackson's status as the commodified form of "imagination" itself. "Captain EO" is the centerpiece of Kodak's "Journey in Imagination," but Jackson's placement there seems less a testament to his powers of imagination than to his condition as embodiment of everyone else's. Finally, because his position is treated as an exception defining the norm, even the potential fantasies circulating around Michael Jackson are felt and lived only in the negative.

This could be said of all the experiences outlined above; they are negative pleasures, wrought from the intricacies of hope and denial. They are also known as making the best of a bad situation. I don't want to underestimate the reality of these feelings as pleasurable; identifying with a dominant ideology and the role it assigns us has long been the source of a lot of happiness for many people. I'm also not comfortable with simply calling this false consciousness. In a culture that has systematically and ruthlessly cut short options and redefined them on the model of consumption and in the absence of a genuinely broad-based and alternative model to counter it, one embraces whatever roles are available. Success or pleasure become, then, playing it to the fullest. This, of course, is all very convenient for Disney World, since its attractions and shows combine to encourage the kind of subject it needs to ensure its own success: what better place to start buying than in the park?

As for avoiding or revamping this position, I'm reminded of several incidents that occurred during my visits to Disney. The first was the presence of groups organized by some criteria other than relation. Disney is populated almost entirely by families: people arrive at the park as families and generally do everything there together—eat, watch the shows, tour the grounds, shop, and leave. I saw two exceptions to this. One was a group of seriously displaced skinheads. Walking around in high urban mode—boots, black leather, pale skin—they seemed genuinely at a loss as to how to do the park without betraying themselves. The best they could produce was to convert specific areas into their own urbanlike space: instead of resting or eating at designated tables and benches, they would stretch out on stone walls or steps, self-consciously refusing to sit where they were supposed to. They did not, however, do this on the steps

leading up to Cinderella's Castle, where they would be a real hindrance to traffic flow, but off to the side, by themselves, safely avoiding any openly disruptive behavior.

The second exception to the families-only rule was girl-groups. These were not spring break revelers in from the beaches for the day, but younger girls—thirteen or fourteen—old enough to know the pressures of the park's gender and sexual definitions and young enough to not yet feel compelled to fulfill them. They traversed the park in varying numbers, usually five to seven, and in general were the most uninhibited people there. This was true even compared to younger children, who one expects to make scenes. Waiting in the long line for "Space Mountain," they brushed and arranged their own and each other's hair—a species of eroticism, not vanity—composed and sang songs, played what they will later discover are drinking games, and in one case planned revenge on "the biggest sexist in the class." This later was a joke prepared for the next school day about the "miracle birth" at a local hospital: a baby born with a penis *and* a brain. Elsewhere they demanded attention from whomever they could get it—posing elaborately for strangers' photographs, calling attention to one girl's birthday, and compelling the crowd assembled for the start of the midday parade to sing "Happy Birthday" to her.

This kind of behavior may be characteristic of girls at this age generally; it certainly was of me. Perhaps it is also a function of their sexually exclusive groups. The presence of men or boys with young women only slightly older had the disquieting result of rendering them silent or bland. Perhaps it is also a liberating effect of the park's otherwise total exclusion of them. Throughout Disney, the perspective through which we are asked to see the world is almost exclusively male. Most of the attractions are narrated by men, or the narratives they construct are explicitly from a man or boy's point of view. "Cranium Command" discusses the human brain by taking us inside that of a twelve-year-old boy. A film about the workings of the imagination begins with a group of children of both genders and various races playing in the grass, but focuses again on the (white) boy to develop its themes. The same move takes place in the Kodak film relating reproduction to photography: it begins with photographs of all kinds of babies, but shifts to the white boy, then the adult man, to tell the story. Beyond images of children, African Americans pop up in attractions only irregularly and then strategically. And while black women appear in several places, adult black men are rare. But it is young girls of any color who are the most absent party in all of the attractions at Disney. Their lives, activities, and thoughts are simply not represented except by implication or analogy. Rather than leave them out, however, this oversight seems to have freed them up. Perhaps one of the bigger shocks at Disney for the uninitiated is how few people actually appear to be having a good time. While either patiently waiting in line, methodically making their way between lands, or staring stony faced at one extravaganza or another, many people just look anxious or bored. These girls, for whatever reason, were immune to boredom; they were the happiest people I saw.

One other story: In "Germany" I met a woman seated on one of the outdoor benches, drinking a Coke, doing nothing. This is itself a mark of difference at Disney World; all guidebooks to the park reiterate the importance of careful planning so as to see and do everything, with the consequence that most everyone looks slightly frazzled. But this woman was using the park her own way. A resident of Orlando, she has a year pass to Disney World and comes to the park frequently, particularly to EPCOT's World Showcase. "I enjoy coming out alone," she says. "I come out alone quite often and people watch. You never know who you'll run into. There are people here from everywhere." It is likely she bought the Coke in the park, and it is also likely that she might otherwise identify with the consumer model everywhere on display, but she did not have to participate as a consumer to enjoy herself. In fact, she made this explicit:

"I just wander around, and I don't have to buy anything." The irony, of course, is that the luxury of being in the place without having to "buy anything" is itself purchased annually for $190—the price of a year-round ticket.

On this occasion, she was using the park the same way many people use a mall: as an open and seemingly public space where one can go and take part, or not, in the activities for which it is ostensibly designed. Anyone who has been in a mall lately knows the number of people of all ages and types who are there for reasons quite other than shopping, only one of which is people watching. This is part of John Fiske's argument (after Michel de Certeau and ultimately Henri Lefebvre)[15] that since the site of surveillance and control is no longer production but consumption, we should look for oppositional social practices in how people actually use the culture they're given, ignore what of it they don't or can't get, and remake the balance. While one can still claim, as many have, that "poaching" and other guerrilla tactics intended to subvert a culture of buying only reinvent it for a new generation by confirming again the centrality of consumption, the accuracy of that conclusion is perhaps in direct proportion to its limitations.

Consider her preference for World Showcase: this hardly seems accidental, nor does the fact that she prefers to go alone. Besides "Germany," she usually stops by "France" for a "fix." In his guide to the park, Steve Birnbaum warns his readers they won't find the "real" countries at EPCOT Center, only their "essence, much as a traveler returning from a visit might remember what he or she saw."[16] What he means is what he or she might have bought. In EPCOT the eleven countries—Western Europe and miscellaneous allies, although one anticipates the inevitable introduction of some conglomerate of Soviet states—are signified by culturally specific, generally clichéd, but usually marketable attributes. All the countries are finally defined by where you can shop or what you can buy. Disney training manuals are quite explicit about this: "World Showcase represents what people would expect to find on their travel rather than what they actually will see in a given country's shops."[17] Hence, rather than tripe, "France" roughly equals perfume and makeup, wine, baked goods, Impressionism, prostitutes, and dancers on the model of Toulouse-Lautrec (the latter are not for sale; they're part of the "essence").

On the one hand, this woman was well aware of the distance between the actual Germany and the statue of St. George in the center of the pavilion. "If you're into reality," she said, "this is not a good place to be.

I don't deal with reality, so I'm right at home." On the other hand, she knew that this was not quite the whole story. The above comment was followed immediately with an abrupt conclusion: "Of course, that's not true either." The point, I think, is that she is very much "into reality," and so her willingness to enjoy the fake indicates not a readiness just to make do with an available copy—much less a preference for it—but a passionate desire for the real thing and a stark awareness that the circumstances of her own life make it unavailable. Perhaps this real thing is the kind of communal values enshrined at World Showcase though effectively eliminated from it. Or perhaps it is just a place cut off from the domestic and work-related pressures she feels subject to. She told me that coming to EPCOT is "like going into another world. You can go out and hide. The phone won't ring. Nobody will want me." Perhaps even the real Germany to which EPCOT's copy refers is itself significant to her not in its own right but in its status as representative of a host of other things: travel, for example, or the changes in her life that would either make travel possible or the desire for it unnecessary—another job or no job at all, a different cultural background, a different life.

I'm making this point in part to counter what seems to me a continuing trend in critiques of Disney's brand of postmodern simulation—and perhaps it has slipped into my own—to degrade visitors to the park and cast them as an unreflective band of consumers eager to enjoy the benefits of a simulated world. Disney may very well be an example of Baudrillard's "techno-luminous cinematic space of total spatio-dynamic theater,"[18] but if we are to understand the desires that are exploited there and begin to find other ways of fulfilling them, then glib generalizations just won't do. For all the talk in the park about opportunities for fantasy and imagination, this woman's story is the best instance of it I found, and where there is genuine fantasy, there is also at some level acknowledgment of the problems that fantasizing seeks to overcome and the potential for doing so. While we might shake our heads at her sitting in EPCOT rather than actively working to change her life, at what appears to be complacency in spite of self-knowledge, at the fact that Disney is still, even in negation, the model by which she shapes and understands her own fantasies, we cannot, for her sake and ours, ignore the extent of her desires or the self-consciousness with which she is pursuing them. For the distances Disney World purports to take her are finally not that great, and if her world is small now, living in this world can only make it smaller.

STORY

TIME

· · ·

From then on, men and machines can proliferate. It is even their law to do so—which the automatons never have done, being instead sublime and singular mechanisms. Men themselves only started their own proliferation when they achieved the status of machines, with the industrial revolution. Freed from all resemblance, freed even from their own double, they expand like the system of production, of which they are only the miniaturized equivalent.—Jean Baudrillard

Mechanical dolls were an invention of bourgeois culture. Ironically, if playing with dolls was originally the way children learned the nurturing behavior of adult social relations, it has become a training ground for learning reified ones. The goal of little girls now is to become a "doll." This reversal epitomizes that which Marx considered characteristic of the capitalist-industrial mode of production: Machines which bring the promise of the naturalization of humanity and the humanization of nature result instead in the mechanization of both.—Susan Buck-Morss

In his masterful study of Walt Disney, Richard Schickel claims that pacing is what Disney could do well. Unable to draw—he had to be taught the Disney "signature" and even how to do a quick sketch of Mickey Mouse for autograph seekers—he was supposedly brilliant at making decisions about the plots of his films.[1] From "Pirates of the Caribbean" to "Splash Mountain," it is precisely the plot or narrative sequence that is most often pointed to as the distinguishing characteristic of the rides in the Magic Kingdom. The Disney enthusiasm for storytelling gets expressed in several aspects of the resorts: as Scott Bukatman has noted, the

forced perspective architecture, the walkways, the themed costumes of the "cast members" are all an attempt to place the "guest" into narratives.[2] It is impossible to escape interpolation at one's hotel, restaurant, ride, or shop since each is essentially a themed backdrop against which one is invited to act out roles scripted by many small stories. The overall experience is of a three-dimensional cinematic event that includes processions, sets, costumes, sound effects, and props.

The use of narrative at the parks has changed over time, however, and this has more than a little to do with both the death of Walt Disney and the influence of postmodernism. In what Hal Foster calls its "neoconservative" vein, postmodernism hails "a return to narrative, ornament and the figure. This position is often one of reaction, but in more ways than the stylistic—for also proclaimed is the return to history (the humanist tradition) and the return of the subject (the artist/architect as *auteur*)."[3] Foster distinguishes this nostalgic postmodern reaction from what he terms "poststructuralist postmodernism," which is "profoundly anti-humanist" and, one could say, antirealist. Disney's vision is of course more akin to a humanist postmodernism—to a dependence upon some version of history, however incomplete and bowdlerized it might be—and an antimodernist aesthetics. His active dislike of modernist abstraction was demonstrated on the occasion of his seeing a Soviet cartoon in the 1930s that consisted of purposely flattened and skewed figures. At the conclusion of the film he could not help but exclaim, "Jesus Christ, you want me to make pictures like that?"[4] The Disney studios in California went on to make ever-more naturalistic realism their goal and, indeed, Disney was originally the Ibsen of the cartoon, without the social commentary, in that he brought the technological refinements necessary for realism to a medium that was, until his innovations, unable to be anything but unrealistic. Once achieved, the Disney brand of realism had to be protected from further innovations. Realism was the prize; Disney could not abide any other goal: every leaf must quiver and every blade bend in a Disney movie. The same obsession is evident in Disneyland. He continued to tinker with the park until he died, but his pet project was the creation of the Audio-Animatronic automatons that he first introduced in the form of the "Enchanted Tiki Birds" at Disneyland and which the Disney Imagineers continue to make new generations of today. Not robots, simply the perfection of the human-miming puppet, these creations are the embodiment of Jean Baudrillard's idea of hyperreality in their extension of a naive realist aesthetic:

The hyperreal represents a much more advanced phase [of realism], in the sense that even [the] contradiction between the real and the imaginary is effaced. The unreal is no longer that of dream or of fantasy. . . . To exit from the crisis of representation, you have to lock the real up in pure repetition.[5]

Yet as a metonymy for the goals of the park's design, the implications of this meeting of aesthetics and technology are much graver than one might think, since they represent the insidious aspects of realism as it is deployed in the park: "The only weapon of power, its only strategy [is] to reinject realness and referentiality everywhere, in order to convince us of the reality of the social . . . and the finalities of production."[6]

Walt Disney's investment is still jealously guarded (as are his eccentric wishes that a train always surround the Magic Kingdom because he loved model trains, that men who work at the park have 1950s-era haircuts, etc.) and embalmed in each new replication of the Magic Kingdom. "Realism"—even in its postmodern versions—continues to pay, even though the Disney "real" continues to rest on the myth that we all strive to be wealthy, WASPish, and white. Now global in its reach, the hyperreal space of the Magic Kingdom exists as an "innocent" antithesis to Le Corbusier's desire for a modernist utopia like the Ville Contemporaine, Plan Voisin, or Ville Radieuse. With the opening of EPCOT Center in 1982, however, a new paradigm was introduced: a futuristic space that unabashedly bathes itself in retro-aesthetics, hyperconservative ideology, and imperialist iconography.

"Do you know what 'E.P.C.O.T.' stands for? 'Experimental Polyester Clothes of Tomorrow.'"—Tram driver at the EPCOT Center

What does one do with EPCOT? As Steve Birnbaum's guide to Disney World notes, the Magic Kingdom's "Tomorrowland offers a picture of the future that is a little less than wonderful, since the architecture looks a bit too much like yesterday's version of Tomorrow."[7] In fact, the Anaheim Tomorrowland was unfinished at the time of the park's opening in 1955 and has been updated many times since then;[8] at the Orlando Tomorrowland the simulated space flight to the moon has become the "Mission to Mars." The Disney Company has had to make frequent changes to its futuristic sections and is currently planning the most extensive upgrades so far: the Tomorrowland section at Walt Disney World will soon become "an intergalactic space port for arriving aliens," and Future World, one of the two main sections of EPCOT, is also slated for improvement.[9] Perhaps it is not surprising, then, that at the recently opened EuroDisney, Tomorrowland has been renamed Discoveryland since the future, as a theme, has caused Disney more problems than any other. As an indirect critique of the present, the future easily catches up with Disney: it is a much more difficult place to hide one's agenda than the past. If the Disney future is in need of frequent revising, then might there be a problem with its thinking about the present? Why, one must wonder, would Disney decide to create EPCOT, a billion-dollar version of their weakest resort creation in the first place? And now that it exists, how can it ever be anything but an obsolescent view of the future? Of course, it exists in part because Walt Disney willed it—almost literally. Before his death (or freezing, whichever occurred) he envisioned the 28,000-acre Florida property as containing not only the Magic Kingdom but also an entire city encased in a dome and consisting of homes and a city center with showcases for leading-edge capitalist-developed technology and products from around the world: an Experimental Prototype Community of Tomorrow. What resulted over twenty years after his death was another resort park whose characteristics resemble a conventionalized rendering of only the city center part of his plan. Instead of a capitalist beacon of hope and opportunity, it is an urban simulacrum whose goals seem to be not to thrill or entertain, but to sell things and distract as many (or bore as few) people as possible in a given day. Disney's dream of a city may yet be realized to some extent in the Celebration project—a town where houses will be wholly owned by Disney. But the futuristic present that he imagined has been transformed into a digital theme park of hands-on computer games (Communicore), corporate narratives of impossible futures (Future World), and second-order simulacra of the parts of the global village most visited by the United States tourist (World Showcase).

Unlike the rest of Walt Disney World, EPCOT is not only a spectacle in Guy Debord's sense of the term but also a model, as Baudrillard defines the word: a self-contained processor of circular information.[10] In an attempt, perhaps, to be more participatory and educational, the park is filled with interactive computer games and information stations. Most of these, however, simply replay the same limited information from the same limited number of choices and combinations. The experience of these devices is similar to the experience of many of the rides. In "Horizons," for instance, one may choose to view several possible futures— living underwater, in the desert, etc.—yet the choices are controlled and the resulting information so basic as to seem ludicrous. The information about the future that is generated at Future World involves, like public opinion polls, the manipulation of *"that which cannot be decided."*[11] As Baudrillard explains:

> Do [polls] give an exact picture of reality, or simple tendencies, or the refraction of this reality in a hyperspace of simulation whose curve even is unknown? True, false, undecidable. Their most sophisticated analyses leave room always for the reversibility of the hypotheses. . . . The internal logic of these procedures (statistics, probability, operational cybernetics) is certainly rigorous and "scientific"; somehow though it does not stick, it is a fabulous fiction whose index of refraction in any reality (true or false) is nil. This is even what gives these models their forcefulness. But also it is this which only leaves them, as truth, the paranoid projection tests of a case, or of a group which dreams of a miraculous correspondence of the real to their models, and therefore of an absolute manipulation.[12]

What is supposedly offered in the narratives created by Exxon, AT&T, Kraft, and other multinationals is either objective projections of our future based upon statistical fact or, as in many of the computer games one can play, the opinions of either the majority or the expert. What is actually occurring, however, is the transference of one or another type of impossible ideal back to the visitor—an ideal that one may never have had but in which one is invited to believe. As with opinion polls, this process short-circuits any possibility for imaginative thinking, since one becomes involved in the process of believing in the choices while at the same time unknowingly giving the poll-taker or the field scientist exactly what they want.[13] Because the choices are prepackaged, yet presented as "personal" preferences, participants are alienated from themselves in the very act of asserting themselves. EPCOT epitomizes this process by giving visitors the illusion that they can choose their desires for themselves from an unlimited supply.[14]

One effect of this alienation is the death of the singular, the original. As Baudrillard notes, the World Trade Center is radically distinct from the

Empire State Building because the former consists of two identical build-ings.[15] At EPCOT, this same effect is symbolized in the repetition of the two Communicore buildings that lie at the heart of the park. In fact, their design is mirrored in the circularity of the geodesic sphere and park layout, as well as in the ubiquitous styling of the buildings. Future World parallels the distinguishing features of pop art in which repetition and serialism evoke a simulation as distinct from the idea of the counterfeit copy as Warhol is from a Renaissance painter. The mechanical and tech-nological reproduction of opinions, of futures, and of the experience of the city runs rampant at EPCOT where, with time, one can repeat the same ride, the same film, the same visit endlessly in an orgy of plasticity. What one can never do is suppress the boundaries of capitalism as it invades every area of one's consciousness and represents itself as a desire about to be fulfilled. The boundaries of the Magic Kingdom—Frontierland, Ad-ventureland, Fantasyland—are here made into one neat binary: a nation-less space (the future) where companies replace countries, or a memory of or desire for travel to a country whose image is already so encrusted with fictionalization as to be no more real than a film or legend. Borders are replaced with a temporal stage between the eventual capitalist take-over of the world and the pseudoreality of current late capitalism.

If EPCOT's design foregrounds time, the Magic Kingdom's can be said to focus on the experience of space. As Louis Marin suggests, in the arrange-ment of lands into a starlike pattern, the Magic Kingdom suggests a map.[16] The historically specific type of map, I* would argue, is not a mod-ern map of "geographical form" brought to "birth of modern scientific discourse" but resembles instead the medieval maps described by Michel de Certeau that "[mark] out ... itineraries (performative indications ...), along with the stops one was to make."[17] One begins at the entrance to the Magic Kingdom and then, by visiting each land, one enjoys a set of preordained emotions much as one might in a staged pilgrimage of re-ligious ecstasy, only here one is not crossing a real terrain but an artificial one through one's own childhood (Fantasyland) or national memory (Liberty Square). However, as de Certeau theorizes, a frontier "does not have the character of a nowhere that cartographical representation ul-timately presupposes. It has a mediating role. So does the story that gives

*Shelton Waldrep

it voice."[18] The frontiers of the Magic Kingdom—the various lands and their borders—are about communication between zones, contacts, encounters, and struggles that require stories in order to be passed on. The *frisson* offered the visitor is the excitement without any of the (real) hardship. The experiences are of the body—the threat of danger, pain, getting lost, the thrill of making it through. The use of theatrical procession—of architecture as time or narrative—is central.

The monorail is the resort's primary symbol, the embodiment of movement through space and time that culminates with the arrival at the lobby of the Contemporary Hotel's Grand Canyon Concourse. As de Certeau notes, "[i]n modern Athens, the vehicles of mass transportation are called *metaphorai*. To go to work or come home, one takes a 'metaphor'—a bus or a train. Stories . . . every day . . . traverse and organize places; they select and link them together; they make sentences and itineraries out of them. They are spatial trajectories."[19] In the Magic Kingdom, narrative is used metaphorically to transport the visitor out of one world and into another. Rather than fixing space, the boundaries between lands actually create the possibility of its movement, its ambiguity via narrative.[20] Realistic detail is needed to protect the illusion begun by the story itself. In the "Jungle Cruise," the automatic elephants that spray water on the guests must look real in order not to disrupt the metaphorical ride of the story literalized in the movement of the boat. And passing through various "barriers"—from South America to Africa, for example—is brought about by the (racist, sexist, and colonialist) banter of the pilot: border crossings verbally "literalized" and staged by an actor whose script even demands that he pretends to get lost.

The many opportunities to participate (however passively) in these stories at the Magic Kingdom—to *enter* "20,000 Leagues Under the Sea," "The Haunted Mansion," etc.—provide the park's primary enjoyment. Visitors cross over into realized fantasy. At EPCOT, on the other hand, the narratives or stories fail to present any border other than the one between the "now" and the "will be." The only story is that of capitalist expansion masquerading as science fiction in which the heroes of the next century are not people but machines, with faith placed not in courage but in technology. Lacking the stories that Disney took from his films and used as narratives for the rides at the Magic Kingdom, EPCOT represents the failure of space to articulate narrative. There, stories substitute playing to the market for the tensions that empower fantasies. As de Certeau remarks, "[I]n order to discern in [spaces] the modes in which . . . distinct operations are combined, we need criteria and analytical categories—a necessity that leads us back to travel stories of the most elementary kind."[21] At EPCOT a sense of place is lost and, with it, the possibility of stories. In fact, the only narrative that remains intact is the official myth extolling the wonders of what can be accomplished without the state. The creation of a stateless utopia—no land—ultimately removes any possibility of communication between and among groups. Just as the architecture of the various "countries" of World Showcase are kept apart rather than connecting as the "lands" of the Magic Kingdom do, EPCOT represents the monadic separation and alienation of people from each other and from themselves.

Why should we be obliged to prefer a nostalgia for the future to that for the past? Could not the model city which we carry in our minds allow for our known psychological constitution? Could not this ideal city, at one and the same time, behave, quite explicitly, as both a theatre of prophecy and a theatre of memory?—Colin Rowe and Fred Koetter

Critical culture depends on political culture, and our political culture is reactive in its anxiety about the present.—Hal Foster

In an essay on Walter Benjamin's *Passagen-Werk,* Susan Buck-Morss notes that for Benjamin "utopian desire was based on memory, not anticipation."[22] She proceeds to quote Benjamin quoting Kafka's description of the singing mouse Josephine in one of his stories: "Something of our poor brief childhood is in it, something of lost happiness which can never be found again, but also something of active present-day life, of its small gaieties, unaccountable and yet real and unquenchable."[23] The re-creation of desire for the memories of one's childhood is central to Benjamin's examination of the Paris arcades which were, at the time he was writing, mainly a distant memory of a crumbling edifice from the age of Napoleon III, the bourgeois king who brought Paris its boulevards and sewers. Buck-Morss sees Benjamin's great project as an attempt to find nothing less than the origins of modernity in the transformation of mass culture that took place after the arcades were closed. The story his text would tell, therefore, would not be a canonical one: "Told with 'cunning,' the *Passagen-Werk* would accomplish a double task: it would dispel the mythic power of present being . . . by showing it to be composed of decaying objects with a history. . . . And it would dispel the myth of history as progress (or the modern as new) by showing history and modernity in the child's light as archaic." Benjamin likened the structure that would contain this twofold purpose to a fairy tale. His consistent objective, however, was to present the material—as opposed to the mythological—explanation for the arcades and the objects in them.[24]

The arcades caused Benjamin to "once again live the life of our parents and grandparents." His fascination with the old-fashioned items that were preserved for sale there is perhaps not unlike the feeling one has at EPCOT upon finding brochures that suggest teaching schoolchildren about the marvels of nuclear energy. Although lacking the decadent appearance of Benjamin's arcades, EPCOT is also caught in a hopeless dialectic of decay in which one can only relive ideologies now so fragile as to crumble upon the slightest brush with thought. The theological status that consumerism occupies at EPCOT parallels in an ironic way the enlightenment that Benjamin hoped would occur as people became aware of the true nature of the shift in consciousness that had taken place. By becoming a storyteller much like Disney, he hoped to bring material history back to the analysis of culture, but in order to aid in a very different kind of revolution.[25]

If the arcades function as an ancestor for EPCOT in terms of the technological development of mass culture, it is in the examination of childhood memory that they act as a precursor to the Magic Kingdom. In terms of scale alone the construction of the various sections of the park functions differently in order to provoke various psychological reactions. Although most of the fiberglass facades use forced perspective—the buildings are nine-tenths normal size on the first floor and eight-tenths after the first floor—Frontierland looks "grown-up," so that one can more easily enter into the scene as a participant, which is impossible to do at Fantasyland where the adult, at least, experiences the rides from a wistful—therefore more distant—mental state.[26] The section most recently added to the park, Mickey's Starland, makes this subtle use of scale obvious: the entire area is proportioned for young children (mouse-size) so that they can play in a section built not to accommodate their parents' memories and imaginations but their own feelings of uniqueness—the equivalent of what adults feel in the rest of the park. To say that the reason for this is at least in part so that they may better ape and strive for the condition of adults is finally to miss the point. As Buck-Morss notes, "From the child's position, all history, from the most ancient to the most recent past, occurs in mythic time. No history recounts his or her lived experience. All of the past lies in an archaic realm of 'Ur'-history."[27] The rest of the park may be an attempt to recreate this childhood state in the older consumer[28] as the planners tap into a "collective unconscious with innate archetypes" or what Benjamin referred to as the "world of symbols." The "child's reception of objects" accomplishes what adults cannot, which is to "discover the new anew." The Magic Kingdom is an attempt to recreate in adults at least the memory of this discovery and to fuel the original process in any child who visits the park and drives a miniature racing car or bops through Fantasyland.[29] In EPCOT, however, the function of objects in relation to the mythos of childhood is quite different; indeed, EPCOT acts as the anodyne to the Magic Kingdom, becoming the place where "the bourgeois ideology of historical progress does its best to overwhelm this childhood intuition of even the most recent history as archaic and mythically distant, by substituting for it the image of history's triumphal march, which submerges the new generations in its 'irresistible' tide."[30]

The displacement of children that occurs in the movement from the Magic Kingdom to EPCOT is part of a general trajectory away from childhood that seems to be taking place in the Disney constructions completed since the opening of the original Disneyland. Richard Francaviglia, in his comparison of the Main Street, U.S.A. sections of the Anaheim and Orlando parks, accurately delineates the change from the first streetscape with its "softened and romanticized . . . image of the small town" to the "ornate, almost burlesque quality [that] pervades the design" of its counterpart in Florida.[31] Especially in World Showcase, EPCOT seems designed for nostalgic adults and the desires that are peculiar to them. In this sense the German beer hall, posters for Parisian follies, and pseudoscientific rides bring to mind Fredric Jameson's idea of the historicist, as opposed to the historical, in that they form "an allusion to a present out of real history which might just as well be a past removed from real history."[32]

The Disney-MGM Studios Theme Park, the newest addition to Disney World, is even less childlike in that here the point to almost every "attraction" is to celebrate the loss of innocence by seeing firsthand how movies are made. Most of the MGM park is devoted to showing visitors how something is done: stunts, animation, set design, and special effects; the mood is one of mellow realization that it is all sleight-of-hand. This mood is achieved in large part by the park's carefully planned deco architecture, which evokes a nostalgia for a Hollywood of the 1930s, and the restaurants, which embody the wry sense of humor of television couch potatoes of the baby boomer generation. With an emphasis on eating, shopping, and nostalgia, the park's ethos is even more distinctly aimed at adults than EPCOT's.[33]

Although the manipulation of memory is paramount to the functioning of all three parks that make up Orlando's Disney World, in many ways the MGM theme park contradicts the paradigm established by the Magic Kingdom. If the first park existed—like the TV show of the same name—to sell Disney products, one cannot help but be struck by the various trademarks and copyright symbols on the pages of the official brochure describing the rides at MGM: "Star Wars," "Indiana Jones," "Teenage Mutant Ninja Turtles," "Jim Henson's Muppets," not to mention as yet unincorporated real-life stars such as Chevy Chase and Robin Williams. Here Disney has as many tie-ins with other peoples' products as with its own. Like the Magic Kingdom, the MGM park advertises Disney products— from the latest shows on the Disney Channel to the newest Disney animated or live-action film—and does so in a much more naked manner than in the original Anaheim park. But the MGM park also champions rivals, and does so by copying another competitor's paradigm, Universal Studios, for the very form of the park itself.[34] By and large the park celebrates the cultural product created and nurtured by someone else under the putative theme of celebrating the history of movies in general.

Of course, Disney is not unique in copying itself—there is an entire chain of Six Flags parks—or even in copying other parks as the differences between theme parks, hotel complexes, malls, etc., are eroding rapidly. But in the pairing of MGM with the Magic Kingdom at the same resort, Disney seems to be in competition with its own history, its own stories about itself. The MGM park does not strive for a total approach to aesthetics the way the Magic Kingdom does: Disney conceived of Audio-Animatronics as the combination of all of the arts, and the cinematic feeling of the Magic Kingdom recreates the feel of his films.[35] MGM, in contrast, does not place its emphasis on rides. Instead, there is a tendency in the attractions to replace automation with live action. This trend takes various forms, such as inviting different celebrities to the park each day, presenting shows and demonstrations (some with audience participation), and having cast members act out parts (such as autograph seekers who come up to guests). Narrative, the mainstay of the Magic Kingdom, is replaced with skits and characters that are free-floating, or, more specifically, function only as advertisements for current products or as stereotypes in a Hollywood "that never was." The overall effect is to undermine the strategy of the Magic Kingdom—to cheapen the illusion it creates.

The one ride at MGM that does resemble those at the Magic Kingdom is entitled, self-consciously, "The Great Movie Ride." Containing some of the least interesting yet most technologically advanced Audio-Animatronic figures, it has no story to tell; it is similar to the rides in Future World, which, in lieu of stories taken from films, present either a pastiche of "educational" information and corporate self-congratulation, or muddled metanarratives, like "the ascent of man." For all of their datedness, the earlier "dark rides," as they were called when in development, present passengers with a seamless effect that taps into various psychological tropes.[36] At MGM Studios, however, the feeling is one of entering a world of commercial allusion that references only that which is available on cable TV and within the recent memory—or at least exposure—of the Reagan generation.

Much of the MGM park is boring. The backstage tour contains such stupefying attractions as "The Studio Showcase—Here before your eyes are the actual costumes, props and set pieces worn, handled and utilized by today's biggest stars." Any real imagination has gone somewhere else, mainly into the creation of an intriguing version of Hollywood Boulevard circa the 1930s and 1940s and restaurants that make dining a pointedly postmodern experience. The architecture is not so much Disney's own special brand of pastiche canonized by Venturi as it is a classically postmodern variety consisting of references to actual historical examples, such as " 'California Crazy' architecture," or to TV culture as in the Sci-Fi Drive-In Dinner where, according to one guidebook, you can "[s]it in booths designed like vintage '50s convertibles and watch scenes from campy science fiction films while dining on burgers and sandwiches." With the MGM park Disney has created its own comment on postmodern culture, including the manipulation of tone ("campy") and distance ("designed like"). The odd combination of the straight-faced and the surreal that dominates the Magic Kingdom and EPCOT is here effaced. A park for the video generation, it contains the Michel Eisner ethos of new product hustle: money is what dreams are made of.

For myself, and for others of my generation, the effects of television on the Magic Kingdom could be discerned mainly in the way that theme parks and TV used the same strategies to sell themselves via the selling of other products. With the advent of the MGM park, TV and video seem to dominate and largely replace the stories that rides are based upon—or the references that tourists collectively understand. Movies, Disney almost seems to be saying, have lost the battle with TV. In a videotape produced by the Walt Disney Company and used to promote the park under the ostensible function of "planning" one's vacation to Disney World, the introductory segment to the MGM park says that "all the major television networks play a popular leading role at the Disney Studios." Although the use of TV was an early and successful strategy of Walt's that has always been a part of the Disney parks, it is ironic that TV has a special formal relationship with the MGM park. It is truly an acknowledgment of a shift in consciousness to see TV as the cultural glue uniting the visitors rather than the innate stories of adventure and romance, that one sees re-hearsed—however insensitively—at the Magic Kingdom. An extreme ex-ample of TV as common cultural referent occurred to me at Universal Studios, Florida, when I first walked through "Hollywood" and heard the theme to *LA Law* playing everywhere as the aural marker for this portion of the park. Hollywood—a nostalgic place physically residing in Los Angeles—was represented by a television show about modern-day Los Angeles. An area of an amusement park that referenced a fictive discourse about film and power was given its subliminal identity via a reference to a TV show from the present. Across the "street," actors dressed as Lucille Ball and Desi Arnaz walked toward me. At MGM the celebrities often invited to the park are usually stars of TV, not film. Here, however, were actors portraying TV stars. The effect I experienced contained so many levels of cultural reference refracted through each other that the result seemed hardly describable by the concept of postmodernism. Increas-ingly, in discussions of "high" as opposed to "low" cultural production, scholars are already talking of effects that are somehow beyond post-modernism—or that seem a further intensification of it. If a cultural change has occurred, I would argue that it first happened in Orlando when MGM Studios opened and was soon followed by Universal.

What MGM and Universal tell us about changes in theme parks spe-cifically—especially Disney's—is somewhat difficult to pin down. The designers of Universal are in some ways luckier than those in charge of MGM in that they are free to cram into one space all of the ideas they can

copy from Disney World whereas MGM must—at least to some extent—avoid competing with its other parks in order to maintain the illusion that each is separate and unique. Universal has compounded this advantage by opting not to mimic the Disney image in everything. Although Universal seems to uphold the Disney standards of cleanliness and crowd control, it does have rides that are bigger on thrills and attractions and shows that are more daring in their use of sexual innuendo and in acknowledging difference within and among people. Disney, in rushing to open MGM before Universal, seems to have built a park before they really had a clear idea of what they either wanted to put in it or even what type of image they wanted for it.

Perhaps befitting Disney's film tradition, MGM trades mainly on atmosphere rather than thrills. By contrast, Universal pushes the adventure movies that made money in the 1970s and 1980s: *Jaws, Back to the Future,* the remake of *King Kong, E.T.,* and, surely to come in the 1990s, *Jurassic Park.* Universal Studios is more likely to reference a broader range of movies and other types of media—one sees clips of the Beatles while waiting in one line, for instance—than does MGM, which focuses instead on a putative tradition of great moviemaking. MGM seems to have doomed itself into a defensive posture by attempting, as Fjellman says, to become the "spoiler" by opening before Universal; if the park has a strategy, it has taken on the job of educator—much like EPCOT—and left the thrills mostly to Universal. When MGM opened, it was by far the smallest of the three main Disney World parks; however, it has added "Star Tours"—MGM's version of Universal's "Back to the Future" ride—and is about to open the "Twilight Zone Tower of Terror." Both rides are heavy on thrills. MGM is also adding another section—Sunset Strip—to its cramped space. An equally important sign of change is the fact that one can now find fresh fruit stands in the park, although these concessions to changing times coexist with shops that sell toy guns to children in a jungle-themed area near the "Indiana Jones Stunt Spectacular." While some things change at Disney, much else never does.

MGM has to its advantage over both Universal and the other Disney parks the fact that it is do-able in less than a day. Similarly, there is a relaxed atmosphere to this park that makes it feel less overwhelming than either the other Disney parks or even Universal. Whereas Universal's park is organized into a large gridlike pattern, at MGM the curved, compact streets and alleys are fractured and laid out in an irregular pattern so that one has a greater sense that one is exploring. MGM's designers have used its relatively small size to create an urban design that emphasizes twists and turns, unexpected juxtapositions, nooks, and vistas much like the better pedestrian effects in the Magic Kingdom. The shopping areas of MGM are similar to Main Street, U.S.A. in their blend of merchandising and nostalgia. By focusing on TV, however, one is made aware that this is a postmodern version of the golden age of Hollywood: from the black and white TVs in the 50's Prime Time Cafe to the monitors that broadcast prerecorded instructions while you wait in the numerous lines.[37]

In a sense, MGM's thesis seems not to be that one can go home again—as it is in the Magic Kingdom—but that the past has been replaced by the media through which we now generally access it. Hollywood is only available via the visual media, especially television. Like an apotheosis of Marshall McLuhan's tenets, MGM asks that one acknowledge the difference between Walt's vision of the past and a newer version historically available only to people the age of his children and younger. From MGM to the ubiquitous Disney Stores now in every mall, Disney seems to be placing an emphasis on marketing the villain, which has come back into prominence in the last three Disney animated hit movies. By banking on this type of character, Disney seems to be betting on an adult interest in camp or queer sensibilities—that is, on a generation that doesn't take their products straight.

With a section of the park devoted to presenting Europeans with American regional styles in the form of hotels—Hotel New York, Hotel Santa Fe, etc.—designed by leading postmodern architects, EuroDisney completes the process of postmodern comment begun at MGM. Euro-Disney reflects an image from across the Atlantic of our own cultural process by leaving nothing sacred, nothing unabsorbed. The technique of representing European capitals as shops and restaurants in EPCOT is here neatly reprocessed and combined with the postmodern style of the 1990s. Undoubtedly, American tourists in Paris will flock to see EuroDisney in order not only to have done another Disney resort, but to comfort themselves with the idea that they can now place the Louvre in perspective.

Whatever the future holds for the Disney parks, it is certain that they will have company. An explosion in Disney-inflected entertainment complexes is on the horizon, with everything from an Elvis park in Tokyo to a quasi-Buddhist playground for attaining enlightenment in Niagara, Canada. Resembling Jim Jarmusch movies more than county fairs, these extravaganzas parallel the more recent changes in Disney resort history. The original antimodernist aesthetic and technological vision Disney had for the Magic Kingdom, which metamorphoses into a postmodern version of a modernist nightmare at EPCOT, has finally resulted in the properly postmodern cash cow that is the MGM theme park. As the themed environment becomes more and more commonplace, Disney will struggle to redo its formula and reinvent its continuing commentary upon both its own origins and its current distance from them.

This historical metanarrative that Disney authors for itself seems poised at a point of contradictory impulses: modern and postmodern, narrative and spatial, xenophobic and open-minded. The response to the contradictions might be a new commission-based approach whereby the Disney company comes more and more to resemble a franchiser with a line of products (that includes resort parks) and less a collection of artists, as Walt Disney imagined it. Indeed the "Disney Decade," as Eisner has proclaimed the 1990s, may become a decade of crisis as the enterprise attempts to adapt and profit from the uncertainties of a cultural and economic situation that Disney could not have predicted. We are already witnessing the increasing displacement of the "interrelated and sequential" themes that provide park visitors with a detailed, relatively unified sense of place and "story." The "themes" planned for new parks ("animals," "ocean") promise to abandon narrative and enter an era of high-concept production: the simpler the idea, the greater the draw. All that is needed are special effects and big stars.[38]

What one may ultimately be left with are neither stories nor parks but simply products replayed and remarketed at different times and in different forms in an endless loop for every new generation. The planners, meanwhile, attempt to give their resort one of everything: one wave pool, one campground, one punk disco, one haunted house, one tropical hotel. To occupy the space between the EPCOT hotels and World Showcase, Disney is now planning its own version of the boardwalk in Atlantic City. It will, naturally, be filled with shops. The choices that one has at Disney, from restaurants to rides to hotels, gives one the illusion that they are all different. Every guest knows, however, that the secret is in the fact that they are all the same. As with flavors of chain store ice cream or Swatch watches or silkscreens by Warhol, the aspect of capitalism that is being underlined is the link between disposability and consumption, product and desire. The point is to eventually do all of them anyway because they are all equally good. Just as capitalism must continually expand its borders and take over new spaces, new stories, Disney must continue to add to itself forever in an endless attempt to provide more of the same, to provide what theme parks are for: a planned opportunity to avoid thinking about the present.

UNdER

tHE

inflUENCE

• • •

Don't get me wrong. I'm not anti-Disney. It's just that . . . well, let me see, how do I say it?" began Bob as he popped a spinach hors d'oeuvre into his mouth.

Bob was practically a total stranger. We were at a cocktail party and had been talking not more than five minutes when he offered me a delectable morsel of folk wisdom about Disney World. I* can assure you that I didn't plan this man-on-the-street interview. In fact, Bob was supposed to be interviewing me. He had literally picked my name out of a hat (well, out of a bowl) as all of us guests had been instructed to do in order to make the acquaintance of a randomly selected stranger and to write impressions in a guest book before leaving. Inevitably then, after a brief introduction, Bob popped the big question.

"So, what do you do?"

My mind frantically scanned a menu of responses that included such things as photographing men at the beach and folding laundry, before deciding on:

"Well, lately I've been involved in a project about Disney World. I'm doing some photography and writing. I'm not a writer. I just kind of fell into this."

"Really? What kinds of things are you writing?" he asked as he took another sip of bourbon.

*Karen Klugman

It was winter, but he was sweating profusely. He periodically wiped his brow with a handkerchief as we spoke. Since he was a little on the heavy side and was wearing a wool sports jacket, I was afraid he was going to pass out. But he needed more information on me in order to write his impression, then leave.

"Probably not what you're thinking. Not travel brochures or anything like that. It's a critical essay, but by critical, I don't mean necessarily negative. In fact, I'm thinking of writing about how it feels to be there, to be under Disney control, if you know what I mean. What specific mechanisms are at work that. . . ."

Bob's eyes darted around the room, then fixed intently on me as he noticed that I had noticed his roaming attention. I realized that I was sounding like a thesis proposal and that poor Bob was going to have to write a topic sentence about me.

"Kathy never throws a party without having absolute control over everything," I heard from another conversation.

"Have you ever been there?" I said, throwing the ball into his court. It was not a long shot. After all, Bob appeared to be in his forties. Chances were pretty good that, by his age, he had found cause to go to one of the Disney parks, whether on a romantic vacation or to take the kids (if he had any). And besides, he was being such a good sport about his obvious discomforts, keeping his jacket buttoned in spite of the heat and keeping his attention on me until he fulfilled his mission, that I concluded that he was the type who toes the party line. The type who, if he *had* been to Disney World, would answer, "Yes, three times now," or "Yes, it's great, isn't it?"

"As a matter of fact, I was just there at a convention," said Bob.

My mind instantly flashed back to the previous year, the setting was the lobby of the Swan or the Dolphin hotels. (Like Tom Stoppard's Rosencrantz and Gildenstern, Michael Grave's Disney hotels exist in my mind as a pair of comic characters with too few distinguishing characteristics to warrant separate identities.) My friend Susan and I had been told to show up there shortly before two o'clock on the chance that a convention would be taking place and that they might have some extra room for us on the Behind-the-Scenes tour. Sitting in the lobby among the plastic Wisteria, we imagined how out of place we would feel in our tank tops and short shorts and carrying backpacks next to a bunch of guys in business suits. It was tempting to spend the next couple of hours just sitting on the lounge chairs beside the hotel pool and so, once again, we reconsidered whether the "underground tour" would be worth the price of admission—$50 per person and two hours of Florida sunshine to see what? A glimpse of a real person inside the mouse costume perhaps? The garbage ducts in the basement of Cinderella's Castle? The nursery for young topiary bushes?

Yes! We wanted all of this and more! With renewed commitment, we marched up to the ticket counter and found that there were indeed a couple of spots not taken by the "Milk Producers of America" convention. We joked to ourselves that since, between the two of us, we had nursed eight children, we fit right in. Expecting to feel like spies in costumes, we decided to go the whole route and wear our Disney Villain caps that Susan had bought at MGM Studios.

The bus was filled with dairy farmers, gray-haired couples in short-sleeved plaid shirts who didn't even seem to notice us. From the back of the bus, we plotted our tactics, what revealing questions we would ask our tour guide. Not too many, so as not to arouse suspicion. Just the important ones, such as "Since Disney prides itself on being in the forefront of technology, how does it handle recycling?" We figured our tour mates were just there for the ride, whereas we were there to investigate the facts.

We had gone just a short distance on World Drive when one of the farmers interrupted our tour guide. "Say, if you guys know so much, why don't you tell us how you handle your garbage?" For any topic you can name, Disney has probably capitalized on it in the form of a money-making product. In this case, they had had their hands in a fertilizer, marketed commercially as Mickey Muck. For the entire trip, the farmers wanted to talk about waste products and to throw around statistics about manure production back home. Every time they said the word "sharn," I smiled and thought of my own experience with it back home. My son had recently added the words "shit" and "darn" to his vocabulary. When I explained that he shouldn't use them because people identify them as swear words, he decided to invent a new word which combined the two, but which people wouldn't recognize. "Sharn" sounded fine to me, but we looked it up in the dictionary and found, by golly, that it meant cattle dung.

So you can understand why, when Susan and I, the dairy farmers, and our Disney guide stood silently together under Fantasyland and listened

as trash whizzed over our heads at 60 mph in Swedish-designed pneumatic tubes, I experienced the Magic. The magic of feeling connected to
other people, to other places, to other times. In this case, a coincidence
regarding waste products had sparked this warm-all-over feeling, a feeling that was soon incinerated by a silly refrain. For, in my mind I could
hear a thousand Audio-Animatronic dolls singing over and over again,
"It's a small world after all."

I wanted to tell Bob about my unconventional convention experience.
He didn't look like the dairy farmer type, but my association with the
milk producers had whet my curiosity about conventions.

"Was your convention by any chance at the Swan or the Dolphin?" I
asked.

"Actually, it was in Orlando. At the Orlando Convention Center."

I was only a little surprised that being in a convention in Orlando
counted as an answer to whether Bob had ever been to Disney World. A
few weeks earlier, I had seen a video presentation entitled "Welcome to
Dislando" in which scenes from Orlando and Disney World were inter-
spersed so that it was sometimes hard to tell them apart.[1] Orlando, it
seems, has been subjected to "Disneyfication," a term not yet in the
dictionary but understood to refer to the application of simplified aesthetic, intellectual, or moral standards to a thing that has the potential for
more complex and thought-provoking expression. So it was with irony
that I recalled the video's reference to the Disneyfication of Orlando as the
attempt to make an urban environment "a life space which is clean, safe,
and entertaining, and distracting."

"It was a convention on fire protection," continued Bob. "I'm an architectural engineer, see, and my specialty is fire safety. The Disney people
came and brought indoor fireworks. Set them off right inside the convention center. Amazing."

Bob made it sound as if the Disney people had casually brought along
some fireworks in their pockets as my Aunt Dorothy used to do when she
would show up at wiener roasts with a pocketful of cherry bombs. But of
course the Imagineers had arranged every detail of their "surprise" entertainment in advance with the convention planners, Orlando officials, and
the fire marshal. You have to wonder if any other institution associated
with pyrotechnics could have obtained this permission. The convention
organizers had to insure, after all, not only the public's actual safety, but
the public's feeling of being safe. Imagine how you might feel, for exam-

ple, being in an enclosed space with the topic of fire in the air and hearing an announcement that the NASA people had brought some indoor fireworks?

Accidents at Disney World never make the national news. Unless you live in Orlando and watch Channel 6 or know someone who works at the parks, you have probably never heard of any problems. I personally witnessed only two incidents that, with a stretch of the imagination, you might call equipment failures. The first involved a tall man in the Surprise Celebration Parade who had trouble with one of his stilts. I wasn't even aware that anything was wrong until an assistant appeared out of nowhere to adjust it. For a brief time, maybe one minute, the crowd held the magic in suspension as one pant leg was lifted to expose a hairy leg and the failing infrastructure.

The second incident involved my friend's child who, in close quarters with hundreds of other park guests being corralled along the multistory maze toward "Splash Mountain," playfully extended her leg between two posts of a railing and could not get it out. She immediately screamed and kept screaming as her mother tried to free the leg. It was unclear to everyone whether the child was in pain or was having a panic attack, but what slowly took hold of our murky consciousness was that this was an unprogrammed event that might require some initiative on our parts. Charlotte was getting hot and red, was dripping with sweat, and was no longer capable of standing on the other leg so that I took over the struggle with the leg as her mother supported her weight. Meanwhile, no one left his place in line to get assistance. Perhaps, like me, they fantasized one of the eighteen-year-old "mountain guides" arriving first to check out the situation. We certainly did not expect that a Disney cast member dressed as a frontier logger and carrying a chain saw would show up anytime soon. By and by, the others moved past us in the line. Then, in an admirable example of what I call female technology, a woman who was probably ten minutes ahead of us in line but, in fact, was located on the floor just below our balcony, tossed me a bottle of Johnson's baby lotion and, over the piercing screams, told me to rub it on the leg, like WD-40. Three minutes later, the leg, now dripping with pink lubricant, was still stuck and the woman asked to have her bottle of lotion back so that she could move on. By now, it was clear that we were regarded as just another passing "attraction." Out of desperation, I suppose, my friend and I used logic to solve the problem. The leg went in. Therefore, it should be able to come out. Maybe, as with the Chinese finger puzzle where you slip your fingers into a tube and try to get them out by pulling, the secret is to push them in farther in order to release the pressure. Since it was impossible to convince Charlotte to push her leg in farther, we had to fight against her pulling and forcibly extend the leg, which then easily slipped out.

The sudden silence that followed had the effect of a concert by John Cage. Previously anaesthetized senses began operating on full power, so that it seemed as if someone had turned up the volume on the piped-in Muzak. My first thought was, "My God, Disney goofed!" The episode of the wedged leg had been a minor mishap, really, and, in any other public place, I would not have expected every railing on the property to meet crib-test standards. Yet it was a reminder that other details might not have been tested for borderline cases like Charlotte, who had just barely passed the height test for "Splash Mountain." Had Disney test-driven the eight-seater logs down the waterfall, for example, with four crash dummies weighing over two-hundred pounds all sitting on the right? Since our group of eight would occupy an entire log, we discussed seating permutations right up until embarkation time. The three teenagers, who were trying to maximize the thrill, couldn't decide between getting the biggest jolt in the rear seats or the biggest splash in the front. I, unfortunately, was chosen to complete the foursome and ride in the front but, for the sake of the little ones, I did not reveal my fears. Instead, once we were on the ride itself, I pointed out the cute Audio-Animatronics that were cheering us on. I even felt thankful for the visual and auditory cues that evoked admiration for Disney technology, even as they were building suspense for the climax—a brief, but steep descent that would temporarily take away my breath and the memory of waiting in line for forty-five minutes.

"Only Disney could get away with it," I said to Bob, wondering if his "amazing" expressed awe was for the technological innovation of indoor fireworks or the technological hubris of Disney in bringing them to a convention about fire safety.

"Yeah. They were a big hit," he replied cryptically.

"I need something to drink. How about you? Could I get you some more bourbon?"

Bob accepted the reversal of gender roles gracefully, following me into the kitchen and watching me first pour too much bourbon into his glass, then try to compensate with lots of ice.

I handed him a 16-ounce drink and continued my cross-examination.
"So did you ever actually go into the park?"

"Once. The kids had a great time," he said evasively.

"And what did *you* think of it?" This cat and mouse game couldn't go on much longer.

"It was interesting." Then he spoke softly as if he were telling me a secret. "But once was enough. I hope I never have to go back there again."

Bob waited for me to ask "Why?" before he continued.

"I like my vacations to be more active. Like going to museums in Washington. They supply ten percent, we have to supply ninety. At Disney, it's ninety/ten the other way. Disney does the ninety."

A lot of people go to Disney World expecting to be mentally stimulated. I did. Once. More than anything else, I looked forward to the attractions at EPCOT because I thought that they would provoke thoughts about science, history, and sociology. I imagined that during the trip through time in "Spaceship Earth," billed in guidebooks as depicting history from Cro-Magnon days to the present, I would discuss with my fellow travelers the meanings and significance of the authenticating details, such as the actual hieroglyphics and the replica of a page from the Gutenberg Bible. But, in reality (if you can call it that), it was impossible to sustain even my own thoughts, since history was presented as a series of animated scenarios with a recorded narration telling you how to view them, all passing by in nearly equal time allotments and with equal importance. When I entered the "World of Motion," I fully expected to learn about the history of transportation. But, fourteen minutes and 150 Audio-Animatronic characters later, I emerged stunned and dull-witted.

For thought-provoking detail, I might as well have stayed home to read Steve Birnbaum's guide. It is so enticing that any person with a good imagination might well conclude after a trip to Disney World that the book was better than the movie. True, there were a few surprises in the Disney cinematic version. In the Energy Pavilion sponsored by Exxon, I did hear, as predicted in the book, some oohs and aahs from the audience when the cars began to separate from one another. But not even Birnbaum dared to describe how that same audience would react to coming in for a wide-screen landing onto a panoramic view of what the narrator described as "the majestic port of Valdez"—a snow-white landscape blackened in our minds by our collective television knowledge of the Exxon oil spill.

Guests are not the only people who go to Disney World expecting intellectual exercise. I met a clerk at a shop in "Morocco," a student who had taken a year off from medical school to take this job in the International Fellowship Program because it was advertised as an opportunity to discuss the history and customs of his native land with tourists. Feeling that he had been duped, he was very bitter about working for Disney. He complained that the only question about Morocco that he ever got was, "Where is Morocco, anyhow?"

Bob was not complaining about lack of physical activity, but a mental sluggishness that sets in after a few days of being in an all-encompassing environment of passive entertainment. Critical capacities are replaced with a childlike trust that everything will be handled for you.

Returning home after five days in Disney World, I should have realized the possible dangers of my stupor, when, still inebriated with the illusion of safety, I actually enjoyed the plane ride home. Although the plane was experiencing some pretty severe turbulence, I was relaxed, regarding the jolts as just another ride, like the flight simulator in "Body Wars." If the VIP parking service in Hartford hadn't cleaned the ice from my windshield and warmed up my car, I might have been forced to acknowledge some responsibility for my own fate. But instead, I entered the vehicle,

fastened my seat belt and sat back to enjoy the ride down I-91 as if I were on a track at the "Grand Prix Raceway" in Tomorrowland. On my left, there was a burning van with flames as authentic as those from the exploding gasoline truck in the "Catastrophe Canyon" section of the MGM Backstage Studio Tour. The only difference between my ride and the Disney ride was that, being in the enclosed Subaru instead of an open tram, I couldn't feel the heat from the flames. I was riding along in a high mood until a chunk of ice dislodged from the hood and hit the windshield with a crash. It was then that I started trembling with the sober realization that *I was the driver!* There should be warnings against driving under the influence of Disney.

"Would you care for an appetizer?"

Bob and I paused to admire the tray and to spear some spinach balls with toothpicks. We were having a good time together and I was just thinking how I had been wrong in assuming that Bob was pro-Disney when he said, "Don't get me wrong. I'm not anti-Disney."

In my fantasy, I hugged Bob at this point and said, "It's OK, Bob, you don't have to take back your words. Some of my best friends are anti-Disney. You've probably never met anyone who has admitted it before. But I won't think any less of you. I certainly won't think you're a party pooper. I might even think you're deep."

"It's just that . . . well, let me see, how do I say it? It's just that when I take my family on vacation . . . ," continued Bob.

I was hanging on every word and watching Bob's mouth closely as it took in the vegetable hors d'oeuvre and formed the words:

"I don't like to go somewhere where they chew the food for you."

WORKING AT THE RAT

• • •

Disney's kind of like a duck: on top of the water it looks calm, but underneath, its feet are going a hundred miles an hour.—Jeff

Probably the most obvious thing anyone could say about Walt Disney World is that it's not what it seems to be. In the two years I've* devoted to thinking about the park and to talking to its visitors and workers, I've been confronted with this obviousness: friends, family, and interviewees responding to my assertions and questions with a look I've come to dread, the one that appears when an intellectual has just announced, as though for the first time, something everybody already knows. "It's not real, you know," I confide stupidly. "A simulacrum," I might intimate, just as stupidly, though nonacademics have no trouble understanding this concept. They do know, of course; they've always known. They've been there, after all, or they work there, or they used to, or they know people who still do, or they hope eventually to start or to start again. Disney looms that large in Orlando and its environs; it is the kind of system through which everyone inevitably circulates.

What fascinates me about Disney World is the ability of its inhabitants—the paid and the paying—to entertain contradictory and competing claims about the park and what they're doing in it. They say they know it's not real, that it's not what it appears to be, and then proceed to

*Jane Kuenz

talk about it as though it were. Soap opera culture evidences a similar phenomenon, a more stark version of what can be seen in people's responses to much of TV, at least the parts that still maintain the pretense of proffering fiction. The categories are becoming moot. At Disney, guests know that the park's entertainments are "fake," but claim the fakery doesn't matter. They know that it's "phony," but feel the phoniness is fun, or harmless, or, in some larger way, real, the bigger real, the greater truth. Disney's guests are particularly disinclined to draw conclusions about what is otherwise obvious. They give themselves over to the park. A chef at a Disney resort says, "I tell the ladies, 'Don't worry, you're at Disney World. There are no calories here. It's all part of the magic.' They're like, 'Oh good!' I don't tell them that as soon as they cross that line the calories go boom on your waistline."[1]

This willing suspension of disbelief by the park's guests is neither simple nor simple-minded, but the partial result of a complex negotiation of the increasingly foreshortened list of options available to citizens in a culture that is both commodity-driven and global in reach, a world for which Disney's world is an apt homologue. The "ladies" know there are calories in what they're eating; what they want is not to care, to take time out from a world that demands that a mature woman's body look like that of a fourteen-year-old and that she buy the clothes or diet scams necessary to achieve it or, better, merely continue to try. Of course, when "they cross that line," they reenter a world essentially unchanged and quite likely one that feels a lot worse for their attempt to leave it. They know this, too. The strange combination of assertiveness and embarrassment with which visitors typically recount their experiences at Disney World is a sign of their conflicted pleasure, of their knowingness, and is the very point at which potential resistance in the form of alternate or disallowed desire (the yearning to have hips that are all there) confronts the dominant (the seamless parade of thin blondes in tap shoes) and finds it almost funny.[2]

For the park's employees, this double vision is more pronounced largely because the effort to maintain it is so great and the consequences of doing so are so profound. If there is a consistent theme among park employees it is the desire simply that their work be known, that it be understood as work, not magic, though, even here, many have a curious, vested interest in creating just that—Disney's magic—as if there were no relationship between the production of magic and the invisibility of their labor. On the one hand, they insist on breaking illusions, on reasserting the obvious: Disney is not what it appears to be, they say again and again. One woman turns up for our interview, legal pad in tow on which she has enumerated Disney horror stories: rapes, murders, armed robberies, grisly and freakish accidents involving machinery or wildlife, the resulting lawsuits and settlements secreted away from public view, the occasional suicide in the lake. "Ask Channel 6," she says. "They have video." An attractions host is adamant about making sure I understand the level of Disney's subterfuge, saying that contrary to its popular reputation, the company "doesn't care anything about the public. They don't care anything about the people that work for them. They *really* don't care about the guest experience. . . . They are out for Disney. They are really out for themselves." Or, from another: "They don't have any magic. They're phony. They try to put on a facade, that everything is fine and dandy in the park, that everybody's sweet, but behind the scenes there's a lot of unhappy people." Even local pet names for Disney convey some of this desire to smudge the park's image. A seasonal worker, a CT (Casual Temporary) in Disney parlance, tells me, "A lot of musicians call Disney World the rat, Mickey the rat. They say, 'We're going to work at the rat.'" One hears these things in Orlando: the rat, the mouse, the mousetrap.

But if Disney's employees are eager to break the kingdom's spell, they are also willing to maintain it. For many workers—often the same people who complain bitterly—the park's magic is quite magical, and is so in a way that, almost too perfectly, encourages in them a sense of their own autonomy and distance from Walt Disney Co., the corporate monolith, even as it requires them to perform the tasks for which too many of them are so poorly paid.[3] "Perform" is not used casually here. Understanding Disney's metaphoric translation of workplace, worker, and labor into theater, cast, and performance is crucial to understanding how Disney workers make sense of themselves on the job. This is a place where an entire work force shows up each day, not in uniform, but in costume. Most have internalized this distinction; they *never* say uniform, just as they always say cast, on stage, and backstage. As Shelton Waldrep observes, many Disney employees initially commodify and consume their jobs; they value them and thus themselves in precisely the same terms the company uses to advertise itself: thoroughness, superior quality, "thinking of everything." The language of performance and the fetishistic attention to detail in costuming, scripts, and controlling visibility on stage is evidence to them of the high standards of their work. Only later, and then not consistently, do they come to see it differently—as the thing that hid their labor from view, that which kept visitors from seeing the "real" Disney that they know.

Yet even here, the park is and is not what it appears to be. Within its sphere, performing, acting, and playing take varied forms, not all of them approved or even recognized by supervisors and least of all by guests. For example, cast members frequently play to several audiences at once— including each other. I don't want to overstate the case—Disney's control of its labor force is apparently near total; the workers themselves certainly perceive it as such. But while they are quick to point out that control, they are also quick to claim what they feel is solely theirs. With few exceptions, all the workers I talked to were convinced that they did indeed produce something they were content to call magic; they were equally sure that beyond providing the costumes and sets, the company itself had little to do with this. In fact, what pleasure they got from producing this magic was often seen to be, if not at the company's expense, then certainly in spite of what it wanted.

But, of course, it isn't finally in spite of what Disney wants; though the employees value this magic for its use value to themselves and though they consider it something Disney cannot take from them, the company itself doesn't care and has, in fact, already exchanged it at the rate of $38.00 per head, per day, per park. In other words, Walt Disney World is *really* not what it seems to be, though the nature of its deceptiveness may not be what it seems either. Disney's conceit of theater marshals the creative and emotional energies of its workers and creates a situation in which they are always performing for the company. It is a primary strategy in what Harry Braverman calls "the habituation of workers" to their work.[4] It is also, however, the vehicle for whatever departures they make from it—the determinate structure that brings forth in spite of itself the indeterminate practices for which it nevertheless finds uses.

Team Disney

We have our own security, our own fire department, our own doctors. It's like a town. It's like an army post.—Pam

When Disney's employees arrive every day for work, they enter the world of "property." They are "on property," a phrase conjoining the language of theater with that of real estate. This property extends for almost 28,000 acres—"forty-three square miles of fun," the brochures proclaim. It crosses county lines and encompasses two municipalities, Bay Lake and Lake Buena Vista, both governed by residents, usually Disney employees living in the area, in conjunction with the Reedy Creek Improvement District, a.k.a. Walt Disney Co. Officially recognized as a quasi-governmental body largely independent of state and local authority, this entity is endowed with powers to tax and to regulate such things as its own zoning, fire protection, liquor sales, water and sewage, roads and bridges. While Disney also has the right to determine what to do with its share of the local wildlife, negative publicity about the slaughter of migrating birds—they apparently conflicted with the look of one themed area—has convinced the company to adhere to some outside environmental protection laws.[5]

"Property" is not synonymous with "park." One can be outside the parks, even outside the resort hotels and their recreational areas and still be "on property." For guests who are staying "on property," the effect is to feel always within an environment controlled and made safe for them. They imagine themselves sealed off from the rest of the state, its crime and encroaching poverty, though technically they are not. Anyone can drive on or off property. Properly speaking, "on property" is also not the same as "on stage." "On stage" implies public view and being in contact with guests as an employee and representative of the Walt Disney Co. "On property" means being within the boundaries of Reedy Creek. For Disney's employees, however, this is just a rough distinction; their perception is that any place they might go "on property" is always a workplace whether or not they are actually at work. For them, all of Disney property is potentially a stage. We might think in this context of Michel de Certeau's "*propre*": the realm of strategy, of "panoptic practice"—the "mastery of places through sight"—and of the kind of knowledge made available by the two, knowledge "sustained and determined by the power to provide oneself with one's own place." Part of de Certeau's point is that being able to define and regulate the place of one's authority makes possible the production and control of knowledge that defines and supports it.[6] For those with the power to maintain it, *propre* is a place to stand and look; thus looking—observing, measuring, "including"—is by definition a gauge of that power. For those lacking such a place or the capacity to define one, people like Disney's workers, the realm of property is not a place to be so much as a position to occupy, and a very different one. Stuck in the space of the other, they are always being looked at; for them, "property" suggests the perspective they don't have, the view of someone observing them from every angle.

Disney's property is such a place even, obviously, on the most literal level. Disney protects its borders. When problems occur, something that might require official mediation between inside and out, various cogs of the company's machinery kick into gear. The concern is to let nothing enter or exit the property unregulated or uncontrolled. This includes, apparently, the dead and dying. Says one retail clerk: "If someone was down, say someone had a heart attack in the shop, then you call a supervisor in. They told us we were to call a supervisor and then call the ambulance." (She went on to assure me that she never followed this rule.) Another worker was involved in a car accident caused by a drunk Disney employee who was "fired on the spot."[7] "Within ten minutes," she said, "there were sixty to seventy people there from Disney. . . . An hour and ten minutes later the police were called." Not to worry, however, if this happens to you, since no one actually dies on Disney property. It's company policy: when asked at one of Disney's pricey management seminars whether anyone ever died at Disney World, the group leader, on cue from a supervisor sitting in the back of the room, said simply, "No." If guests have the nerve to die, they wait, like unwanted calories, until they've crossed the line and can do so safely off property:

> We had a guy last summer who went to EPCOT, stood in front of the golf ball, took a gun, and blew his head off. But he didn't die. He stood right there in front of all those tourists and went "cluck" and brains blew everywhere. But he didn't die there. The medic told me that they are not allowed to let them die there. Keep them alive by artificial means until they're off Disney property, like there's an imaginary line in the road and they go, "He's alive, he's alive, he's dead."

This attention to monitoring the "imaginary line" is also directed at employees when they are entering and exiting the park for the first and last time or whenever there is anything out of the ordinary. When hired, they waive their right to discuss in print particulars of their job; when they leave—at least in cases when they are unwilling to go—they are required to sign a "witness statement" detailing the circumstances of their departure. Illness or injury, whether on the job or not, requires their own set of procedures before anyone can come back into the park. According to Pam, "If you go home with a headache, you can't come back until you go to the doctor on Disney property. If he releases you, you can come back to work. If you're in a car wreck, you can't come back until you go to the Disney doctor and he lets you go back to work, although he had nothing to do with the case."

Besides limiting potentially litigious incidents, Disney's strategies for entering and exiting the park—dead or alive—have the added purpose of further defining the nature and basis of its own authority and thus of augmenting it. It appears, for example, that Disney doesn't need state or local regulation because none of the problems that would require it ever seem to occur, or at least the rules monitoring borders do not let it be acknowledged that they have. Thus, no one gets sick or hurt at Disney; no one dies at Disney; no one leaves Disney unhappy or is fired for no reason; and no one writes bad things about the park once they're gone.

But it's not as though these things aren't known. Susan Willis's students might be shocked to learn that the prevalence of kidnapping at Disney is an open secret in Orlando, so much so that some there call it an urban myth, and it's in this corridor between the known/not known that Disney is able to define itself so positively. The rumors fly without ever landing anywhere: the toddler who drowned after crawling under the rope fence at the Fisherman's Wharf; the employee who, in the parking lot of Pleasure Island, pumped five bullets into another in a jealous spat over a third. ("He threw the gun in the lake and went for a beer. Nobody knew for three days." The girl was "carted out of state so she wouldn't get involved. The rule now is if you ever bring it up you're fired on the spot.") There are rapes along the park paths; smashed windshields in the parking lots; beaten bodies in the bushes. There is counterfeiting and armed robbery in the shops (tickets mainly)[8] and the tunnels (cash from the Brinks truck). And there is my favorite—it is so workable—the story of "the first Mickey Mouse" who has since been assigned elsewhere in the company because

> he has a bad skin problem. He has cancer of the skin. He got it from wearing the mask of Mickey Mouse—the head gear. His mother sued for him—he'd never been married—and he has a job guaranteed with Disney for the rest of his life. He's in his late fifties at least. But he has to be behind the scenes because of his skin. Nobody wants to look at him.

Occasionally one of these disasters flashes across the news wires as a reality check, though one that absolves Disney of responsibility. Everyone remembers the girl who fell while trying to jump cars in the Haunted Mansion and sliced off half her face in the process. Or the brother and sister con-team who tried to fake a rape in one of the resort hotels with the hope of cashing in on a negligence suit. No one, however, has ever heard the story of the young mother whose rented paddle boat was sucked into the wake of the *Empress Lilly* where, before the eyes of her gasping seven-year-old, the ship's paddle wheel chopped her quite in half. What one learns from all this discretion and calculated indiscretion is that Disney gets to control its own place because it can and because it can *so well,* even when it does so by defining the terms of its own success or at least the conditions under which that success will be understood.

If the production of magic depends on creating this isolated place and elaborating its architecture, it also presumes not providing a position for those within to see, as it were, the lay of the land. Again, a lot of this is practical, the result of the ever more refined divisions and subdivisions of workers throughout the park. The collective paranoia inculcated in Disney workers from the get go—manifested in the suspicion that there is always another rule one can be found breaking—and which results in their feeling that they are always expected to perform the frequently irritating role of "Disney cast member," is a function of both the tight control that the company exercises over its dominions and a segmented and hierarchical system of relations between management and labor and within labor itself. For better or worse, probably worse, Disney's corporate structure is the model for work in the new world order, its repetitive and service-based jobs subject to the authority not of one head, but a system of specialized functional units, each with its own set of chiefs, all working earnestly at their one task, the left hand oblivious to the right— the CIA model, where one room collects weather data, another trade statistics, while upstairs someone else coordinates so that conclusions can be drawn and the troops sent in.[9] This is a world in which all social planning has been replaced—as every attraction at EPCOT's Future World predicts and hopes it will be—by corporate planning, every advance in social coordination conforming to and confirming the logic of the company's needs.

The divisions of the work force intended by this system include the distinctions between full and part-time workers and those who fall between those categories. Almost everyone aspires to be "permed"—Permanent Full Time—at which point pour down the manna of Disney benefits. "You have better insurance than your parents," says a twentyish man. Everyone agrees: Disney's benefits are great if you can get them.[10] Anyone who's been full-time for three months is automatically eligible, but the trick is becoming full-time, and even that is no guarantee of permanent employment. Many workers simply hope to be rehired every year. One performer spoke of the annual jitters among her crowd: "Even now people are starting to sweat for no other reason than they've gotten a part and maintained a certain type of lifestyle and they could literally say to you, 'Thank you, you have two weeks.'" Short of full-time, one might instead be designated Casual Regular, which is part-time but "regular," that is, ongoing, not seasonal, with some but not all benefits. This is apparently also known by the oxymoronic "Permanent Temporary." For seasonal work, there are the CTs (sometimes Casual Seasonal),[11] the worst of the lot: long hours, though never officially full-time; temporary, but with no assurance of rehire in the following season. The brunt of the entry-level jobs, many of the characters and musicians, sales persons, hotel and restaurant staff, reservationists, etc. are staffed by CTs. Many return year after year, hoping to get back their old job; others hang on in whatever capacity they can, hoping to move up to full-time. During the summer, up to half of the park's employees may be CTs; many others—the high school crowd—are Casual Regular.[12]

The dividing and subdividing of Disney workers and their jobs continues in their placement: they can work on property or off,[13] on stage or backstage; they may be assigned to a department (e.g., Entertainment or Retail), which is further divided by park (Magic Kingdom or MGM), by area (Frontierland or Future World), and by attraction ("The Living Seas" or "20,000 Leagues"). Then they are given a specific position within the attraction, shop, or restaurant. Some workers are rooted in one area all day while others may canvass several areas in the course of it. The life-sized Disney characters—Minnie, Mickey, et al.—may do breakfast stints on the *Empress Lilly* and afternoon atmosphere sets in several areas of the Magic Kingdom, or EPCOT, or MGM. A spieler, one who spiels prewritten scripts, however, cannot leave his or her attraction and wander up and down Main Street. In other words, some workers are identified more by what they do, others by where they are, although all are subject to both and to strict rules about who can appear where wearing what. Being found out of place or time or otherwise out of costume is grounds for automatic dismissal.

The relentless categorizing and subdividing of employees by place, type, and amount of work has the effect of encouraging workers' identification with their area, their immediate group, rather than with other people in the park who might be doing similar things but in different places. The "Pirates of the Caribbean" people hang out with other "Pirates of the Caribbean" people. Chip sticks with Dale.[14] While Disney sponsors what appears to be an extensive network of intramural sports, clubs, and workshops for its employees to meet and mingle (including the Rush Limbaugh Society and the Alliance, a gay and lesbian organization, the latter apparently the stronger), most of the people I spoke with had very little contact with anyone in the park outside of those they worked with every day. As a server in a park hotel puts it, "You have to be identified with your area, and because of that you tend to stick with those people. I don't know anyone in the hotels who runs around with someone in the park." In other words, labor at Disney is themed along with everything else; one is not just a restaurant server, but a server in a particularly themed restaurant in a themed area of one of the parks. One's identification is not with other servers or even with restaurant workers generally— much less with CTs generally—but with the restaurant itself.

It's in the reified space of Disney themed work that one loses sense of where one is standing and in relation to whom. Here, any chance of collective perspective is appropriated by Disney under the rubric of corporate "community" and subsequently disabused of any liberatory potential.[15] This project is boldly announced at Team Disney, the company's corporate offices in Florida. Disney's notion of community is well known; it is cited by employees as one of the initial attractions of the job, and consists of several implied or stated commitments: promoting from within, thus giving every employee the opportunity to advance, and, as a corollary, giving each employee a valid and equal voice in the doings of the company—the sign of "equality" being an informal familiarity among employees regardless of rank. In practice, however, the relation among these elements engenders the contradictions that render suspect any community they were intended to promote; certainly they work at cross-purposes for the bulk of Disney's workers, for whom "community" specifically excludes their perspective as it invites, and indeed requires, confusing the personal and the corporate.

For example, internal promotion at Walt Disney World is usually in the form of the promotion of someone to the position of lead. Leads are hourly workers selected from among their peers, sometimes with senior-

ity, sometimes not, to work as the first line of supervision. They are not supervisors or management, however, and, while they earn more per hour than the others in the area, they aren't salaried either. They are given a high profile in Disney self-promotional materials—where a leadship is cited as the first stepping stone to upper management—but for many employees leads are seen as permanently submanagement: they've already topped out on their wage scale and have probably been passed over for a promotion to supervisor, much less to area manager. That is, they have to do most of the difficult work of actually supervising workers, with few of the rewards. Many workers feel that very ·few employees advance into real supervisory positions, and the ones that do move up at all become leads and stop there. As one attractions operator put it, "If you're a lead, you're not really going anywhere. It's kind of giving you power but not."[16] Among the park's performers and artists, there is a vague belief that leads are the lesser talents who have risen to their level of incompetence, that they are leads because they're not as good at playing or improvising: "There were certain people who could make up a sentence on the spot." Those who could not were "the bad spielers, the ones that sound like they're reading it. . . . More than likely if you weren't a good spieler, you were a lead."

While supervisors and executives are frequent objects of contempt or hostility ("You're not people of course"), workers' relations to leads are more complex. Some find them helpful mediators: leads are supposed to bridge relations between workers and supervisors. There is a sense, however, that leads are simultaneously discouraged from cultivating any genuine relationship with other employees either below or above them. In certain off-the-clock Disney watering holes—the Big Bamboo in Kissimee, for example, where outdated Disney IDs decorate the wall like so many mounted trophies—Disney employees gather but not together:

> You'd see that the people who were going out together weren't the leads. They weren't going out with you. They were staying away from us. You didn't really understand why. The leads would have their own little pack. The supervisors would have their own little pack. And nobody interacted in between. If you were a lead that hung out with your operators, you were not favored by the supervisors because the supervisors thought you should be with your leads. You needed to separate yourself.

Other workers feel the leads' precarious position relative to supervisors and workers makes difficult if not impossible the kind of community the company says it tries to create. In fact, the word used most often by workers to describe "community" at Disney was the rather less gracious "clique." The uniformity of this particular designation was surprising; the same term was used with equal ease and spontaneity by both the formerly embittered and the currently endeared:

> They treat you like a dog. They treat you like low life. If you're not in a clique, you're out of it. It takes a while to establish that clique. What defines a clique? If you're going to be a brownnoser. That's how you start being.

> It's very very cliquey. If you have a role in one of the primary shows, you're probably going to be doing shows for a lifetime. It's a group of people, and it's very hard to infiltrate. I don't care if you were the better dancer than me, I was there, and you're not getting in.

You can see somebody new. They're in awe. They're welcomed in, but if they don't fit the criteria of your particular group, they become outcasts very fast. There's a very big turnover.

In extreme cases like Karen's, group acceptance is a function in part of the length of time a person works in an area, but is made structurally impossible by the circumstances of employment. Karen responded to an ad for a behind-the-scenes job, was hired in May, told she'd be considered for full-time in three months, then promptly let go in September: "They let about twenty of us go at the same time. After that you'll see an ad in the paper for Disney. All of a sudden it shows up again." Since she and the twenty others who came in with her were hired with the intention of being kept on for only three months, there was no way for her to ever break into one of the groups that would help her secure promotion and consideration for a full-time position:

> We're outcasts. I was outcast for at least two months. That very last month was when I was getting to know people. They don't want any part of you then. Just get your hours in and bye bye, and that's it. It's an invitation-only type thing.

For Karen, any possibility of achieving community with her fellow workers much less the company itself is cut short from the start. For the rest, identification with each other and the perspective on their work it might afford them have been replaced by Disney with a model of community whose interrelations are always one-way. In that model, cliquishness, coupled with everyone's hope of becoming full-time and getting benefits, transforms the otherwise admirable goal of "promoting from within" into unhealthy competition, sycophancy, and mutual distrust. With few exceptions, every Disney worker I spoke with said that favoritism was the primary route to promotion up the ranks. They were sure that Disney's commitment to equal opportunity, Walt's bootstraps ethos, was self-evidently absurd, that in order not just to stay on—many of these, after all, are people who do not have a job guaranteed from one year to the next—but to move into a higher position, they had to be favored by someone above them, which usually requires them to be obsequious, not make problems, not complain:

> You've got to keep your mouth shut. You can't tell them your opinion. You have to do everything they say. The Disney way. Never say

anything negative. Everything's positive. There's never a no. You never say I don't know. If you don't know something you find out fast, even on your own after work.

They look for someone who can follow the rules, be a team player, never rock the boat no matter what the circumstances.

If you made waves, you were a problem. It is very difficult to break in once they know you'll stick up for what you believe in.

They tend to put into higher positions the younger ones. It's very seldom that an older person my age is in those manager jobs. Because the younger ones are more malleable, pliable, and the older ones can see through the bullshit. We're not as easy to make believe something is true that isn't.

That workers lower on a company's scale of value believe blatant sycophancy and problem avoidance are the keys to survival is not inconsistent with the experience of people similarly situated elsewhere, even in the "professions"; consider, for example, the tenuous situation of the lowly assistant professor who daily negotiates the line between self-promotion and self-abasement. What made Disney workers bitter was the gap between their expectations for opportunity with Disney and the eventual reality. When the pixie dust finally cleared, they were not impressed: "That's not what Disney stood for to me. I always thought it was, you know, equal, start at the bottom and work your way up."[17]

Internal promotion contributes to and complicates this cliquishness and consequent favoritism in part because leads are always selected from within the area where they will operate as leads. While supervisors might migrate, no one is made a lead then sent to another area: "They don't bring anybody new in to be a lead. Nobody from the Space Mountain Ride is going to come in and be a lead somewhere else. It's always your same family." Leads are significant to the company to the extent that they *know* their area and the people in them. This is the source of both the respect and contempt given leads. One worker, a sometime Minnie Mouse, puts it in classic Disney-speak: "Leads are someone that wore a head once and forgot what it was like to wear a head. Leads were someone that they put in a polyester costume and they forgot where they came from." If there's anger in her voice, it's double-edged: She is put out with the lead, the person who used to do the kind of work she still does—prance around in a heavy costume all day "wearing a head"—and who apparently has forgotten its difficulties once in the polyester lead costume. But she's also angry with the company that uses the leads' knowledge of worker culture for its own ends:

> To be a better lead, you better tell on someone else or find out what's going on. They'll actually put you out of your polyester and back into a head with me to sit around awhile then you'll know what's going on, what this one's saying about the other. Sometimes you'll be coming straight down to the zoo, so you have twenty-five minutes of talk time, so people sit around and they talk. Here you are a lead, you're back in costume now. Sometimes [everyone else] doesn't know you're the lead inside the costume. So now you know what's going on. Next week you're a lead again. . . . It's like Judas.[18]

In other words, they're spying. There's a lot of this going on at Disney World, though one hesitates to call it spying since everyone knows they're being spied on, except perhaps the guests, many of whom, if they knew, would approve anyway because that knowledge would augment the sense of safety so many of them claim to feel in the park and which appears to be premised on their not caring about a number of things. Besides the kind described above, spying takes several forms at Disney: there are "foxes," those who spy on guests (their name consistent with Disney's menagerie of animal names) and those who spy on employees, the even more aptly named "shoppers." Both dress like tourists. Foxes carry cameras; they keep the peace and hope to curtail some of the shoplifting which, along with counterfeiting and full fledged armed robbery, appear to constitute the bulk of Disney World crime. Shoppers roam the parks acting nasty to see if, like visitors at Buckingham Palace, they can aggravate employees enough to make them step out of character. Or they simply observe how workers interact with other guests; that is, they "shop" them:

> I was shopped one day. She gave me a good report because I'm always friendly to people. I had no idea who she was and still don't know. They come in. They buy two or three things. Disney gives them the money. They pretend they're from Idaho or some damn place, figure no one's ever been there.[19]

One might be tempted by their name to think that shoppers monitor only the shops and resort areas, but they are not so restricted. Shoppers can test anyone in the park regardless of what they do. From an employee's perspective, the effect is to transform all guests into potential *surveillantes*. The name "shopper," by the way, is indicative of Disney's perception of its guests: it's not that there are guests, some of whom shop; all Disney guests are shoppers, either now or in the future.[20]

The surveillance is less inventive backstage. At Central Reservations, several hundred people hooked up to telephones and computer terminals circle a windowed booth in the center of the room in which sit, like Bentham's wardens, the area's leads. Karen says,

> The leads would sit in one little booth in the middle of the floor and watch all of us. If something's really bad, if someone's giving us a hard time, then we'd flag them to come talk, and then they'd plug in [to the phone line] and plug us out. We could not hear what was going on. But the leads for the most part just sat up there and told us when to take a break.

When it comes time to evaluate individual workers, leads "plug in" again to an operator's line, though this time unannounced:

> They say you don't know when they're doing it, but I do. I can hear it click in the back. I can tell when they're overhearing the conversation. You have to really listen closely because they're that quiet. They do not let you know when they're going to listen to you. You never know, but you know your turn's coming eventually.[21]

Both the actual spying and the expectation that it is always potentially present affect worker habits in predictable ways. If the shopper is known, then one may act out accordingly. One performer says, "There are some people who start doing acting backflips when [they know shoppers] are out more so than otherwise, because it is a scary thing." But most shoppers are not identified, and so one is stuck mechanically reproducing the same commodified Disney charm: "You feel like you're a robot after awhile. It's a strain sometimes. It's very stressful, but you just have to."

It's in this context—the surveillance, the status of leads relative to those above and below them, and the culture of mutually generating suspicion and dependence effected by both—that we need to read the cheery familiarity and sense of equality Disney claims to foster between workers and management, but in fact enforces as a matter of policy, a very different thing. For example, everyone goes by first name, including Michael Eisner.[22] Everyone is encouraged to air problems on an area bulletin board, where complaints will be picked up and addressed at larger meetings. Anyone with an idea for how to improve the parks or the work done in them can leave their idea at another drop-off known simply as "I Have an Idea," after which, they will presumably receive credit and compensation for their contribution. But the last is a farce: technically, Disney owns any idea its workers have on property, a fact they attest to when they sign, sometimes unwittingly, a statement to that effect when they turn in their idea.[23] And the efficacy of the second varies with employee status and area: Permanent full-timers brag about their complaint sessions while the more contingent among them fear a trick wherein the meetings serve to isolate not the problems people are having, but the people calling them to management's attention.

As for the familiarity enforced by requiring the use of given names, this is a presumption extended to guests as well: a page from Disney's training manual with the heading "The Disney Difference" instructs employees to call guests by their first names if the name appears anywhere in sight—on clothing, jewelry, etc. "The Disney Difference" suggests that first names, along with smiling and repeating instructions, be used to corral unruly or oblivious guests, meaning they're tactics for crowd control. Similarly, the folksiness of first names is belied in Central Reservations where telephone operators are specifically not allowed to use their own names at all, but required instead to select from a preexisting list a "phony name" (unclear whether the pun is intended), which they use exclusively "in case someone writes a letter about you, and they [leads and supervisors] want to know who's giving that reservation." Furthermore, as with guests in the park, the intimacy of using (fake) first names when confirming reservations masks the fact that the reservationists are pretending to be as helpful as possible when they are in fact required to limit the guest's choices. Susan Willis says that trying to cut a deal on a Disney vacation package is like trying to win when the house holds all the cards, and she's right. According to Karen, phone name "Faith," she is forbidden to suggest more than three hotel options or even to admit that there is any room available other than those three:

> You're only allowed to tell them about three sites. You can't talk more than three sites. You've got to say no even though it shows up on your computer. They don't want you to spend too much time on anyone. They want you to get off, get the next phone call, and get off.

If using first names and cultivating an air of friendly helpfulness is contradicted for guests by the fact of manipulation, this same familiarity and sense of communal engagement is contradicted for workers by rules or customs that render actual worker friendships and cross-area alliances impossible or inconceivable. This is made explicit by regulating break and lunch times:

> You cannot socialize, that's what they tell us. The only time is if you're eating lunch. But they don't let too many people from the same area take their breaks at the same time. So if you check out for lunch with your lead at 12:21 and you're not back in that half an hour, you'll be docked for it. If we were talking—I was coming off break and she was going on—I'd stay an extra minute with her and be late getting back. So you really couldn't. It's like they don't want you to be together.

Or it may be simply "felt":

> If you worked in Entertainment, you'd hang out with Entertainment people; if you were in Attractions, you'd hang out with Attractions people. That's how it was. If you crossed, it was a weird feeling, like you weren't supposed to come through here: You're in Attractions. You're not supposed to be over here talking to us. It was kind of hard that way. You really weren't supposed to cross over the line. It was felt. You could just feel it.

When felt knowledge becomes the sign of internalized practice, it can take several forms: self-conscious rule breaking and self-regulation. What's self-conscious about the rule breaking is that most of it is directed specifically at Disney in its corporate togs and conceived of as sport. A lot of this is so painfully minor that the more workers brag about their accomplishments, the more one measures their unfreedom by them: "Sometimes we steal Cokes," or "No one noticed my lipstick," or "I've broken in line before." Occasionally they slip bottles of Gatorade under their costumes, bring outsiders into the tunnels, don't return IDs. The stricter the rule, the greater the challenge in breaking them. "You can play at work," says an employee on Pleasure Island where a Friday ritual involves switching name tags and thus making a joke of Disney's "friendliness" with every exaggerated misuse of a name. Depending on the leniency of leads, workers in the attractions or anyone employed to deliver scripted spiels may try to make a game out of altering the delivery or content of the spiel:

> Every day when I came in I erased the board [in the break room] and put up a word for the day. Today's word for the day is "casaba." I would write "casaba—n. a sweet melon." Then I would use it in a sentence: "Look at the casabas on that bimbo." That was my sentence that I used on the board. . . . Then every day I'd write, "Please use in your everyday spieler conversation." So you'd hear people say, "So you want to move your casabas all the way to the end of the row, fill in all the available spaces." Or, "We're going to take this guy's casaba and put it right here." We were using all kinds of words— "jocularity" was a word we used. They made us stop because it was not SOP, it was not Standard Operating Procedure, it was not in your spiel. People were hearing these words, which we thought was kind of fun. It helped out with the day, but our supervisors didn't like it. I had a dictionary: I used "animosity" and in the B category, I didn't even know what it was, it was "bannock," something you would not know. I was trying to pick up words you didn't know. Nothing really got out of hand. I think one of the leads said it wasn't very good and then he went to the supervisor and then they told me not to do it anymore.

For the more daring, there is stealing, which may be done for typical reasons if not in typical form, like the woman who nightly donned a new T-shirt and pair of stretch pants under her costume and wore them home. She had stolen upwards of $4000 worth of Disney junk and systematically turned it around for cash at flea markets on the weekends. Or the kid who finally got nabbed when one daily tally approached $1000. Otherwise, "Disney's not going to prosecute you if it's under $2000"; this includes guests.

For others, however, stealing is a kind of game played for less obvious reasons: I steal because I can or I steal from you to remind myself that I am not you. "You'd be surprised what you can get in the pockets of your pants and your costume," says one woman brightly. She's been heisting character watches for three years, giving some away but mainly arranging them around her apartment. One musician points proudly to the pair of very average black sweat pants he is wearing; he got them out of the park by using them to line the bottom of his instrument case. Getting stuff out of the park is particularly prized: it takes some doing when employees must show a receipt or lead-signed statement for everything they depart with, including balloons and empty boxes. As for Lost and Found, well, says one, "that's another story." It's several other stories actually. One hears about the return of a wallet with its $4200 still intact, and then one hears this:

> If you find something you like, you keep it. What are you, nuts? You keep that stuff. You're first week here, you put it in Lost and Found and then you realize that the leads are going through it going, "Hey! Raybans!"

> If you found something that was lost, your job was to go ahead and give it to the lead and say, "This is for the Lost and Found Box." And they'd be like "Take it."

> As a tour guide, or anybody who works with a lot of people, they'd move into the theater and then they'd leave. We were all the time getting cameras, wallets, purses, things like that. Bunch of money sometimes, but you'd turn that in because Investigations could see this.

> My parents have a nice 35mm camera that I found at Disney, via guests. It's kind of like "Eh, it's ours." Because the people at Lost and Found are going to take it anyway. But when it comes to money, you usually turn that in or you would see your lead out drinking on it that night. If you found a wallet and it had identification and it wasn't a foreigner, you gave the money back.

It's not really that hard to square these tales with Fjellman's figures for theft in the park; he claims 35 percent of all lost items are returned to their owners, but then lists among the contents of that 35 percent sunglasses, Cabbage Patch dolls, and false teeth, not, particularly in the last instance, the kind of thing you'd want to keep.[24]

Stealing might come as a revelation to Disney guests who are so pumped up on feel-good hype about safety and mutual happiness that they can't see literally what's going on around them. Perhaps they would be surprised also by the presence in this inventory of alternative worker practices of two old favorites, sex and drugs. The latter can be, and apparently is, done "anywhere":

You can get high right on property. There's a lot of places. Lots of people get high. Disney doesn't drug test you. They can't afford it. They've got 35,000 people working here. They're not going to drug test anybody, so its sold on property. It's done right there on property. No problem.[25]

Drugs seem to be more common among costume characters and CTS generally, who are partial to amphetamines, legal and not, which they use to pump themselves up in order to work overtime and thus earn more than their usual $5.60 an hour. For CTS overtime is paid for hours worked over each eight-hour shift, not time over each forty-hour week: "After eight hours, you could go home or you could stay and get paid time and a half. After sixteen hours, double time. If you want to work those hours, you take pills or cocaine. Speed up." One might want to remember this next time these characters are seen bouncing among children on the Disney Channel.

As for sex, the underground tunnels and elevators appear to be a big attraction both during and after park hours. Mickey and Minnie, sex unclear, have been found "doing ungodly things to each other," so "un-godly," in fact, that "a little girl walking in would have been scarred for life." Or consider the people who sneak back into the park at night in pilfered custodial costumes and head over to MGM's "Wheel of Fortune" where they can be found going at it "right there on the wheel."

But this is the good news. The bad news is that for a great many Disney workers coping with rigid rules and potentially hostile worker relation-ships means adopting forms of self-monitoring and regulation. For some, this requires avoiding contact with anyone: "Your best thing is to stay by yourself at Disney. If you want to keep your job, do your work, keep your mouth shut, stay by yourself." Others advise finding a group as quickly as possible and start making the ties with leads and supervisors that will help if there is ever trouble in the future. Finally, some had begun regulat-ing each other—becoming, in effect, another kind of Disney shopper. When asked what they did if and when they went to the park on their own or with friends and family, most said they seldom went—current employees don't want to be there and former ones can't afford it—but those that did described their main activity and *enjoyment* as watching other workers, usually people doing something analogous to what they do. Either they simply made mental notes for their own improvement or they approached and "advised" their coworkers. Says Annette: "Sometimes if I see something I don't personally think is very symbolic of what this park's about and the concept of Disney, I personally would take it upon myself to go to that person and say 'I can tell you're having a bad day,' or whatever."

It's difficult to know how to judge Annette's comments—e.g., the ominous "or whatever"—where the attempted empathy of "I can tell you're having a bad day" belies its opposite: not the fact that she knows, or doesn't, what a day like this is like, but that she knows the other's work is not "very symbolic of what this park's about." While her repetition of "personally" is consistent with the personal understanding and concern inherent in her capacity to recognize the difficulties she presumably has also dealt with and empathize with the other who is dealing with them now, it also betrays her. Finally, what she feels personal about is not her coworker, her own work, or her helpfulness, but the "concept of Disney," one tenet of which invites as a management strategy the habitual confusion of the personal with the corporate.

The skeptical among us will say I'm overreading, and perhaps I am. It's easy after talking to Disney workers to fall into their habits and specifically into the suspicion and paranoia many of them feel within the park and, for some, even outside it. What this example indicates is the extent to which Disney attends to the space of its own authority: apparently, its surveillance includes employees monitoring and tutoring each other off the clock and across the space of the property where their encounter might take place. But the requirement that workers observe rules and each other while they are "on property" at least in theory offers the possibility that they can eventually be "off." It's difficult, however, to see where this off property place would be, if, as one worker put it to me, "Your outside activity from work is taken into account at work," by which he meant not even what he actually does off the clock but whatever his leads and supervisors perceive to be his character when they aren't around. According to him, their thinking runs like so: "If you're wild out there, you're going to be wild in here. We can just tell. That is one of their things." Or, consider the ruminations of this person who was convinced one of Disney's "things" was that it could and regularly did gain access to police and bank records, which it used to summarily fire anyone whose private activities could be seen to threaten its image:

[Working at Disney] feels like being a prisoner almost twenty-four hours a day. It's a concentration camp. If you don't carry your ID with you, and nobody knows you work for Disney, it's fine. But if they find out you work for Disney and something bad goes wrong and you're involved—it's not the Disney way. Just do not let them know you work for Disney. The best thing is not to carry your ID. But if someone asks you who your employer is, then you're stuck anyway. I don't know how Disney finds out. It just pops up somehow. If it's a police report. [pause] I don't know if they do surveys about us or what, if they search from one place or if the bank reports it to Disney [e.g., a bounced check]. You feel like someone's watching you.

The free-floating anxiety palpable in this rambling comment—and it is the most extreme of its kind—reflects the ease with which she imagines Disney's potential or inevitable presence in any aspect of her life, the suspicion that she could at any time do something that is "not the Disney way," that Disney might "find out" because news of it has "popped up" somewhere. Why or how Disney would have routine access to bank records and police reports was unclear to her and finally didn't really matter; she was certain that the company did, that should something go wrong in town her ID card was as much a liability as it is otherwise a benefit when used for discounts. Certainly Orlando residents believe that Disney's reach is long: one employee from Universal Studios, disappointed not to be included in my interviews, informed me that "Disney and the *Orlando Sentinel* are in bed together."[26] Not too many residents, however, actually believe the company is in league with the banks, though they might want to continue to assess that relationship. For example, Sun Bank, a prominent Florida bank—Disney's bank, in fact, for which, the urban myth goes, thousands are employed just to count the park's daily take—has imported the idea of using leads to manage and train other employees.

But this is all in the spirit of business, team work, Walt might say, and who in fact did say that his most rewarding experience was not, alas, seeing the happy faces of delighted children but just "the whole damn thing, the fact that I was able to build an organization and hold it."[27] Walt Disney's conception of his contribution to the daily work of his employees, his idea, that is, of "holding it," hovers tellingly between the cartoonish and the erotic. When asked by a child what he actually does since he does not draw Mickey Mouse, or write the jokes, or even, incredibly, sign his own name, he tells the young innocent, "Well, sometimes I think of myself as a little bee. I go from one area of the studio to another and gather pollen and sort of stimulate everybody."[28] This stimulation continued after his death and became at that point rather more perverse. Knowing that he was dying, wanting to ensure not just the success of his new park in Orlando but the compliance of his staff with his vision for it, and apparently supremely suspicious of the motives, talents, or enthusiasm of those he was leaving in his stead, Disney recruited a camera crew in the months before his death and made a series of films in which he continued to stimulate his workers from beyond the grave. In the films, he conducts staff meetings to an empty conference table with the intention—and apparently the result—that they be shown monthly to his senior staff after he's gone. "What he did," said one local county commissioner,

> was to hold conferences right through the 1980s. I think it's once a month these fellows sit down and view the film. And there's Walt Disney saying, "Bob, this is October, 1976. You remember we were going to do this or that. Are you sure it's underway now?" I think that demonstrates his remarkable attention to detail.[29]

Though his plans for the Orlando park were not followed to the letter, though EPCOT is pretty much exactly not what he wanted, not a real "community," prototype or otherwise, but the permanent and permanently anachronistic nightmare that it is, such was not the case for Walt's lack of prudence in trying to oversee his employees. Like the company that survives him and that bears his name, the one that calls itself a "team" yet cannot see its way to playing fairly, Disney is always watching. He seems, like it, to be nowhere and everywhere, the imaginary line of his existence finally quite permeable and fluid as he extends his reach into the present in this last attempt at total theater. He talks to no one—a vacant conference table—yet is continually invoked in conversations about future plans: "What would Walt think?" the executives coo. "Would Walt have approved?"—as if the chances are always good that he might appear in the room with them, disagreeing and scolding, a talking corpse whose legacy is the "remarkable attention to detail" that haunts his followers in the guise of their own commitment to reproducing it.

Shiny Happy People

TED: *Let's say you were like Pluto, and you were the person in the costume. See, I would never say that to anybody that would write that in the paper, that there was somebody inside the costume. These kids come up and hug you and you sign the autographs and plus, you know, it's just something you have to experience, because you are the cartoon. You become Pluto. You have to experience it to understand.*
JK: *Is the "experience" the becoming Pluto or the interaction with the kids?*
TED: *The interaction with the kids.*
JK: *I see.*
TED: *As Pluto.*

At one end of the hole under Disney's Magic Kingdom, under the "Carousel," backstage, lies the "zoo." Here, mice and bears, the whole Disney menagerie, gather between their public appearances to kill time without being seen. They must arrive early for their shift to pick up and put on the heavy costumes they negotiate above ground for $5.60 an hour. Inside the huge heads, the heat of a Florida afternoon builds. Some say it gets as high as 130 degrees. All peripheral vision is cut off. Some of the heads are so unwieldy or the body of its wearer so small that a metal brace is worn on the shoulders with a post extending down the back and up into the head to keep it aloft. Without this, a child's overzealous hug might throw the characters off balance and send them, like grotesque babies, following the head to the ground. The working conditions are so bad that the characters are supposed to go above ground for only 20 to 25 minutes at a time, though in peak seasons they may stay longer. Even then, it is not unusual for the characters to pass out on stage. If you know what to look for you can see them around the park as they wait for a lead to scurry them back to the "zoo," where they can finally remove the head. Leaning against replicas of eighteenth-century lampposts or propped against a float's lit backboard, their inhuman heads flashing a permanent smile, they wait, half conscious, hand raised from the elbow, waving absently to no one in particular.

Apparently the costumes alone can make wearers sick or, in conjunction with drugs and the Florida heat, can be so painful that wearers are more susceptible to heat exhaustion. Disney has an elaborate roster of height requirements for each kind of costume character: the costumes are built to the specifications of a particular body height and type, although not—as is the case for some performers in MGM Studios—to specific bodies. The bears, for example, require not just height, but strength because of the brace supporting the head. Problems arise when, in the crunch of the summer season, people (usually women, teenagers, and some younger kids) are put into costumes they are not equipped physically to handle:

> When you put a head on, it's supposed to fit on your shoulders. That's why there are height requirements for each individual costume. I have found kids that were 5′ given costumes that should have been given to someone who was 5′4″. So to hold that costume on, they strap the brace on you to make the shoulders stick out. This is how they're walking around for anywhere from 25–45 minutes. I've seen children being hurt by it. They are tired; they're fatigued; their backs, their necks are hurting. And if you were to say "I can't wear this costume," then you can be sure you won't be working there for very long. Your hours would be cut, or you're just not one of the favorites.

> It sounds crazy. The gummy bears costumes do not fit somebody that was 4′10″ and they were putting 4′10″ people in them. It was still too large and too heavy for the shoulders of someone with that frame. I played Sunny Gummy and Scruffy—that's the little mean gummy. The heads dig into your collar bones. When you're dancing or even if you're on the moving float, you are in pain. That's metal. There's no way out of it, and there's no relief when you're in it.[30]

It's unclear how many of the Disney characters pass out on a given summer day, though everyone is sure that they do. One man reports that during the summer a goodly part of his job is devoted to driving around retrieving characters where they fall. One day he picked up three at one stop—Donald, Mickey, and Goofy: "All of them had passed out within five minutes of each other. They were just lined up on the sidewalk." This is in EPCOT which, unlike the Magic Kingdom with its system of underground tunnels, has a backstage behind the facades of the park's various attractions and to which the characters can escape if they have to. If they are in the Magic Kingdom, however, or on a parade float, they must simply ride it out or wait until they've recovered enough to walk to a tunnel entrance in costume and under their own steam. This can get a bit dicey. Passing out is sometimes prefaced by (and probably directly caused by) throwing up inside the head, which cannot be removed until out of public view:

> You're never to be seen in a costume without your head, *ever.* It was automatic dismissal. It's frightening because you can die on your own regurgitation when you can't keep out of it. I'll never forget Dumbo—it was coming out of the mouth during the parade. You have a little screen over the mouth. It was horrible. And I made $4.55 an hour.

> During the parades, I've seen many characters in 90° heat vomit in their costumes and faint on the floats and were never taken off the float. There's so much going on during a parade that people are not going to notice if Dopey is doing this [slumps] and he's not waving. . . . I've never seen them take a character off a float.

In one instance described to me, Chip of Chip 'n Dale fame passed out where he stood at the very top of a float, mounted to it by a post that ran up one leg of the costume and into the head. While this was a precaution to keep him from possibly falling off when the float jerked or hit a bump, the visual effect was crucifixion: Chip held up by a post for public exhibition, head hanging to one side, out cold.

The cardinal rule among Disney costume characters is never to be seen out of character and specifically out of the head or, alternately, never to let the costume be seen as a costume. Costumes must be black bagged when the characters travel to do work in town or out of the park: "Everything is black bagged. . . . God forbid if that black bag has a tear in it that you didn't know about, and a nose is sticking out of there. You're in trouble." The characters must follow rules about how to and not to move. They can't back up, for example, for the obvious reason that they can see only whatever is straight in front of them and even then only at eye level. They also cannot feel anything around them because the costumes stick out from their body and distort their sense of space. Sometimes these conditions provide the occasion for delight, as when Minnie Mouse came undone on stage: "I'm walking by the railroad and my pantaloons were around my ankles. You don't feel it because you have so much on you. People were hysterical. Finally, a lead came out, 'Minnie, Minnie, your panties have fallen.'" The fate of Winnie the Pooh, however, is also instructive:

One time somebody dressed up as Winnie the Pooh backed up. When she backed up she hit a bush and the head popped off. The head popped off Winnie the Pooh, and all the kids see this girl walking around in a Winnie the Pooh costume. And she's fired on the spot because her job is to be the character. And she didn't follow the rules. She should have turned around and walked out. Instead she backed up.

Her job is to be the character, and it is on this injunction to "be" a Disney character that the rule not to lose one's head is grounded. Apparently losing her panties is in character for Minnie; Winnie, however, is fired immediately for losing her head, the same way Dumbo would be fired immediately for taking off the one he had just thrown up in because both actions destroy the park's magic, the illusion that the characters are real. One person I spoke with refused for an hour to acknowledge even that there were actual human people inside the Disney character costumes: "That's one of the things I really can't talk about. Not because I work there, but because it keeps it kind of sacred." "Snow White *is* Snow White," another explains. Thus, when she goes to receive an award at a local hospital, Disney officials will not allow her to publicly accept it out of costume. Instead, she must appear as Snow White so those either assembled for the occasion or made privy to it later will not be disillusioned by her transformation into a regular person. In an attempt to impress upon newly-hired employees the significance of the rule not to break character, one management type recounted in a training session the story of taking his visiting niece into the tunnels to find that same Snow White. When they met her, she turned on them, cigarette and Diet Coke in hand, and told them "Get the hell out of here. I'm on break." The child was crushed, the spell broken, and a future shopper permanently lost. It's not a true story, of course—no one can smoke in the tunnels—but it's used apparently to great effect to confirm for new employees the importance of their work and what's at stake—a child's "dream"—in maintaining the company's high standards: "I was very much an idealist about it, about the job, and the whole Disney magic thing that they try to project to the public. I felt that all that magic and happiness was embodied in the character."

The extent to which Disney workers seem actually to become their roles and thus embody magic and happiness—and this includes everyone, not just those in head costumes—is one of the most remarked and generally praised aspects of the park and is said to be the thing that distinguishes Walt Disney World from its neighbor down the street, Universal Studios: "Why is Disney a happier place? Because it's Disney." For those not in character costumes but nevertheless cast and in costume, the transformation to "Disney" via "embodiment" amounts to a kind of leveling out of difference wherever possible. "They deliberately hire blondes," confides one brunette apparently not concerned with reconciling this contradiction. The perception is that they do hire blondes or recreate them as blondes either with wigs or, in one case, enforcing a rule not to have two-toned hair: one woman wanted to stop coloring her hair and let it go gray, but was prevented from doing so by a rule designed to weed out those tending toward fashion experiments.[31] It was okay to be gray; she just couldn't let it go gray. She was left with no choice but to continue coloring it the same honey blonde she had when she came in. Generally, however, it doesn't matter who or what you are when you come in since, once in, you will become whatever you were cast to be: "They have your personality waiting for you. That's literally true: Check it at the door."

It's uncanny, in fact, the way Disney's workers once through that door seem not to stop being their roles. One woman explains how it's hard for her to step out of character when she's in the park on her own time:

> I sometimes find myself smiling at people. They're like, "What are you smiling at me for?" I know they're thinking that, but it's because I still feel like I'm constantly this character. I have to say, "Oh, no one notices me, no one recognizes me. It's okay." It's strange sometimes. I'll smile at people or if a child falls down, I go to pick him up, and people probably don't understand that, but I forgot.

During our interviews, many Disney employees would break in and out of character as they spoke, beginning first in a descriptive or narrative mode and switching at some point to direct address as though I were a park guest they encountered in the course of the day. Moreover, their training at Disney University has left permanent marks on their memory. They and the half of Orlando that has worked in the park at some time or another can spout off Disney fun facts at will. How many spots were used in *101 Dalmations?* 6,469,154. How do you remember the names of the Seven Dwarfs? Two s's, two d's, and three emotions. What kind of popcorn is used in the park? Orville Redenbacher. There's a Disney library and a Disney trivia line for emergencies, but many still have this stuff down years after leaving their jobs. They are information machines, walking advertisements for the park.

Apparently this transformation to Disney product is what many of them want when they apply to the park in the first place. These are frequently people who have migrated to Orlando specifically to work at Disney, often with exceedingly high, perhaps naive, expectations about the park. While these expectations are sometimes only vague notions that Disney must be "the epitome of the fun place to work," at other times they reflect a high level of personal investment with the park and with its power to raise the innocuous or mundane lives of average people into the fantastical and magical existence of the Disney cast member:

> I came down in the summer. I told my parents I was going to work for Disney World, and they said, "Sure you are." I said, "No, really I am. I'm going to go down and work for Disney." They said, "No you're not." And I said, "Yes, I am." So, me and two friends of mine came down—I was just turning 21—in March or April. As soon as you walk in, you are so excited just to be there. Especially me. I'm from Dalton, Georgia. I was a little guy who'd never known anything or been anywhere, and I just decided to come down and do what I wanted to do.

> I had six kids in my family. We didn't have a lot of money. But I saw that the park was the one place I saw my parents be relaxed, be kids again. So the park was basically wonderful. What was amazing for me to see would be my dad. He's a truck driver, but he would wear this Goofy hat when he was there. He wouldn't wear it after he left the park, but he would wear it there. And I would see them smile and relax, unlike their usual lives. I saw the behavior change. That is what said to me, "There's something special here."[32]

> I was going through a divorce after seventeen years of marriage. I was a dancer many years ago, and I never got the opportunity to do the craft again because I was raising children. I was out of New York. Never knowing what I was going to do and still in the process of raising children, I decided I was going to go to Disney. Why, I don't know; it was a fluke. When you fail at sixteen, it's okay. When you fail at thirty-six, it's kind of rough. It took me seventeen years to get out of my house and get on I-4 and have the courage to go down and

apply for something. Well, I go, still never telling anybody, especially my ex-husband who'd said, "What are you going to do? Who's going to want you with three kids? You never worked a day in your life except in the family business, blah, blah, blah." But I thought to myself, I have to do this at least for something just for me.

I was always kind of sentimental about it. I had never been to the park before I worked there. I had just moved down here to Florida from northwest Indiana, the Chicago area, in August 1988, and I got hired in September. It was a very quick thing. It was my senior year in a new school. I didn't know anybody. There was this great opportunity to do something. I picked the character department because it seemed like a lot of fun—the whole concept of "Hey, I'm Pluto."

This is who they are: a twenty-one-year-old homeboy from small town southern Georgia for whom the park represents escape from his parents—their arguments and negative dismissals—so that he can "do what [he wants] to do"; a young woman from a working-class background led back to the park by memories of her parents living one day that is "unlike their [and her] usual lives"; a woman for whom Disney represents a new life and opportunity and the chance to prove she can make it on her own; a seventeen-year-old who finds a place for himself in a new environment at a difficult point in his life by adopting the identity of Pluto. What these stories have in common is the hope that Disney World will provide people with a clean slate and something to write on it; here they can become part of the magic—a Disney item, familiar and reproducible. The park is the site for this transformation, a place where the past—and particularly past identities—is erased, where all bets are off because here a divorced mother of three can and does audition with sixteen-year-olds decked out in their "matching socks and headbands" and get selected over them because, as her director explains, "when she danced, she danced all over."

These narratives should be read alongside the various legends and myths that are told and retold in the park and Orlando about miscellaneous millionaires and former executives said to be ladling lemonade at Aunt Polly's Landing. I encountered many tales of these people—though no one who fit the description—who are supposed to have abandoned their former lives either permanently or on a twice-weekly basis to work at Walt Disney World: a former journalist for the *New York Times*, stock

analysts in flight from Wall Street, semiretired doctors of various spe-
cialities, including a former emergency room doctor from "a New York
hospital" (she "couldn't handle the trauma"), bank presidents, disillusioned heirs, and leisured women who jet in from the islands (which they
own) for some quality time with the general public. Some of these are the
$1-a-year-salary types: "Nothing for me, please. I'm just doing it for the
children." Others are said to have walked out of their earlier lives (read:
the money, the status, and their attendant problems) to refashion themselves in this new Disney environment. While some of these stories may
be true, the veracity of individual cases is less important than the Disney
truth produced by the circulation of them: Walt Disney World is the place
where truck drivers' daughters work alongside corporate executives in
their common mission of producing magic. Furthermore, it's important
to see that both the firsthand accounts and the Disney myths trace the
same narrative movement. Whether seen from outside as a rise or fall in
status or morality, inside the world of Disney they are all the same story,
Disney's story, in which everyone moves not up or down—since these
implied inequities don't matter or exist in the park—but toward and
within the place where each is remade in such a way that anyone can and
would want to say "Hey, I'm Pluto."

It's the "Hey, I'm Pluto" factor I want to address here, the "experience"
of getting to be the Disney cast member so completely that one "embodies
the magic." This experience is not just playing with kids, it's playing with
kids "as Pluto." I want to be clear about this lest anyone think I've been
unfair, misleading, or too one-sidedly negative: in the main, and in many
ways quite understandably, Disney employees like their work. They don't
particularly like the Walt Disney Co.: they find its rules and policies
unbending, silly, and degrading, but they love working at Disney World.
Without a single exception, every person I spoke with found something
good to say about their time at the park, and without a single exception,
every person I spoke with identified that something in similar terms: it
has to do with being in public, with being performative, and with the
kind of transformative potential many feel is generated—though not necessarily carried through—by the two.

Sometimes this is as simple as allowing people to be something they
find themselves otherwise incapable of being: outgoing, confident, or
happy. Though he certainly likes them when he's in character, Ted (Pluto
above) never visits the park when he's not in costume because, he says, "I

don't like crowds." Pam tells a similar story about her job in retail: "It's the only place I know where I can go and make a total fool of myself and have a ball." Guests tell her that she is "more fun than going out to one of the shows." She makes this connection to performance explicit by comparing and at points confusing her work in the store with her earlier career as a pianist in a cocktail lounge:

> I played the piano for years, so I'm used to talking to strangers. Yet if I was not playing the piano and there were a table full of men executives I would never say hello to them. It's different. If I'm on stage I have a persona that I can get away with. If I'm privately there I'm much too shy to go up and say something to them. But if I were playing that night I would go up and ask them for songs, where they were from, did they get away from the wife for two weeks, my god, give me their address I'll write them and tell them what you're really doing. I kid with them. As long as you're on Disney property, you can do that.

Terry, who finally left her husband and headed down I-4, reveals in her job preferences just how her work is helping her negotiate the gender roles and definitions evolving with the changes in her life. As a character performer, Terry prefers being Minnie "because I relate to her." She has "a problem" with Mickey "because he has to use that macho stance." Finally, though, it's Pinocchio who's the real favorite "because you can be a girl, except you are a little boy, and the boy can be a little bit feminine." When I suggested to Pam, perhaps in warning, that a bit of this play acting goes on for all of us—I'm a teacher and a writer, after all, poseurs both—she was careful to distinguish between those inside and outside Disney and even within the Walt Disney Co. itself. The operative category again was property: "If it were a Disney store in the mall, you'd still have the persona of being on stage and part of Disney, but it wouldn't feel the same because you're in a mall in Illinois. It's totally different." Annette concurs: "The majority of people that I have found who work in front of the public in merchandising, selling things—we play with them [she's an improvisational actress] and they play with us—and that's something you don't get in a mall, even if you're doing retail. So that changes every day."

It's telling the way both women understand and anticipate the comparison to and criticism of their work as "mall jobs." In neither case had I mentioned malls. It's taken for granted that such jobs are awful, that their awfulness is the result of an ungainly combination of place (the endless Midwest small town that is ironically the source of Disney's Main Street and the layout of every mall in every town in the country), routine (the job that doesn't "change every day"), and, most especially, the lack of Disney "play." In the absence of play, what's left is the brute fact of the work itself, selling usually, requiring for its success not the persona of the Disney World cast member but someone who merely works. The horror of the mall job is the horror of fading into such a creature, disappearing, as it were, into the woodwork of the counter behind which one stands for eight hours a day.

Yet disappearing is exactly what happens at Disney World. Here the possibilities for play lie precisely in becoming so visibly a part of the park, its life and well-being, that one must of necessity be rendered invisible in other ways, as when, for example, no one notices that you've passed out. But it's not only in these instances, nor only when the lesser or former self left behind in the other world is no longer apparent. In general, and as a matter of policy, workers are not seen or allowed to be seen by guests as anything other than the roles they've been cast in and sometimes not seen at all. "Where's Smiley?" asks a guest at the Polynesian, sarcastically converting a buffet server into one of the Seven Dwarfs and thus translating the server's discontent or bad mood into the language of a fairy tale where it can be effectively hidden or ignored. The guest's cue is picked up by Smiley's lead who tells me, "I can be Grumpy too, but I try to put on a smile and change my attitude. Put on a face."

This smiling attention can be taken only so far, however, because, while Disney workers must be visibly concerned with the pleasure of the park's guests, they must remain invisible to guests as persons themselves. One woman talked about almost losing her job in a park resort hotel for "being nice to a guest":

> [A fellow employee and I] were waiting for the ferry, and a honeymoon couple came out. They're very lovely people. They began to talk to us and said, "Why don't you take us through the park and be our guides? You guys are so funny." So we went through and spent eleven hours with them. We had dinner with them that night. [My supervisor] found out and tried to fire us. What they don't want is for you to get to a guest and tell them the dark side of Disney. They're petrified of that, that their secrets might get out.

These were people she had already met and presumably helped in the course of her work; what causes her problems is the extension of that prescribed familiarity into a genuine intimacy. The very closeness she develops with her new friends is what brings her to the attention of her supervisor: "They wrote me letters, they sent me pictures, and they wrote a letter to Disney and thanked them for the wonderful day they had with Katy and Dawn." What she should have done is smile, "put on a face" of friendly and concerned interest, and politely refuse. She should, in other words, stay in character, making clear that, even among those in the park whose work puts them directly in front of the public in seemingly un-scripted and unpredictable roles, all roles at Disney are scripted and should be predictable. The further irony is that, as someone working with the public, her role is scripted for "naturalness." She plays the part of the helpful and friendly hosteler one should expect to encounter on Disney's Main Street: "Be yourself," she's told, "otherwise act authentic."

For the bulk of the park's employees engaged in the repetitive, often mindless, if not idiotic tasks that together produce Disney's magic, the putting on of happy faces is daily work.[33] "We have a hard time," says David, an attractions host, because

> you go out in public and be this boy scout for eight hours a day. When you come home, you're a mess. You're a maniac. You're angry. You're tired. You have to get rid of your anxieties. You start teaming up with people because you could all talk about the day's events. So you go out and get as drunk as you possibly can, pass out, and the next day get up and go to work. You're just like, "I can't take this anymore."

If reciting the same scripted spiel every fifteen minutes to a new, yet somehow ever more familiar audience is difficult, it is at least made bearable by Disney's rotation system. Ostensibly—and this is its advertised benefit—rotation exposes each employee to the work of those around him or her; this is, in fact, what it does, but only to the extent that the employee is kept going through the shift. Without rotation, says one, "you'd be just sick to death. They tap into a good thing there by moving you around. It does get monotonous as all get-out even then." At a typical Disney attraction, rotation consists of a series of fifteen-minute or half-hour minishifts in which a worker is bumped from monitoring a line outside, to ushering crowds into a theater ("Walk all the way to the end of the row please"), to spieling itself, and back again to the line. In other words, they're not really learning other aspects of the park or of the company's business, but how the particular machinery of their attraction works and how they can function interchangeably as cogs at various points in it. Guests don't register this, of course. What they sense is functionality in its pure and purely invisible form.

Functionality can backfire, though, as when remaining in character and following Disney routine do not prepare one for any contradictions they might engender. For example, Disney workers cannot embarrass a guest, and while that sounds simple enough, it is more difficult in practice when one has more than one guest not to embarrass. Kevin recounts such an incident taking place in Gasparillas, a "little hamburger joint" which, because it is adjacent to the hotel pool and stocked with video games, attracts daily the hotel's entire male guest population between the ages of eight and fifteen and their mothers. Into this den walks one morning a woman—a "Brazilian"—in a thong and something attempting to pass for a bikini top. She is not, apparently, a little girl. Kevin describes the scene thusly:

> When she bends over to pick up something, everything swings forward. Mothers were grabbing their kids and dragging them out. We can't go up to this lady and say, "Excuse me, could you please put a T-shirt on?" because that would embarrass her. She's not embarrassed. We couldn't do anything except pray that she'd walk out and go back to the pool.

They also can't do anything when "a group of Brazilian kids ages nine to eleven . . . all boys" proceed to chase each other around the lobby of the Grand Floridian playing what is politely known as grab tag. Eventually one of the boys opens the piano and bangs on it to the delight of his fellow ruffians. The hotel staff is at a loss:

> The concierge and front desk are trying to ignore them. This goes on for about twenty minutes. I can hear the kids speaking, but I can't make out if it's Spanish or Portuguese. I can see these other people ["Americans"] getting annoyed. It's like, "Why don't they do something?" They're banging on the piano and nobody comes up to do anything. So the guest gets up, and he goes over and says, "Excuse me, but that's not your piano. You shouldn't be banging on it." And

they look at him and say, "No speak English." The guy goes and sits down. He's thoroughly upset. You're not supposed to embarrass a guest but this other guest who's paying is thoroughly upset. *I* could have said something because I was on my off time, but it's not my job. Security finally goes up and says something.

Kevin understands the staff's problem: while there are two sets of guests to accommodate, they can't satisfy one without insulting or displeasing the other. He senses that age and means might give the "other people" priority, but even so imagines being able to handle the situation himself only by being "on off time" and out of his Disney role. He doesn't say anything, however, even when he is "on off time"—which apparently means still "on"—because "it's not his job." What he means is it's not his *role*. Neither is it the concierge's role nor that of the front desk staff; thus, they do nothing but stand and watch. It is security's role, however, and, indeed, eventually security arrives to play its part by "saying something" to the boys and ushering them out.

This problem of negotiating the needs of different guests with Disney's needs to cater more to some of them is also handled linguistically. At work, Kevin distinguishes between PXS and VIPS. A PX is a very important guest, as opposed to a VIP who is just anybody. Although presumably all Disney guests get special treatment, PX is used by employees among each other to distinguish those guests "one level above VIPS" who do get special treatment. The term offers a way to refer to these people without making other guests feel less important or even know that distinctions are being made:

> We're not supposed to single any guest out above any other guest. If we happen to be in a guest area, we say PX because other guests don't know what we're talking about with PX. If we say the VIP is in Room 102 and another guest hears it, they're like "Oh, so that's a VIP that's staying up there. What am I?" It's so we can single out the very important people without making the VIP regulars seem regular.

Examples of PXS, in descending order, are Mrs. Eisner, Michael (Jackson or Eisner), and any vice president.

Though at work Kevin is on stage—a half-wall and glass separate him and the kitchen from hotel guests who frequently stop to watch and chat—compared to workers in the attractions, the street vendors, and many others, he has relative flexibility and creative freedom. For the park's self-identified artists and performers, disappearing on the job is understood to be the erasure of just that creative input in the performance of tasks which either by their sheer repetition and monotony or the inanity of their production render employee contributions null. A bad day at MGM Studios, says Annette, is when "it's like a Broadway show that's been on tour for three years. Then it feels like nine-to-five theater. You show up and do acting." A professional musician, full-time and permanent, describes playing in a fourteen-piece tuba and bugle band for a convention of four people at 8:00 in the morning while trying to convince himself he's not a "theme park musician": "They had the entire convention center, a 100,000 square foot room with one table in it with them eating breakfast. And tubas were the entertainment." While the incongruity of this particular incident provoked his reaction, the same response is occasioned at other times by the kind of evacuation through repetition described by Annette. The worst thing about the job, he says, is "when it becomes a theme park job, when you've played the Mickey Mouse March a thousand times. It gets to you." But finally the repetition itself is less a problem, or at least a more manageable one, than the lack of an appreciative audience either because the one available is incapable of recognizing and acknowledging what you're doing or because there is no one there at all:

> It's nice to have big crowds. That helps. It's a sad thing to go out and there's nobody there. We play and nobody's there. That feels like the true theme park musician. You're not there for yourself. You're there for the job. You're there for Michael. You're there for the mouse. That's kind of bad.

Those who literally do "put on a face" by putting on a character head routinely claim that park guests seem by their actions not to realize that there are people inside the costumes; guests seem not to see *them*. I find this frankly incredible, but their stories are consistent. A character lead says that "adults and children really believe what they're seeing. . . . Even adults, they believe that's Mickey. The kids go right on with it. That's Mickey that they see." One result of guests temporarily forgetting that Mickey is filled out by a living person is the threat of immediate physical danger. The little kids "pretty much consider you to be a large stuffed animal and treat you the way they treat their stuffed animals at home."

You can imagine the possibilities: either they "spot you from twenty yards away and come rushing toward you saying, 'I love you Donald' " or they "hit you, punch you, kick you, bite you." "They think it's fun," he continues. The kids think, "I've seen it in *Home Alone* where the guy gets kicked in the groin and everyone laughs, so, hey, I'll try it with Goofy." Apparently "adults are pretty much like the kids":

> You get the ones that are happy to see you even though you assume that they know better, that I'm not Goofy, that I'm a man wearing a costume that looks like Goofy. You get some that are just really happy to see you just like the kids. They want to get their picture taken. They want to get your autograph. Then you get the adults that are assholes. It's like "Yeah, you're Goofy. I'm going to mess with you." They punch you. I've gotten punched a few times. Punch punched.

Other than picking on Goofy for whatever thrill that provides, the more common response to the Disney characters is simple overexcitement, the kind that encourages guests not to think about the people inside the costume and what they're doing to them. Overexcitement is a bit of a euphemism; as Susan Willis argues, a top priority of Disney guests is to get the right pictures that will document the success of the trip and thus the coherence and happiness of the family so captured in them. Most of the workers understand and are sympathetic to these feelings:

> When people come to Disney and they leave, they don't say, "Oh yeah, we rode Space Mountain, and there was a really nice guy who helped us in line" [in fact, people do say this]. No, it's "We went to Disney" and before they get to anything else they say, "We saw Mickey. We got our picture taken with Mickey."

> Visitors are hyped up by their travel agents, and they show them everything they'll get—Mickey and Minnie. These people forget. I really don't believe that they think there's something under the heads. They've got to take that picture home. They need that touch with the characters.

This last was told to me by a young woman who, appearing as Minnie, encountered a crowd that apparently needed her touch so badly that it knocked her down and eventually quite unconscious:

I was taken down by two gentlemen, pulled off the conga line, knocked down to the ground—those heads are very heavy. I lost my balance. The bodice on the costume is wire, and if somebody were to push on that, it will go directly into me. Well, they bent down to help me up. Now there's a crowd of probably fifty people standing around looking at Minnie laying on the floor on Main Street. I was dragged about ten feet. At this point I don't know what's happening. I just think, get me up, get me out of here. That's a mob scene. It's very very frightening. All I know is that this gentleman must have bent down to help me up and his knee hits the body which hits my ribs. At this point I was locked into this head and could not breathe. I thought I was stabbed because there was pain in my side. It's black. There's no way for me to see if there's something sticking out of me. It is horrendous. They left me on Main Street for about fifteen minutes while they were trying to get security. I had passed out. Never to take off my head on Main Street, they took me underground on a stretcher, costume, head and all, and then took it off. I had contusions in two ribs and was out of work for quite a while.[34]

I suppose it would be difficult to overestimate what people will do in a place like Disney World where everyone is encouraged to re-achieve the giddy innocence of childhood and, in any case, treated as though they have. A trumpet player complains that during a street performance "a group of Brazilians" held hands, surrounded the band, and ran in circles around them singing songs. This was potentially disastrous because "if somebody bumps into you while you're playing that could really hurt." The problem is that when people really do take Disney at face value, that is, when Disney's magic really works, it's at the expense of recognizing either the limits or the vulnerability of the people making the experience possible. Of course, park guests should not have to worry about whether or not Minnie Mouse is being impaled by her costume. My point is that the same "magic" that makes the characters effective, so effective, in fact, that people "really believe what they're seeing," can be abstracted to other workers in less unusual circumstances, those on the "front lines" as one employee—himself not on the front line—put it, where "really believing what you're seeing" means not seeing at all:

> I've had people that I knew for years who when I was walking through the park going to break in a custodial costume would walk by and not even look at me, not because they didn't know it was *me*, but because of the costume I was wearing. It's like you're invisible. People do not pay attention to you whatsoever. You wouldn't believe that until you actually put it on and go, "Hey, you going to talk to me?" They're like "Oh my gosh! What are you doing?" They would never talk to you. You would be invisible to these people in those costumes. We were invisible to you. We were just part of the scenery.

If you listen hard you can hear the resentment, couched and muted in the pronouns shifting uncomfortably at the end of this statement. There's very little of that among Disney employees for the park's guests, and what little there is is filtered, as this comment is, through the park itself or, in a real bit of magic, projected and transformed into something else. What, for example, is going on with all those Brazilians? They turn up everywhere in worker narratives, always playing the part of the out-of-line guests who use language or ethnic difference to excuse unacceptable behavior. If the employees are to be believed, Brazilians wreak havoc from one end of the park to the other: they leap over store counters in a fury when credit cards are refused; waltz into restricted areas in the path of oncoming conveyances; invite their boy-children to relieve themselves in the line of the "Great Movie Ride"; grope aspiring actresses in their starlet costumes at MGM; and amuse themselves by trying to toss coins into tubas as if the band were a dime game at the county fair. It was not the case that just any ethnic or national group could be substituted in these stories; it was always Brazilians, obvious and identifiable, even by people who can't distinguish Spanish from Portuguese, even by people who don't know Brazilians speak Portuguese. Even factoring in employee gossip and the routine racism of central Florida where Latin Americans are openly perceived as cultural invaders, the identification of Brazilians as problem guests was pervasive enough to suggest that it was functioning for workers in some capacity other than the obvious.

Yet, except for these, there are few other real complaints about guests among Disney workers. "For the most part," says a former employee otherwise embittered by her experience, "people are nice. They really are." And those who are not, are Brazilian. In other words, "Brazilian" is the sign of the difficult Disney guest—all of them—and their frequent appearance in employee tales should be read as a measure not of their actual presence or destructiveness in the park, but of workers' desire to rename and limit any other difficulties with guests they encounter there. By so doing, Disney workers "other" the problems associated with guests onto a particular national group made mythical by the tales of their exploits. What this leaves is the "typical" Disney guest who is not Brazilian and who, therefore, does not create problems of the sort that require workers to acknowledge the routine self-negation their work asks of them.

A similar kind of denial shading into ambivalence surfaces in conversations with people otherwise content with their work. When questioned about what made for a good day at the park, employees frequently respond with something like "rain," meaning anything that would keep the crowds down or, in some instances, prevent work altogether. What's interesting about this is that rainy days don't mean that they—in this case, outdoor musicians—can stay home, only that they don't have to go into the park itself. Instead, they camp out in break areas all day, sleeping, reading, playing cards, or watching TV. One musician talks about retiring to his band's trailer when they couldn't perform in the park:

> Sometimes a really good day is when it rains all day, because we don't perform. We just do whatever we want to do, sleep in the trailer, read books, or whatever. We all hang out. Most bands don't, but we all

hang out. We're a group. There's a lot of other musicians, but they're in other bands. Some people try to transfer into our group when someone leaves because they don't want to just punch a clock. It's not our trailer. It's Disney-owned, but we made it our own. We bought a fooseball table, a VCR and TV. We hang out and watch videos all day or play Foosball. There's a bagpipe group that hangs out at our trailer somedays, but it's really our trailer. There are decorations on the walls.

Elsewhere you can see worker ambivalence in descriptions of work punctuated by elaborations of their opposite, something on the level of "This is what's fun about my job, but it's more fun when I'm not doing it." For example, though she speaks glowingly about the children she sees in the course of the day, one costume character also let it be known that she prefers doing atmosphere sets in EPCOT to the Magic Kingdom because there aren't as many kids there, and those that are are more subdued. An attractions host describes something akin to this desire in his area where everyone got a week when, rather than drive their shuttles, they monitored them from a distance:

> We had something called Shuttle Watch. Usually with the shuttles, you'd drive a shuttle and spiel and you'd load guests. But they had something called Shuttle Watch where one week you got to go out and watch the shuttles all day. It was great. You got to get away from the crowds, be in the grass. Nobody wanted to be around you when you were on Shuttle Watch because you were dirty. You'd been watching the shuttles all day.

There are two things to note here: the first is the tinge of smugness in the musician who fancies his band the elite among such outfits by virtue of their superior trailer and the kind of subculture they've developed in it. The second is the way the last speaker uses the invisibility of his position to affect personal satisfaction otherwise unavailable in the straight shuttle job. He wants to be alone. This is also, of course, why randy couples choose custodial costumes to wear when they sneak into the park. In other contexts, workers use their own invisibility as cast members to act where they are otherwise unable:

> We have to smile at a guest no matter what he does. It's really a way of controlling what you're really feeling. That smile has to be there.

But it's also the one way we can fight back. For instance, if someone's really snotty with a credit card you can take all the time in the world because their signature doesn't match. "Oh, gee, I'm going to have to see some kind of ID." You know.

Another worker calls this strategic badgering with kindness "friendly force" and concludes his description in a mock Disney voice: "'It's been our pleasure to serve you.' We always use that word. 'It's been our pleasure.'" When these two notions converge—using the Disney costume against itself and creating a subcultural group—they can make for the most interesting performances in the park. In those instances, it is the very disappearance into their roles and subsequent embodiment of Disney's magic that allows some workers to create and sustain an alternate culture within the park capable of critical engagement with its primary text. That culture is queer, and its text is family.

It is no secret in Orlando and among Disney workers that Walt Disney World is gay-friendly, and decidedly so. By "Walt Disney World," they do not mean the company or its policies—though many do include the company—but the people working in the park itself. Casual estimates made to me of the park's gay and lesbian population ranged from 25 to 75 percent, depending on department.[35] On what basis people were making these determinations was unclear; certainly every person I spoke with believed there was a strong queer, particularly gay male, presence. "You're guilty until proven innocent," laughs one after telling me the same joke I'd already heard three times that week. Q: How many Disney straights does it take to screw in a lightbulb on Main Street? A: Both of them. "It's very open," says another.

> Disney wants to say it's not open, but it's quite open underground. You have to curtail it. It's prevalent to us, the people down there, but if anybody sees that, of course, they'll start trouble for you. That makes headlines and Disney doesn't like headlines.

How well they are curtailing it seems to depend on how well anyone watching knows what to look for. As I said in the beginning, not all forms of performance in the park are approved or recognized by supervisors and guests, and when cast members play to each other it's frequently by way of camp. Whether they know it or not—and some of them did not—many of the in-park cultural practices described by Disney workers are adapted from gay cultures. This is particularly the case in the Entertainment Department, where one can find a number of alternative shows posing as "family entertainment": a female dancer lets a male musician perform in her stead and in her clothes, thus transforming a Christmas pageant on the steps of Cinderella's Castle into a drag show for knowing employees; the four Teenage Mutant Ninja Turtles vogue and pose Madonna-like to each other and to anyone in their audience able to recognize their moves. It may be difficult to recognize some of these moves when they have been coded solely for exchange among employees. A common term in the Entertainment Department, for example, is "thu," a lisping version of "through" used to signify exasperation, fatigue, irritation, or insult. It can be used alone or with a hand sign to describe oneself, to tell other employees or leads that a guest or situation is growing tiresome, or to tell another employee that he or she is being irritating. When on stage, the gesture alone signifies being thu. It can be subtle or campy:

> If someone were really annoying you, if you were annoyed, if you were tired, if you were exhausted from working a lot of overtime, you were thu. It was convenient because there was an accompanying hand sign so you could do it in costume. So if we saw someone do this, it wouldn't necessarily mean, I'm in trouble, but I'm really over this [places the middle and index fingers on the cheekbone]. I'm through with it, over it. I've had enough of this person, of this situation. I've had it. I'm tired. If I don't want to speak to you anymore, and I don't think this is getting anywhere or it's not doing me any good, I would say, "I'm thu" or "This is thu."

Elsewhere one can see a life-sized, costumed Donald Duck whispering seductively, "fag," as he walks by other Disney employees while the latter watch Donald flirt same-sexly with the park's oblivious—or not—male guests. "If you were watching the characters," says one such employee,

> and there was a guy in there, you could see him looking at the men. Not too much, but you would know. But if you were in the park, everything would be tasteful. Nothing would be done so that anybody could say "Oh my god, there's a queen in this costume."

But apparently there is a queen in the costume, and her performance as well as that of the many other members of Disney's "family"—recognized far and wide in Orlando as Disney slang for the park's large gay and lesbian contingent—camps Disney's notions of family values even as it represents them.[36] They work the park, making the dominant function, as Certeau says, "in another register."

But for how long and to what effect? While they certainly make the day go faster—and I do not underestimate the value of this—alternative practices at Disney do not significantly alter the park's ideological plots nor the status and value of those whose labor is used to produce them. Donald Duck is still Donald Duck. Pam is not a pianist anymore, but a clerk in one of Disney's stores, where her performative flirtations sell ice cream by the gallon. The very thing that brings her out of herself— she told me her coworkers are "the only family I have"—is just the thing needed in the shop. Ironically, it is often when workers try not to do the Disney thing that they most completely do just that; they end up, in spite of themselves, playing the role the company's written for them. Though they may hope otherwise, the pleasure they garner from their actions, though still definitively their own, is just what the company wants.

One woman tells me her favorite Disney story about giving a stuffed animal to a blind child in a wheelchair. She gets, as she says, "one of the little ones so he could hold it" in his crippled hands. It is classic Disney, "the kind of story," she says, "Disney wants out." "But," she continues, "we don't tell them because they don't deserve it." With this disclaimer, she reiterates the important point: "I could have given him a bigger one, but it wouldn't have fit in his hands." This, then, is the thing she will claim as her own: the fact of her attention, of her noticing what was needed by this child, at this moment—not the poster-ready big animal, but the small one, the one he could hold without calling attention to his awkwardness and his difference.

Or consider the reservationist who bragged about straying from company policy and sending a park brochure to a family on her own. "I used my own stamp," she says. That this is something to brag about should be taken as a measure of how strictly Disney controls its workers' relations to its guests. She sends it herself because Disney requires her to tell guests that the brochure will get there in two weeks when she knows it'll take four, too late for them to prepare for their trip. She's proud of this story because (1) she knows her employers will not like it, and (2) she feels she's actually doing something helpful for people, presumably the very thing she's supposed to be doing in her job, but which she feels she's prevented from by the company itself. She says, "I put a little note in it: 'I hope you have a great time at Disney, signed Faith.' I did not tell Disney that I did this. I did this on my own. I know the people appreciated it. I'm sure they did." Perhaps they did. Meanwhile, Disney simply doesn't care as long as the family gets to the park and spends its money. "Faith"'s actions have only made it more likely that the company that won't even allow her to use her own name will nevertheless benefit from her work, as though the more she tried to make her presence felt, the more she faded from our view.

As for our custodian, he at least knows it's the costume that renders him part of the scenery and easy to ignore. To guests and even to his friends, it makes him part of the pneumatic tubes sucking trash backstage to underground incinerators. He's not entirely right about that: his is work that is normally difficult to see; the costume only makes it doubly so. But while he still wanders unseen in this world, others, those who cannot be made to disappear behind a costume or into the seamless scenery of the park's stage, never leave that other world of tunnels and backstage lots:

> You don't usually see a lot of greasy, unkempt type people working in front of the crowd. They're usually very clean-cut, very army-type people, very well organized, very focused. The other kind of people usually work in food, inventory, everything else. That's just an observation I've made.

> The third shift employees are looked down upon, the graveyard shift, the cleanup crew that works when the park is closed. Some of them don't have all their screws. They're a little distant. They do hire people that aren't completely mentally stable. It's good that they do that, but sometimes they're made the butt of jokes.

> If you go to Disney World and you're walking around the park, you never see any black people, any African American people. I didn't realize that until I walked around and really looked at the areas, all the parks, and they're not in the areas that I know of. In Attractions—I never see them. You might have four or five in your area, and that's it. But if you go over to custodial, or to culinary, or to foods and beverages, there are more. Not an extreme amount, but it is obvious that there are more people there in the background, backstage. I'm not saying Disney is prejudiced.

Disney employees frequently follow admissions with disclaimers or qualifications. Like most people everywhere, they want to be proud of what they do. But it's more than that. As I said earlier, what's so striking about the park's guests and workers is their double-vision, the way one view screens out the other. It's in the way guests register the absence of racial and class difference among on-stage workers and themselves as the form and sign of the park's "safety." It's also there when the last speaker tries to accommodate what otherwise seems to him to be the obvious racism of Disney's hiring and placement practices by denying intention. Later, concerned that I will draw the wrong conclusion, he returns to this subject by telling me the story of "James," an African American who'd been working at Disney "a real long time": "He's a lead, and I don't think they're going to let him go anywhere else. It's not because of his color, it's because of his attitude." With this he tries to explain the practices he had just described by naming them something else. Falling unconsciously into the perspective of the supervisors he has condemned, yet exonerating their motives in the process, he questions the integrity of his friend and calls it "attitude." It's a telling criticism, a damning one at Disney, of someone whose excessive self won't go finally away: James has too much attitude—he's too black, one fears, as one fears the kind of adjustments necessary to make him less so, while what cannot be made less so is pushed underground and out of sight.

The disappearance of labor and the people doing it is built in at Walt Disney World at the level of architecture. The winding tunnels under the Magic Kingdom whisk away trash as easily as they send up the people who do the work that makes the place a success. "Underground is the whole world of Disney," says David; down there in break areas and cafeterias, locker rooms, storage areas, garages and roads, life goes on apace. Probably a number of the park's visitors know about the underground tunnels; fewer, however, know that "underground" is not underground at all. Because Florida's ecology and water levels cannot support the kind of digging that would have been necessary to create such an extensive basement, the park itself is actually the second floor, not the first. Propped like Metropolis over an invisible city, the Kingdom reigns seemingly unaware that there is anything holding it up. It floats there, oblivious of its own scaffolding, like a castle in the air.

At a corner table in one of Orlando's twenty-one Denny's restaurants, Terry is finishing her fourth cup of coffee. She has been trying to impress upon me one final point and has, in her effort, sometimes repeated herself, her comments winding around to their beginning, as though everything led inexorably back to the one point. "I would like people to know," she begins again, leaning closer and speaking into the recorder between us,

> that what they see in the World itself takes a lot of people to make up what they're enjoying, and sometimes it takes too much out of the people doing it. I don't think people realize how much of what they're enjoying is taking a lot of feelings out of other people, at their expense. It's just not a show; it's real life for some people.

Real life is the academic's joke. The next morning I'm sitting on a green and gold sofa in an apartment complex off Orange Blossom Trail with Joyce. As a behind-the-scenes CT, Joyce had worked split shifts from eight in the morning until ten at night. She got a fifteen-minute break and a half hour for lunch, though the split shift meant "lunch" could come at odd hours or not at all. Joyce was let go from her position at the end of her second season when admissions began tapering off. She now works elsewhere for $4.25 an hour; a brown uniform with orange trim waits draped over a kitchen chair. She regrets not getting back in with Disney, though she had tried. Biding her time until the peak season came back around, she returned to Central Casting to reapply, at which point she was told she could not be rehired because she was "too fat."

Short, heavy, and dark, a single mother—divorced, I think—maybe early forties, maybe late thirties, Joyce knows how and on what terms she is excluded from Disney's success, though even the knowing has not dulled what she wanted and still wants for herself: "I just want to do my job to the best of my abilities and go home and still be favored and feel that I'm a competent person on my own merits." Now, however, she feels "stuck": "I moved from Daytona Beach to Orlando just to get a job at Disney and now I'm stuck in Orlando is how I feel. I really do feel stuck." Her bitterness is palpable; it assumes shape before me as she speaks:

> He was a tall, blond-headed fellow, and he came right out and told me, "You don't fit our qualifications. You're too fat." It's called casting, and they do get away with it. You want the role, lose some weight. And it was behind the scenes. . . . If you're pretty, and you're young and have a good little figure, they put you up front with the

executives. Secretary types. I think some of these blonds don't even type, but because I'm older, I feel I didn't get them [other jobs].

In illustration, she begins a story about one "secretary type" who's hired after her and soon promoted to a better area. Unconsciously, perhaps, she uses my name in the telling: "Then, say, Jane comes in. She's only been there two months, but she gets picked ahead of you. It's the same. They go for the good looking, cute little hourglass shaped figure. It's mostly blonds they like, even the boys." She pauses as though distracted and, reaching toward me, lightly touches the delicate earring dangling by my chin. "You couldn't wear those at Disney."

Her son walks in. They have a short exchange before he leaves again. I wonder, briefly, why he isn't in school at 11:00 on a Monday morning. It is getting time to leave. I ask her directions to Lake Eola, the site of my next appointment. She begins drawing a map, then changes the subject. She asks me if I have a husband. I tell her no, and she nods her head in approval: "And you're not looking for one, are you? Smart lady." She asks about Duke and what I do, mentions the name of her high school, quizzes me about the ratio of single men to women in North Carolina, jokes about the dearth of men in Orlando. She contrasts my life favorably to hers and openly admires what she rightly perceives to be my relative freedom. Perhaps I look distressed. She leans forward, laughing, and shakes my arm playfully. "Don't worry," she says, "you're okay."

I start gathering my stuff on the sofa. It is getting time to leave. She's still laughing as I move to the door, thanking her and wishing her good luck, uncomfortable and self-conscious in my purple coat and black pants, my blond hair and youth, my Duke credentials, all of it conspiring to make me the image of the woman she will never be. I pause at the door long enough to notice the church calendar tacked to the wall beside it. St. Francis leans improbably on the trunk of a smiling elephant. Below him, several days of the month are marked in green ink: "Food Stamps" I read and walk out.

An hour later, I'm waiting for Annette downtown in the bandshell in Lake Eola Park. Constructed in 1988 by Disney, the bandshell is the cornerstone of downtown Orlando's revitalization effort. The company offered the city a choice of that or a homeless shelter, and Orlando's leaders chose the former. Rows of metal benches surround the bandshell in a half-circle, while behind it the placid water of Lake Eola shimmers in the sun. There is an attendant at the lake's dock where lovers are supposed to rent swan boats for the afternoon. A bridge and food court are planned for future construction.[37] I sit among the lunch crowd and marvel at the metal squirrels arranged where Orlando's homeless used to sleep.

I spot Annette among the flowers. She floats toward me like a goddess, on air. I don't know how I know it's her. Tall and thin, blond curls spilling lazily down her back, she has the beauty and carriage of the future star she plans to be. "I'm an improvisational street theater performer," she told me over the phone. "A comedic actress. We do one-on-one with the guests." She is eminently likable: smart, ambitious, no nonsense. "I have a lot of ideas," she says. Before being hired at Disney, she had been to the park twenty-one times; she is at best in her late twenties now, probably closer to twenty-five. Now, after seven years there—a year and a half of that full-time—she is moving on to Los Angeles, next week in fact, to meet up with a friend, someone who's already "hooked up out there" with "Sally Struthers and a couple of other stars." About her time at Disney, she has "nothing bad to say." Like many of her fellow workers, she uprooted herself after high school and moved to Orlando specifically to work for Disney, preferably as an actress, but at least "in some capacity." Unlike Joyce who feels "stuck," Annette "moved here, and everything inevitably fell into place." She loves her job; she thinks it's "very fulfilling"; she "can't believe" she's "getting paid for this." She loves the company; she makes $500 a week with full benefits, an enviable salary for an aspiring actress in the middle of Florida. She recognizes that others complain, but she has no patience for them: "The bottom line is that as a performer you have to decide what you want. No one owes you anything. You either want Disney or you want something else." To her, it is a question of having a work ethic.

Her work ethic is on display at MGM, where she is part of the "street atmosphere" of 1940s Hollywood Boulevard. She plays a starlet on that street, "Vanessa Veneer," and her job consists of being Vanessa Veneer for five hours at a time by improvising with guests and with the other eight characters that make up the cast of each shift. "But we're not Audio-Animatronics," she reassures me as though I might have taken her for one. "We're people. We don't do a scripted show." She brags modestly that the lack of a script makes her troupe "Disney's risk." "Who knows what we're going to do," she says. This is an elite ensemble, and she knows it. Disney has invested in her: she has three of the same costume, each custom-designed and fitted for her at $1000 each. "I even have custom shoulder pads." She works a twenty-five-hour week and gets paid for forty. She would be first in line for in-house auditions had she any reason to want them. As it is, she has been selected, sans audition, for performances elsewhere in the park. She says that sometimes there's not enough time or money to hold an open audition. Leads and supervisors accommodate her work schedule so she and her coworkers can audition for other temporary or permanent acting jobs outside the park. She had a brief stint with Miller Lite. She thinks of Disney as a "training ground," where daily improvisation has kept her "fresh" and where she can network and "hook up" with now and future "stars." She has a sense of responsibility about her position, can calculate what she's gained and what she owes. "Right now," she says, "I'm going. I want something more. I've already done this. I'm going to make room for another performer to come in and experience what I've had."

What she has had is the opportunity to "recreate the forties for the guests." She does this with the help of a steady diet of historical trivia and cultural references fed to the actors by leads and directors. Though this information is provided and updated regularly, they use it as and when they want. Their primary responsibility is to develop their characters and, in her words, "to reveal who we are as people within the bounds of our character." Though there are three casts of nine characters, any one of whom may be on Hollywood Boulevard at a time, each character is unique to each other. Thus, while there are three starlets, there is only one Vanessa Veneer: "You don't rotate these jobs at all. I would always be *my* starlet. No one would ever be me. I'd be myself, which I created, the character, for seven years." While it's unclear in this formula where "myself" ends and "the character" begins, Annette's experience of becoming her character is fundamentally different from other enactments in the park both because of her creation of it and because rather than disappear behind her character, she and her fellow actors use their roles to "reveal who we are as people." She's quite explicit about this: "When [guests] meet my character, they have no idea where my character stops and where I start. Because of our training, we have our fears, vulnerabilities, and insecurities right up there so people can identify." Unlike other people working in the park who can be confused with Audio-Animatronics, Annette gets to be creative; she has responsibility: "When you don't have a script, you become the one who's responsible for the finished product." Moreover, when Annette has a bad day, she doesn't have to "put on a face"; instead, she can incorporate her negative feelings into her act by pouting on a city bench all day and crying out about how bad she feels and how her "career is in complete shambles." She continues talking to me about happiness and choice, two items Disney provides her in quantity. Her job is great because she is "surrounded by people who are of basically my same make up. Everybody here's happy. Everybody's here because they want to be. They're choosing to be here."

I resist the temptation to say something snotty. I really do like her. She's so upbeat and modern. There's nothing like her where I come from. So I ask her about auditions and hiring, and rehiring and firing. She says people get to stay as long as they want, unless they're not rehired, but that would only be "if they find someone better." Even then, they try not to just axe you, but move you to another position, as happened to Diamond Lil. Twenty years ago, Diamond Lil was the resident party girl at the Diamond Horseshoe Review. "Now she plays a cleaning lady for our team." In fact, it seems like all the cleaning ladies, and the gossip columnists, on her "team" are former starlets from the same group. Annette tries to explain:

> We've got girls who used to play starlets but now play gossip columnists, so in case they wanted to do that character, they could because they already have the costume, but due to the fact that they went on an audition tour and found me, so in this case I would be the starlet this year. She could be a gossip columnist, because we lost a gossip columnist or something.

I count up those seven years, as I suspect she has, and pass up the opportunity to ask by what logic she has decided to avoid the unhappy fate of Diamond Lil by risking instead becoming her generation's Sally Struthers. Her decision to exchange one Hollywood Boulevard for another has taken on a different cast. She seems finally aware of the same gender restrictions that plague Joyce, but this truck driver's daughter is intent on and so far has the means to avoid them. She is planning ahead. All those "ideas" are for "entrepreneurial ventures." She presented some of these to Disney's Imagineers, but "they said, 'These are too big for us right now.'" So she's filing them away for California and beyond. "All of my mental time I spend on my own projects," she says. I ask her if she ever takes vacations. Her hair shines white in the sun. "This is a vacation."

THE ALTERNATIVE RIDE

• • •

As you enter the Magic Kingdom, you are really entering a theater peopled with cast members and scripted with visual, auditory, and even olfactory cues that create the unmistakable impression of being in a small town in America sometime around the turn-of-the-century. From the Town Square you can see the train depot, city hall, the fire station, and Victorian buildings that look like houses but are actually shops and restaurants. Subtle rhythms seep into the senses as gradually and predictably as the smell of popcorn penetrates the air. The toot of the train departing for Mickey's Starland and the ding of the horse-drawn trolley leaving for Cinderella's Castle punctuate the low-key conversation at regular intervals, confirming a sense of orderly activity. Every morning at eleven o'clock, the Walt Disney World Band marches down Main Street to the Town Square, where wire chairs and stands complete with books of sheet music have been arranged for a concert. Few people pay much attention to this performance, however, for there is always so much going on in this area of the town that the music seems merely part of the atmosphere of the place, which can be described as jovial at any time of the day or night.

The marching band was just approaching when I* was seated on a bench in the Town Square, my face red and wet from crying. My two daughters and my son were also crying. Only my husband was not, but

*Karen Klugman

that is because he never cries. We had been in Disney World only one full day, the first time any of us had ever been to a Disney park, and already we were feeling like a failed family. The argument had started over a necessary, but unexpected purchase of a pair of shorts and it was growing more complex as time went on. The twelve-year-old who needed the shorts had been insistent that they not be decorated with pictures or logos. Having learned the hard way that when it comes to kids' opinions on clothing, there is no disputing taste (which, in this case, I happened to agree with), I had been determined that we were not going to spend money on clothing she would not like. And so we had gone up and down Main Street looking for the impossible—a characterless bargain—before we reluctantly gave in to spending $40 for a pair of shorts with a small Mickey on the seat of the pants. My other daughter argued that she ought to be able to buy something too, and that she would be easy to please since anything copyrighted would be fine with her. To make matters worse, my son begged to go back to the Caribbean Beach to watch TV. Meanwhile, my husband, who is instantly put into a bad mood by any shopping anywhere, was upset about spending so much unbudgeted money so early on our trip and by unappreciative, uncompromising children. The argument reached a climax when the band took its place near our bench and began to play "Dixie" as background to my husband's suggestion that we spend the rest of our vacation in our hotel room with no television allowed.

> Oh, I wish I was in the land of cotton
> Old times there are not forgotten
> Look away, look away, look away, Dixieland.

I knew that if I looked away I would feel even worse. What I needed was a dose of ironic humor that recognized our problem. Something like a photograph of a family crying in the middle of the Magic Kingdom.

That was when I started my journey on the Alternative Ride through Disney World, an activity that I recommend to anyone who, in the presence of constructed joviality, feels like a cultural misfit. It puts your critical faculties to work *for* you, not against you, enabling you to participate in the magic on your own terms. Instead of feeling like an anonymous peasant with particular interests that are not recognized in the vast kingdom, you can think of yourself as the court jester.

The Alternative Ride is a method of constructing visual drama that mocks a vision that is prescribed and stereotyped. It takes the backside

view of life, one that recognizes that fantasy and reality do not always match. Focusing your attention *not* on the scene that is attracting other people's interest, but aiming it, instead, 180 degrees the other way, this backward vision reveals the social process that occurs during the interludes between the memorable events—the unposed forgettable moments—when people are eating, waiting, watching, or shopping. It's these commonplace acts, not the Disney-approved attractions, that can provoke thoughts about history, science, technology, and sociology. But they don't just pop out at you like plastic dinosaurs in the "World of Energy." You must think of yourself and other people not as passive consumers of entertainment but as individuals acting out a larger social drama—one that takes into account how contemporary cultural issues interact with the highly programmed culture within Disney World. In selecting the people who will serve as actors in your play, you will be running your own casting studio. In choosing the gestures and relationships that impart private meaning to public events, you will be acting as choreographer and director. While other people take home memories of constructed situations in which Disney is orchestrating what to see and how to remember it—whether a street performance or a picturesque view—you can construct more personalized memories that reveal your own responses to the invisible hand of Disney.

Surmounting the subtle control of the Disney's total environment begins with a recognition of it. It is essential to see the infrastructure of Disney World as not merely a support system for the rides and attractions, but an intentional subject itself. Sometimes taking the form of details that are so insidious that you might easily overlook them, stationary elements such as architecture and food can play as crucial a role as cast members. Throughout the parks, for example, rows of Mickeys, in an unabashed admission of the power of simulacra to affect our lives, decorate the paper cups and plates, uttering simple superlatives about the status quo. The multiple Mickeys have only a limited repertoire of messages, but they can be applied to any situation. "Wow! This place is the best surprise I've seen yet," they say cheerfully, whether they are entertaining a six-year-old customer who has just learned to read or are sitting in a pile of french fries on their way to the trash can. Sharing a thought balloon, the Mickeys always speak in one voice, the universal "I" that insinuates itself in our minds as Disney-speak: "Wow! There is so much to do here, what'll I see next?" Or, "I'm thirsty! What do I want to drink?" Your eye is led to the bottom of the cup, where it rests on the logo for Coca-Cola. Their words are never so bold as to take the form of a command, nor do they express altruistic motives. It is inconceivable that their slogans, like anonymous bumper stickers, would encourage us to "Practice random acts of kindness." Rather, the Mickeys, who exist to serve their creator, assure us that we have made the right choice in coming to Disney World.

On the Alternative Ride, character simulacra that usually work as Disney operatives can be employed by you as independent contractors in turning even the most ordinary situations into ironic social commentary. When their inflexible grins contrast with the sober expressions of park guests, wink back at the little characters to indicate that you recognize that their happy countenance belies the range of moods in the land of magic. When their features are distorted by bellies wearing them as T-shirts, misshapen by hands that are crumpling them on napkins, or beheaded by mouths that are eating them as ice cream and candy, see those features as corporate logos being transformed and consumed by individuals. While each reproduction of Mickey has passed inspection to meet Disney standards, what people do with the character is another story.

I first recognized that I had transcended Disney magic and had entered another world of make-believe, where I was at the mercy of my own imagination, when I came across three dwarf Minnies. Their practical shoes (they all wore matching sandals instead of trademark high heels), their appearance in public in multiples (Minnie wouldn't be caught dead with a double, let alone as a triplet), and their nonstandard form (we would probably detect even small deviations from the norm, but these shoulderless Minnies were downright differently-statured) combined to create a satire of the stereotyped, old-fashioned Minnie. But the joke is less on Minnie herself, than on the Disney Corporation for which she stands. After all, Minnie's appearance and lifestyle originated long before feminism and, since she never claimed to represent the modern woman, it would have been out of character for her to change with the times. The broader issue that underscores the humor of the Minnie impostors, however, is the contradiction between Disney's thoroughly controlled productions and the constantly changing social environment in which we view them.

The Disney enterprise, which has always portrayed itself to be on the

threshold of the future, has been criticized for its sanitized versions of history and science that gloss over or entirely ignore conflicts. Unlike textbooks that have been rewritten to take into account present knowledge of past events, most Disney narratives remain unaffected by revisionist interpretations. As Disney World begins to respond to the criticism, some of its educational entertainment demonstrates an effort to acknowledge the diverse interests of its audiences. Instead of ending so many attractions with a shot of a rocket blasting into space, vaguely suggesting that technology will solve all of our problems, Disney is attempting to ground some of its lofty ideals by putting them into practice.

The "Hall of Presidents," for example, updated to include an Audio-Animatronic President Clinton, features a film in which abstract notions of freedom have been refined to convey more precisely the notion of racial equality. Even more encouraging than the film's many quotations from historical figures who emphasize that we have not achieved freedom until we have achieved equal opportunities for *all* people is the achievement signified by the narrator's voice itself. For, as headlined in a banner over the building's entrance, the film is narrated by Maya Angelou, the poet who wrote and delivered Clinton's inaugural poem. Throughout the film, the familiar deep voice with the extended consonants reso-

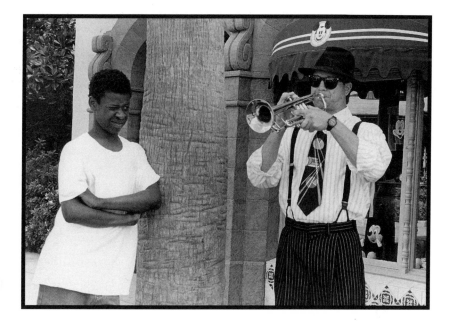

nates with significance, confirming a new milestone in the struggle for equality—that a black woman has authorized a Disney history.

In other attractions, as well as on the streets of Disney World, however, discrepancies between Disney narratives and the facts of real life still abound, providing plenty of opportunity to fill in the blanks with constructive irony. You can perceive the Dixieland band at MGM Studios, for example, only as Disney would have you see it, as representing happy times in the history of the South. Alternatively, you can broaden the context by applying the 180-degree turn-around rule and including the current audience in the frame. Just as smiling character reproductions are transformed in the hands of consumers, this street performance seems ironic in the presence of a young black man who grimaces at the trumpeter as if he were playing out of tune. Surrounded by Disney paraphernalia, the musician is not supported by historical references, but instead stands beside Mickey, a representative of the corporation. In the same way that John Berger suggested that we can discover assumptions about gender representation by imagining men substituting for women in traditional images of nudes, we can discover assumptions about racial representation by simply reversing the roles of audience and performer in this traditional scene. That this improvisational exercise produces the surprisingly unfamiliar picture of a black musician at Disney underscores the fact that jazz played on street corners by African-American solo performers or in groups (like this all-white band) are not a part of the United States history package at MGM, on Main Street, U.S.A., in Frontierland, or at the American Pavilion in EPCOT.

It is a relatively new idea to extend the frame around any production and suggest that its meaning might be affected by the social factors surrounding its creators and viewers. Not long ago, art photography was judged by a set of formal criteria having to do with the medium itself, qualities such as composition, framing, rendering of detail and print tones, with little or no questioning of the meaning of its subject matter viewed within the social context of its production. A photograph of an African-American family seated on a bench outside Tony's Town Square Restaurant in the Magic Kingdom might have been appreciated for its pyramidal composition of forms, recalling those in Renaissance paintings of Madonna and Child. (Nevermind the assumptions challenged by the Da Vinci analogy in which Virgin Mary is a large, black woman, Jesus is a young black girl, and Mickey Mouse plays the part of the Holy Ghost.) In a slightly less absurd structural reading, the image might have prompted a discussion of tonal contrast—of how well detail is rendered in the shadow and highlight areas of the print—without mention of historical and cultural associations triggered by the contrast of a black family on a "plantation" that is, in the context of Disney World, both figuratively and literally a white space. Likewise, the dresses might have been regarded only as designs contributing to the internal cohesiveness of the image by reaffirming the close grandmother/grandchild relationship. Such a formal reading would have ignored things external to the image, such as the fact that most contemporary Disney guests wear crumpled, prefaded, oversized, unisex casual wear. Read in this social context, the well-pressed, brightly colored dresses might indicate another kind of cohesiveness—a class or cultural style, by Disney standards a couple of revolutions back on the "Carousel of Progress," in which the women do the ironing and wear their Sunday best in public. But if their clothing does indeed signify social difference, then it must also be noted that they are wearing an item of clothing that, by any standards, serves as the great leveler of social distinctions, be it class, race, ethnicity, gender or age—the white sneaker.

Perhaps because we are eager to take a vacation from the real world,

most of us still comment on the formal structures of Disney World and its ability to regulate large groups of people without making obvious associations to social issues. Most of us collaborate with Disney in portraying the park as a collection of scenic views indicated by photo spot signs as willingly as crowds admiring the emperor's new clothes. Not, however, the ten-year-old boy I met at EPCOT who was leaning over a bridge and timing how long it took his spit to reach the lagoon. "Disgusting," he said. I thought he was referring to his spit, but then he pointed to where it landed and continued his unsolicited comments. "And they call that water! Do you realize how much junk falls in there every night from the fireworks? That lake is polluted. You'd better believe it."

I believed it. I also believe that if you let your awareness of other contemporary issues come into play, Disney looks a lot like the rest of the country. When I first saw guests sit or lie down on the sidewalks on Main Street, U.S.A., I expected a Disney official to tell the squatters to "Get up and keep moving." As the sprawl of people increased, this turn-of-the-century town began to look like a whitewashed version of main streets in any city in the United States. Incredibly, Disney seemed to have a homeless problem. But, as I soon found out, it was an hour before parade time and people were claiming curb space for a good view. In spite of the interruption to pedestrian traffic, they were allowed to stake out territory until twenty minutes before the procession began, when traffic regulators appeared out of nowhere to rope off crosswalks and shepherd the crowds.

In scenes similar to urban homelessness, exhausted people collapse in more rural areas of the parks and inadvertently create environmental portraits that are most familiar to us as promotional ads for social welfare programs. Recalling documentary photographs from the depression era, a family on a bench in Frontierland suggests the need for a modern-day version of the James Agee/Walker Evans study—"Let Us Now Praise Famous Mice." Draped in bright yellow raincoats with optimistic Mickeys, they are probably just suffering the adversity of bad weather in the "land where the sun always shines." Had they chosen a more picturesque resting spot, such as the bench in front of the "Swiss Family Treehouse" or the arbor near "Bwana Bob's," perhaps they would not look so pathetic. But, flanked by empty strollers and in the stark environment of the early pioneers, three slumped figures present a view of a family in Disney World that would never make it into the travel brochures.

Another urban drama—the issue of gun control is played out everyday

on the streets of Frontierland, where the Disney-staged gun fight between the good guys and the bad guys is upstaged by numerous domestic arguments involving guns. For here, as well as near other principally male attractions such as "Indiana Jones," "Pirates of the Caribbean," and the Canadian Pavilion trading posts, little boys beg their parents to buy them a souvenir gun. The moral dilemma raised by the availability of guns in a place that offers an otherwise pretty innocuous selection of fare can come as a surprise. And for most people, the decision of whether to allow a child to buy a gun is no Mickey Mouse matter. In no time at all, a verbal battle between parent and child can become physical, for the guns are lined up within easy reach of their targeted buyers and the very sight of a gun held by their child can embarrass, if not frighten, a parent. On the Alternative Ride, you can see them arguing or even wrestling with one another over the weapons in a much more convincing drama than the daily Western shootout at the saloon.

In niches off the beaten track, you will find parents resting while allowing their children, who have probably been warned against pointing their guns at people, to finally point them at one another. A generation ago, most parents would have responded with pride when other people noticed their children engaging in behavior that was considered reas-

suringly gender-appropriate. But, in today's climate of crime awareness, even if parents privately regard their sons' gun play to be a natural if not inevitable stage of development, they are aware that, like smoking, it is viewed by many people as socially unacceptable. As awareness of real world problems is increasingly affecting how we view play, Disney's attempts to recreate the innocence of childhood is at risk. Whether you watch a little girl selected from the audience to join the row of tall and thin, multicultural Barbie and Ken look-alikes in the outdoor theater at the American Pavilion or a little boy aiming his rifle into a crowd on Main Street, knowledge of the social consequences enters into the play.

A couple of years ago I saw a teenager on Main Street, U.S.A. pointing a gun teasingly at the head of his friend. It was a western-style pistol that, to the untrained eye, could have been mistaken for a street weapon. Although the sight of a gun in the hands of a young man was mollified by the common knowledge that crime at Disney World is practically nonexistent, the image was loaded enough with real-life associations, even back then, to make you wonder. To wonder if crime was really low or, like the garbage, just swept out of sight too quickly to be noticed. To wonder about how easy it would be for someone to carry around a real gun there. In the two years since then, the man/gun image has been increasingly associated with locations that were formerly considered to be safe havens— malls, commuter trains, churches, and one's own car. Today, faced with a realistic looking gun in the hands of a teenager, people would no longer stop to wonder about the possibility of crime at Disney World. The issue of crime so permeates U.S. culture that even a poster of a man with a gun could blow holes in Disney's illusion of safety.

Disney, like the rest of the world, has been forced to acknowledge concerns about crime. The guns they sell are now labeled with bright yellow stickers that warn "if traveling by air, check with baggage" and, like toy guns everywhere, the tips are painted or plugged with plastic that is orange-red. Over the last several years, the types of toy guns available has decreased as fears about real guns have increased. Except for the multi-sound laser blasters in Future World, the only choices left are a couple of western metal pistols and old-fashioned wooden muskets and rifles that are obvious frontier relics.

I know the gun market because I saw the parks through the eyes of an eight-year-old boy who, when told he could buy just one souvenir, chose (in spite of having a closet full of weapons at home) to make it a gun. Thus, our itinerary included stops at all of the weapons outposts so that, by the last day, he would be sure that he had covered all the possibilities and could quickly return to make the optimal purchase. As a tennis pro might handle a selection of rackets, Seth compared the guns for their length, number of movable parts, and sounds made when cocking and releasing the trigger. He was disappointed to find that, with one or two exceptions, the offerings at EPCOT and MGM were the same as those in the Magic Kingdom. Being used to a broader free market system, he was surprised to discover that identical models were sold at the various "stores" for the same price. By the time that he finally decided to buy a rifle, he could have written a *Consumer Reports* article about firearms in Disney World, yet he was not satisfied until he had dutifully held and fired each of the fifteen identical-looking rifles that were lined up like soldiers on the display rack. Lo and behold, the sounds made when the hammer struck the plate were in fact distinct, so that when he finally chose the gun that made the loudest click, he felt that he had completely shopped

the market. The bottom line is that, as long as there are consumers like Seth, there will be guns for sale at Disney World.

Like boys playing with guns, screaming toddlers are no longer automatically assumed to be a family matter. Not since child abuse began to appear in national headlines. Not since people found themselves studying pictures of missing children on milk cartons as they eat their cereal. Not since a two-year-old was murdered after he had been dragged out of a mall in front of scores of people by ten-year-old boys claiming to be relatives. At the ice cream shop in my hometown, a woman came running in, frantically wanting to know if the man in the parking lot wrestling with a screaming child had been in the shop, had treated the child well and called her by name. Satisfied with the answers, she left with the words, "You can't be too careful these days."

Yet, trained by my own experiences when I was the parent of toddlers, my sympathies still go out to the parents in such battles. I will never forget how misunderstood I felt when, one day in the supermarket my screaming daughter held her breath until she turned blue, then white, and finally passed out on the floor while I followed the instructions of our pediatrician to ignore this behavior. Back in those days, people observing the attempts of an adult to subdue a protesting minor might have disapproved of the childrearing practices, but would never perceive such a fight as other than a private domestic quarrel taking place in a public place. But these days (outside of Disney World, at least) we are conditioned by news events to see disputes as a policeman might, with the same paranoia and civic response of the woman in the ice cream shop.

How do Disney officials respond to the increasing fears for children's safety? The same way they have always responded: they actively ignore it. Promotional advertisements for Disney World never mention its reputation as an enclave of safety in an increasingly dangerous world. In fact, it is in part because of this intentional omission, not in spite of it, that the reputation continues, for anything that might call attention to the issue of safety might trigger our watchdog responses. Thus, in park brochures the category of "Lost Children" is casually mentioned in a list of "What You Need to Know" with the same emphasis given to "Lost and Found" and "Disney Dollar Exchange." This low-profile presentation of a potentially explosive issue has the effect of defusing it in the minds of parents, which in turn creates a more relaxed atmosphere in the parks, which in turn contributes not only to the reputation for safety, but probably to actual safety as well. Aware of the effectiveness of this positive feedback system as well as its inadequacies, Disney maintains a nonchalant facade about the handling of lost children, while undercover cast members scan for distraught parents and banks of video screens monitor park exits for kidnappers. In terms of maintaining a public image of safety, the Disney Corporation would surely agree that "You can't be too careful these days."

While it is difficult to find tangible evidence of crime at Disney World, it's a good bet that the problem exists as surely as the streets in the Magic Kingdom are strewn with litter after the parade. And, although the anti-crime forces are out of sight, they probably stand as ready as the litter control squad to remove every sign of transgression at a moment's notice. On the Alternative Ride, the post-parade cleanup can be viewed as an allegorical play about magic and is an attraction not to be missed. In the midst of thousands of pedestrians scattering after the parade, white-clad cast members firmly but politely maneuver through the crowds, pushing trash into little piles that disappear before your eyes into gigantic motorized vacuums. Finding a tray overflowing with leftovers on the ground nowhere near the restaurant from which it came, a young cast member grimaces with a hint of disgust as he stoops to remove it, but says without a trace of sarcasm, "Excuse me, ma'am. Are you finished with this?" Searching every niche for popcorn and food wrappers, this is a truly

efficient crew. About as fast as the pedestrian population returns to its normal level, the curtain closes on the final act and the people in white scurry underground with the garbage. The streets are once again remarkably clean. You can almost believe that people do not litter in Disney World.

That is why it was such a surprise to find, fully thirty minutes after the parade had ended, a subversive Mickey, peeking out from a paper cup stuck between the boards of a bench. A fellow traveler on the Alternative Ride, he too had escaped the highly-controlled, Imagineered illusions. But even if he managed to survive the next round of surveillance after the Electrical Light Parade that evening, the night crew would surely find him when they arrived to hose down the park and perhaps even repaint his hideout. I wanted to immortalize the spirit of this Mickey's defiance and to honor his last act on earth. And so, before I sat down to rest on the bench, I took his picture. After all, on the Alternative Ride, you can't just sit back, relax, and let Disney do the rest.

public use/

private

state

• • •

I* recall a discussion with four or five women friends on the subject of shopping malls. None of us was pro-mall, so our talk tended to highlight those aspects of malls that most annoy us, like obligatory photos with the Easter Bunny, the polysemous but universally greasy stench of the food court, as well as the overall Muzak-infused ambiance. We were having fun condemning malls for their morgue-like artificiality and we might have continued into the night with a litany of complaints had we not turned the conversation to the question of practice. What do people do in malls? The elderly and indigent find climate-controlled relief from the extremes of winter and summer weather, teens hang out, parents practice aerobic walking and leave their kids to amuse themselves in the mall's safe, suburban plazas and walkways. Such generally cited positive uses of malls left us bored and searching about for less common examples. At that point one of my friends described an incident which is so horribly banal as to be unforgettable. She had gone to the mall to buy the Sunday paper. It was noon, so many of the stores were not yet open and there was only a scattering of shoppers and strollers. She was in a hurry and might not have noticed them—they were in fact so normal a family: mother, father, and two children, dressed in their Sunday clothes—except that they were preparing a picnic, spreading a blanket on the cement next to the mall's perfunctory fountain. They had brought food from home in a

*Susan Willis

real picnic basket. This was an ordinary Sunday picnic—in the mall. We were stunned, mildly appalled, and sat in silence until one woman ironically remarked, "No muggers." More silence until another took the cue and commented, "No rain!" The final observation was given in deadpan cynicism: "No ants."

The family's Sunday picnic in the mall and our response to it have everything to do with current debates in cultural studies about public practice and private property. As a cultural form, the picnic draws on a long historical relationship to communally defined public spaces such as town greens, church lawns, and public beaches and forests. In moving this picnic into the mall, the family was imposing its public practice on corporate private property. This encroachment underscores an interesting thing about malls: their resemblance to "towns" encourages people to transport public social assumptions and practices into the private sector.

The dominant school of criticism in cultural studies, derived from Michel de Certeau and promoted by John Fiske, sees these public infringements on the private as subversive acts. De Certeau applauds the secretary, for example, who makes use of company time and technology to write a love letter to her boyfriend on the office typewriter. Both de Certeau and Fiske catalog a number of instances whereby capitalism's disenfranchised "poach" on the system that exploits and oppresses them. From this point of view, the family picnic in the mall is a classic example of "poaching." While they didn't steal the king's rabbit, the family made use of corporate property and refused to buy from the legally sanctioned food court menu.

Characterizing the family picnic in this way elevates it to the heights of subversion but fails to account for the banality of the episode and the cynicism of my friends' comments. What's lacking in this celebratory form of criticism is a recognition of the limitations imposed by private property and commodity culture on the range of activities (both real and imaginary) available to people. Notwithstanding their resemblance to towns, shopping malls are highly developed sites for social control. Outside of Disney World, there is no better example than the mall of the wholesale use of architecture and decor as a means for promoting consumption—in an environment where there is probably more surveillance per square inch (both technological and human) than in any of today's underfunded public prisons.

Many young people who are coming of age in this era of privatization

have no clear sense of the distinction between publicly funded spaces and private property. Yet this distinction fundamentally defines our social practices and relationships. Only at moments when the dominant order is challenged or disputed can people begin to realize the constraints imposed by property relations and privatization. Such was the case in the early weeks of 1991 when the United States prepared to wage war against Iraq and many young people joined in protest on the steps of post office buildings and marched in candlelight vigils through downtown streets. Shopping malls, ripe for leafleting and demonstrations, were off limits— to bring free speech into a mall is to commit trespass.

It's no wonder that young people have difficulty conceptualizing the distinction between the public and the private at a time when public education, the most important public institution, has been undermined by the inroads of privatization. Decimated by the Reagan/Bush cutbacks, public schools have opened their doors and classrooms to corporate investment and business tie-ins. Computer companies offer schools "good deals" on (educationally limited) business-oriented learning programs. Insurance companies package and sponsor interdisciplinary "problem-solving" programs whose not-so-hidden ideology attacks the liberal justice system. And fast-food chains promote tie-ins with public schools whereby sales to students eventually add up to playground equipment for the school.

"The biggest contribution business can make to education is to make education a business."[1] This was the goal of Chris Whittle, head of Whittle Communications and promoter of Channel One, a media package heavily promoted for public school use during the Bush administration. Channel One offered to lend schools the necessary hardware—VCRs, TVs, and satellite dishes—and made its profit on the paid commercial messages included in the programming. Channel One was actually just one strategy among several promoted by the Bush administration and big business aimed at making the American workforce "competitive." Quoted in *The Nation*, Arnold Fege, director of government relations for the national PTA, said that corporate America "is becoming involved because the public schools are not producing the types of student that business needs."[2] To supply business with what it needs, President Bush proposed the formation of new schools, funded by private industry start-up grants. These were to be exemplary high-tech proving grounds whose very existence would threaten the potential of already existing public schools. Meanwhile, to meet industry's expanding need for a docile, low-skilled workforce, many states have implemented youth apprenticeship programs at the high school level. These programs assign high school juniors and seniors to twenty-hour-a-week jobs (95 percent of which require mindless, repetitive labor) and offer a curriculum that features watered-down math and pro-business ethics.[3] Although the Bush era may be over, the swing toward privatization has not been reversed, and many corporations maintain toeholds in public education.

I recently asked a class of undergraduates to name the public places or publicly defined activities that had shaped their daily lives. All were at a loss until one student named playgrounds. Communally funded town parks and recreation halls are a remnant of a public sector that may soon be wholly erased. Indeed, youngsters today don't need to wet their behinds on rain-spattered sliding boards or swing over muddy puddles or skin their knees on the town's grass-bare playground. They can go to the "Discovery Zone." Here, for the price of admission, they can play in a "safe" climate-controlled indoor amusement play area, where nothing is left to accident or imagination. Play becomes a class act, reserved for those who can afford it. Such is the privatization of fun. "No muggers," "no rain," "no ants."

At Disney World, the erasure of spontaneity is so great that spontaneity itself has been programmed. On the "Jungle Cruise" khaki-clad tour guides teasingly engage the visitors with their banter, whose apparent spontaneity has been carefully scripted and painstakingly rehearsed. Nothing is left to the imagination or the unforeseen. Even the paths and walkways represent the programmed assimilation of the spontaneous. According to published reports, there were no established walkways laid down for the opening-day crowds at Disneyland.[4] Rather, the Disney Imagineers waited to see where people would walk, then paved over their spontaneous footpaths to make prescribed routes.

The erasure of spontaneity has largely to do with the totality of the built and themed environment. Visitors are inducted into the park's program, their every need predefined and presented to them as a packaged routine and set of choices. "I'm not used to having everything done for me." This is how my companion at Disney World reacted when she checked into a Disney resort hotel and found that she, her suitcase, and her credit card had been turned into the scripted components of a highly orchestrated program. My companion later remarked that while she found it odd not to have to take care of everything herself (as she normally does in order to accomplish her daily tasks), she found it "liberating" to just fall into the proper pattern, knowing that nothing could arise that hadn't already been factored into the system. I have heard my companion's remarks reiterated by many visitors to the park with whom I've talked. Most describe feeling "freed up" ("I didn't have to worry about my kids," "I didn't have to think about anything") by the experience of relinquishing control over the complex problem-solving thoughts and operations that otherwise define their lives. Many visitors suspend daily perceptions and judgments altogether, and treat the wonderland environment as more real than real. I saw this happen one morning when walking to breakfast at my Disney resort hotel. Two small children were stooped over a small snake that had crawled out onto the sun-warmed path. "Don't worry, it's rubber," remarked their mother. Clearly only Audio-Animatronic simulacra of the real world can inhabit Disney World. A real snake is an impossibility.

In fact, the entire natural world is subsumed by the primacy of the artificial. The next morning I stepped outside at the end of an early morning shower. The humid atmosphere held the combination of sun and rain. "Oh! Did they turn the sprinklers on?" This is the way my next-door neighbor greeted the day as she emerged from her hotel room. The Disney environment puts visitors inside the world that Philip K. Dick depicted in *Do Androids Dream of Electric Sleep?*—where all animal life has been exterminated, but replaced by the production of simulacra, so real in appearance that people have difficulty recalling that real animals no longer exist. The marvelous effect of science fiction is produced out of a dislocation between two worlds, which the reader apprehends as an estrangement, but the characters inside the novel cannot grasp because they have only the one world: the world of simulacra. The effect of the marvelous cannot be achieved unless the artificial environment is perceived through the retained memory of everyday reality. Total absorption into the Disney environment cancels the possibility for the marvelous and leaves the visitor with the banality of a park-wide sprinkler system. No muggers, no rain, no ants, and no snakes.

Amusement is the commodified negation of play. What is play but the spontaneous coming together of activity and imagination, rendered more pleasurable by the addition of friends? At Disney World, the world's most highly developed private property "state" devoted to amusement, play is all but eliminated by the absolute domination of program over spontaneity. Every ride runs to computerized schedule. There is no possibility of an awful thrill, like being stuck at the top of a ferris wheel. Order prevails particularly in the queues for the rides that zigzag dutifully on a prescribed path created out of stanchions and ropes; and the visitor's assimilation into the queue does not catapult him or her into another universe, as it would if Jorge Luis Borges fabricated the program. The Disney labyrinth is a banal extension of the ride's point of embarkation, which extends into the ride as a hyper-themed continuation of the queue. The "Backstage Movie Tour" has done away with the distinction between the ride and its queue by condemning the visitor to a two-and-a-half-hour-long pedagogical queue that preaches the process of movie production. Guests are mercilessly herded through sound stages and conveyed across endless back lots where one sees the ranch-style houses used in TV commercials and a few wrecked cars from movie chase scenes. Happily, there are a few discreet exit doors, bail-out points for parents with bored children. Even Main Street dictates programmed amusement because it is not a street but a conduit, albeit laden with commodity distractions, that conveys the visitor to the Magic Kingdom's other zones where more queues, rides, and commodities distinguish themselves on the basis of their themes. All historical and cultural references are merely ingredients for decor. Every expectation is met programmatically and in conformity with theme. Mickey as Sorcerer's Apprentice does not appear in the Wild West or the exotic worlds of Jungle and Adventure, the niches for Davey Crockett and Indiana Jones. Just imagine the chaos, a park-wide short circuit, that the mixing of themed ingredients might produce. Amusement areas are identified by a "look," by characters in costume, by the goods on sale: What place—i.e., product—is Snow White promoting if she's arm in arm with an astronaut? The utopian intermingling of thematic opportunities such as occurred at the finale of the movie *Who Framed Roger Rabbit?*, with Warner and Disney "toons" breaking their copyrighted species separation to cavort with each other and the human actors, will not happen at Disney World.

However, now that the costumed embodiment of Roger Rabbit has taken up residence at Disney World, he, too, can expect to have a properly assigned niche in the spectacular Disney parade of characters. These have been augmented with a host of other Disney/Lucas/Spielberg creations, including Michael Jackson of "Captain EO" and C3PO and R2D2 of *Star Wars*, as well as Disney buyouts such as Jim Henson's Muppets and the Saturday morning cartoon heroes, the Teenage Mutant Ninja Turtles.

The Disney Corporation's acquisition of the stock-in-trade of popular culture icons facilitates a belief commonly held by young children that every popular childhood figure "lives" at Disney World. In the utopian imagination of children, Disney World may well be a neverending version of the finale to *Roger Rabbit* where every product of the imagination lives in community. In reality, the products (of adult imaginations) live to sell, to be consumed, to multiply.

What's most interesting about Disney World is what's not there. Intimacy is not in the program even though the architecture includes several secluded nooks, gazebos, and patios. During my five-day stay, I saw only one kiss—and this a husbandly peck on the cheek. Eruptions of imaginative play are just as rare. During the same five-day visit, I observed only one such incident even though there were probably fifty thousand children in the park. What's curious about what's not at Disney is that there is no way of knowing what's not there until an aberrant event occurs and provokes the remembrance of the social forms and behaviors that have been left out. This was the case with the episode of spontaneous play. Until I saw real play, I didn't realize that it was missing. The incident stood out against a humdrum background of uniform amusement: hundreds of kids being pushed from attraction to attraction in their strollers, hundreds more waiting dutifully in the queues or marching about in family groups—all of them abstaining from the loud, jostling, teasing, and rivalrous behaviors that would otherwise characterize many of their activities. Out of this homogenous "amused" mass, two kids snagged a huge sombrero each from an open-air stall at the foot of the Mexico Pavilion's Aztec temple stairway and began their impromptu version of the Mexican hat dance up and down the steps. Their play was clearly counterproductive as it took up most of the stairway, making it difficult for visitors to enter the pavilion. Play negated the function of the stairs as conduit into the attraction. The kids abandoned themselves to their fun, while all around them, the great mass of visitors purposefully kept their activities in line with Disney World's prescribed functions. Everyone but the dancers seemed to have accepted the park's unwritten motto: "If you pay, you shouldn't play." To get your money's worth, you have to do everything and do it in the prescribed manner. Free play is gratuitous and therefore a waste of the family's leisure time expenditure.

Conformity with the park's program upholds the Disney value system. Purposeful consumption—while it costs the consumer a great deal—affirms the value of the consumer. "Don't forget, we drove twenty hours to get here." This is how one father admonished his young son who was squirming about on the floor of EPCOT's Independence Hall, waiting for the amusement to begin. The child's wanton and impatient waste of time was seen as a waste of the family's investment in its amusement. If a family is to realize the value of its leisure time consumptions, then every member must function as a proper consumer.

The success of Disney World as an amusement park has largely to do with the way its use of programming meshes with the economics of consumption as a value system. In a world wholly predicated on consumption, the dominant order need not proscribe those activities that run counter to consumption, such as free play and squirming, because the consuming public largely polices itself against gratuitous acts which would interfere with the production of consumption as a value. Conformity with the practice of consumption is so widespread and deep at Disney World that occasional manifestations of boredom or spontaneity do not influence the compulsively correct behavior of others. Independence Hall did not give way to a seething mass of squirming youngsters even though all had to sit through a twenty-minute wait. Nor did other children on the margins of the hat dance fling themselves into the fun. Such infectious behavior would have indicated communally defined social relations or the desire for such social relations. Outside of Disney World in places of public use, infectious behavior is common. One child squirming about on the library floor breeds others; siblings chasing each other around in a supermarket draw others; one child mischievously poking at a public fountain attracts others; kids freeloading rides on a department store escalator can draw a crowd. These playful, impertinent acts indicate an imperfect mesh between programmed environment and the value system of consumption. Consumers may occasionally reclaim the social, particularly the child consumer who has not yet been fully and properly socialized to accept individuation as the bottom line in the consumer system of value. As an economic factor, the individual exists to maximize consumption—and therefore profits—across the broad mass of consumers. This is the economic maxim most cherished by the fast-food industry, where every burger and order of fries is individually packaged and consumed to preclude consumer pooling and sharing.

At Disney World the basic social unit is the family. This was made particularly clear to me because as a single visitor conducting research, I

presented a problem at the point of embarkation for each of the rides. "How many in your group?" "One." The lone occupant of a conveyance invariably constructed to hold the various numerical breakdowns of the nuclear family (two, three, or four) is an anomaly. Perhaps the most family-affirming aspect of Disney World is the way the queues serve as a place where family members negotiate who will ride with whom. Will Mom and Dad separate themselves so as to accompany their two kids on a two-person ride? Will an older sibling assume the responsibility for a younger brother or sister? Every ride asks the family to evaluate each of its member's needs for security and independence. This is probably the only situation in a family's visit to Disney World where the social relations of family materialize as practice. Otherwise and throughout a family's stay, the family as nexus for social relations is subsumed by the primary definition of family as the basic unit of consumption. In consumer society at large, each of us is an atomized consumer. Families are composed of autonomous, individuated consumers, each satisfying his or her age- and gender-differentiated taste in the music, video, food, and pleasure marketplace. In contrast, Disney World puts the family back together. Even teens are integrated in their families and are seldom seen roaming the park in teen groups as they might in shopping malls.

Families at Disney World present themselves as families, like the one I saw one morning on my way to breakfast at a Disney resort hotel: father, mother, and three children small to large, each wearing identical blue Mickey Mouse T-shirts and shorts. As I walked past them, I overheard the middle child say, "We looked better yesterday—in white." Immediately, I envisioned the family in yesterday's matching outfits, and wondered if they had bought identical ensembles for every day of their stay.

All expressions of mass culture include contradictory utopian impulses, which may be buried or depicted in distorted form, but nevertheless generate much of the satisfaction of mass cultural commodities (whether the consumer recognizes them as utopian or not). While the ideology of the family has long functioned to promote conservative—even reactionary—political and social agendas, the structure of the family as a social unit signifies communality rather than individuality and can give impetus to utopian longings for communally defined relations in society at large. However, when the family buys into the look of a family, and appraises itself on the basis of its look ("We looked better yesterday"), it becomes a walking, talking commodity, a packaged unit of consumption stamped with the Mickey logo of approval. The theoretical question that this family poses for me is not whether its representation of itself as family includes utopian possibilities (because it does), but whether such impulses can be expressed and communicated in ways not accessible to commodification.

In its identical dress, the family represents itself as capitalism's version of a democratized unit of consumption. Differences and inequalities among family members are reduced to distinctions in age and size. We have all had occasion to experience the doppelgänger effect in the presence of identical twins who choose (or whose families enforce) identical dress. Whether chosen or imposed, identical twins who practice the art of same dress have the possibility of confounding or subverting social order. In contrast, the heterogeneous family whose members choose to dress identically affirms conformity with social order. The family has cloned itself as a multiple, but identical consumer, thus enabling the maximization of consumption. It is a microcosmic representation of free market democracy where the range of choices is restricted to the series of objects already on the shelf. In this system there is no radical choice. Even the minority of visitors who choose to wear their Rolling Stones and Grateful Dead T-shirts give the impression of having felt constrained not to wear a Disney logo.

Actually, Disney has invented a category of negative consumer choices for those individuals who wish to express nonconformity. This I discovered as I prepared to depart for my Disney research trip, when my daughter Cassie (fifteen years old and "cool" to the max) warned me, "Don't buy me any of that Disney paraphernalia." As it turned out, she was happy to get a pair of boxer shorts emblazoned with the leering images of Disney's villains: two evil queens, the Big Bad Wolf, and Captain Hook. Every area of Disney World includes a Disney Villains Shop, a chain store for bad-guy merchandise. Visitors who harbor anti-Disney sentiments can express their cultural politics by consuming the negative Disney line. There is no possibility of an anticonsumption at Disney World. All visitors are, by definition, consumers, their status conferred with the price of admission.

At Disney World even memories are commodities. How the visitor will remember his or her experience of the park has been programmed and indicated by the thousands of "Kodak Picture Spot" signposts. These position the photographer so as to capture the best views of each and every attraction, so that even the most inept family members can bring home perfect postcard-like photos. To return home from a trip to Disney World with a collection of haphazardly photographed environments or idiosyncratic family shots is tantamount to collecting bad memories. A family album comprised of picture-perfect photo-site images, on the other hand, constitutes the grand narrative of the family's trip to Disney World, the one that can be offered as testimony to money well spent. Meanwhile, all those embarrassing photos, the ones not programmed by the "Picture Spots," that depict babies with ice cream all over their faces or toddlers who burst into tears rather than smiles at the sight of those big-headed costumed characters that crop up all over the park—these are the images that are best left forgotten.

The other commodified form of memory is the souvenir. As long as there has been tourism there have also been souvenirs: objects marketed to concretize the visitor's experience of another place. From a certain point of view, religious pilgrimage includes aspects of tourism, particularly when the culmination of pilgrimage is the acquisition of a transportable relic. Indeed, secular mass culture often imitates the forms and practices of popular religious culture. For many Americans today who make pilgrimages to Graceland and bring home a mass-produced piece of Presley memorabilia, culture and religion collide and mesh.

Of course, the desire to translate meaningful moments into concrete objects need not take commodified form. In Toni Morrison's *Song of Solomon,* Pilate, a larger-than-life earth mother if there ever was one, spent her early vagabondage gathering a stone from every place she visited. Similarly, I know of mountain climbers who mark their ascents by bringing a rock back from each peak they climb. Like Pilate's stones, these tend to be nondescript and embody personal remembrances available only to the collector. In contrast, the commodity souvenir enunciates a single meaning to everyone: "I was there. I bought something." Unlike the souvenirs I remember having seen as a child, seashells painted with seascapes and the name of some picturesque resort town, most souvenirs today are printed with logos (like the Hard Rock Cafe T-shirt), or renderings of copyrighted material (all the Disney merchandise). The purchase of such a souvenir allows the consumer the illusion of participating in the enterprise as a whole, attaining a piece of the action. This is the consumerist version of small-time buying on the stock exchange. We all trade in logos—buy them, wear them, eat them, and make them the containers of our dreams and memories. Similarly, we may all buy into capital with the purchase of public stock. These consumerist activities give the illusion of democratic participation while denying access to real corporate control which remains intact and autonomous, notwithstanding the mass diffusion of its logos and stock on the public market. Indeed the manipulation of public stock initiated during the Reagan administration, which has facilitated one leveraged buyout after another, gives the lie to whatever wistful remnants of democratic ownership one might once have attached to the notion of "public" stocks.

Disney World is logoland. The merchandise, the costumes, the scenery— all is either stamped with the Disney logo or covered by copyright legislation. In fact, it is impossible to photograph at Disney World without running the risk of infringing a Disney copyright. A family photo in front of Sleeping Beauty's Castle is apt to include dozens of infringements: the castle itself, Uncle Harry's "Goofy" T-shirt, the kids' Donald and Mickey hats, maybe a costumed Chip 'n Dale in the background. The only thing that saves the average family from a lawsuit is that most don't use their vacation photos as a means for making profit. I suspect the staff of "America's Funniest Home Videos" systematically eliminates all family videos shot at Disney World; otherwise prize winners might find themselves having to negotiate the legal difference between prize and profit, and in a larger sense, public use versus private property. As an interesting note, Michael Sorkin, in a recent essay on Disneyland, chose a photo of "[t]he sky above Disney World [as a] substitute for an image of the place itself." Calling Disney World "the first copyrighted urban environment," Sorkin goes on to stress the "litigiousness" of the Disney Corporation.[5] It may be that *Design Quarterly,* where Sorkin published his essay, pays its contributors, thus disqualifying them from "fair use" interpretations of copyright policy.

Logos have become so much a part of our cultural baggage that we hardly notice them. Actually they are the cultural capital of corporations. Pierre Bourdieu invented the notion of cultural capital with reference to individuals. In a nutshell, cultural capital represents the sum total of a person's ability to buy into and trade in the culture. This is circumscribed by the economics of class and, in turn, functions as a means for designating an individual's social standing. Hence people with higher levels of education who distinguish themselves with upscale or trendy consumptions have more cultural capital and can command greater privilege and authority than those who, as Bourdieu put it, are stuck defining themselves by the consumption of necessity. There are no cultural objects or practices that do not constitute capital, no reserves of culture that escape value. Everything that constitutes one's cultural life is a commodity and can be reckoned in terms of capital logic.

In the United States today there is little difference between persons and corporations. Indeed, corporations enjoy many of the legal rights extended to individuals. The market system and its private property state are "peopled" by corporations, which trade in, accumulate, and hoard up logos. These are the cultural signifiers produced by corporations, the impoverished imaginary of a wholly rationalized entity. Logos are commodities in the abstract, but they are not so abstracted as to have transcended value. Corporations with lots of logos, particularly upscale, high-tech logos, command more cultural capital than corporations with fewer, more humble logos.

In late twentieth-century America, the cultural capital of corporations has replaced many of the human forms of cultural capital. As we buy, wear, and eat logos, we become the henchmen and admen of the corporations, defining ourselves with respect to the social standing of the various corporations. Some would say that this is a new form of tribalism, that in sporting corporate logos we ritualize and humanize them, we redefine

the cultural capital of the corporations in human social terms. I would say that a state where culture is indistinguishable from logo and where the practice of culture risks infringement of private property is a state that values the corporate over the human.

While at Disney World, I managed to stow away on the behind-the-scenes tour reserved for groups of corporate conventioneers. I had heard about this tour from a friend who is also researching Disney and whose account of underground passageways, conduits for armies of workers and all the necessary materials and services that enable the park to function, had elevated the tour to mythic proportions in my imagination.

But very little of the behind-the-scenes tour was surprising. There was no magic, just a highly rational system built on the compartmentalization of all productive functions and its ensuing division of labor, both aimed at the creation of maximum efficiency. However, instances do arise when the rational infrastructure comes into contradiction with the onstage (park-wide) theatricalized image that the visitor expects to consume. Such is the case with the system that sucks trash collected at street level through unseen pneumatic tubes that transect the backstage area, finally depositing the trash in Disney's own giant compacter site. To the consumer's eyes, trash is never a problem at Disney World. After all, everyone dutifully uses the containers marked "trash," and what little manages to fall to the ground (generally popcorn) is immediately swept up by the French Foreign Legion trash brigade. For the consumer, there is no trash beyond its onstage collection. But there will soon be a problem as environmental pressure groups press Disney to recycle. As my companion on the backstage tour put it, "Why is there no recycling at Disney World—after all, many of the middle-class visitors to the park are already sorting and recycling trash in their homes?" To this the Disney guide pointed out that there is recycling, backstage: bins for workers to toss their Coke cans and other bins for office workers to deposit papers. But recycling onstage would break the magic of themed authenticity. After all, the "real" Cinderella's Castle was not equipped with recycling bins, nor did the denizens of Main Street, U.S.A., circa 1910, foresee the problem of trash. To maintain the image, Disney problem solvers are discussing hiring a minimum-wage workforce to rake, sort, and recycle the trash on back lots that the environmentally aware visitor will never see.

While I have been describing the backstage area as banal, the tour through it was not uneventful. Indeed there was one incident that underscored for me the dramatic collision between people's expectations of public use and the highly controlled nature of Disney's private domain. As I mentioned, the backstage tour took us to the behind-the-scenes staging area for the minute-by-minute servicing of the park and the hoopla of its mass spectacles such as firework displays, light shows, and parades. We happened to be in the backstage area just as the parade down Main Street was coming to an end. Elaborate floats and costumed characters descended a ramp behind Cinderella's Castle and began to disassemble before our eyes. The floats were alive with big-headed characters, clambering off the superstructures and out of their heavy, perspiration-drenched costumes. Several "beheaded" characters revealed stocky young men gulping down Gatorade. They walked toward our tour group, bloated Donald and bandy-legged Chip from the neck down, carrying their huge costume heads, while their real heads emerged pea-sized and aberrantly human.

We had been warned *not* to take pictures during the backstage tour, but one of our group, apparently carried away by the spectacle, could not resist. She managed to shoot a couple of photos of the disassembled characters before being approached by one of the tour guides. As if caught in a spy movie, the would-be photographer prized open her camera and ripped out the whole roll of film. The entire tour group stood in stunned amazement; not, I think, at the immediate presence of surveillance, but at the woman's dramatic response. In a situation where control is so omnipresent and conformity with control is taken for granted, any sudden gesture or dramatic response is a surprise.

At the close of the tour, my companion and I lingered behind the rest of the group to talk with our tour guides. As a professional photographer, my companion wanted to know if there is a "normal" procedure for disarming behind-the-scenes photographic spies. The guide explained that the prescribed practice is to impound the camera, process the film, remove the illicit photos, and return the camera, remaining photos, and complimentary film to the perpetrator. When questioned further, the guide went on to elaborate the Disney rationale for control over the image: the "magic" would be broken if photos of disassembled characters circulated in the public sphere; children might suffer irreparable psychic trauma at the sight of a "beheaded" Mickey; Disney exercises control over the image to safeguard childhood fantasies.

What Disney employees refer to as the "magic" of Disney World has actually to do with the ability to produce fetishized consumptions. The unbroken seamlessness of Disney World, its totality as a consumable artifact, cannot tolerate the revelation of the real work that produces the commodity. There would be no magic if the public should see the entire cast of magicians in various stages of disassembly and fatigue. That selected individuals are permitted to witness the backstage labor facilitates the word-of-mouth affirmation of the tremendous organizational feat that produces Disney World. The interdiction against photography eliminates the possibility of discontinuity at the level of image. There are no images to compete with the copyright-perfect onstage images displayed for public consumption. It's not accidental that our tour guide underscored the fact that Disney costumes are tightly controlled. The character costumes are made at only one production site and this site supplies the costumes used at Tokyo's Disneyland and EuroDisney. There can be no culturally influenced variations on the Disney models. Control over the image ensures the replication of Disney worldwide. The prohibition against photographing disassembled characters is motivated by the same phobia of industrial espionage that runs rampant throughout the high-tech information industry. The woman in our tour group who ripped open her camera and destroyed her film may not have been wrong in acting out a spy melodrama. Her photos of the disassembled costumes might have revealed the manner of their production—rendering them accessible to non-Disney replication. At Disney World, the magic that resides in the integrity of childhood fantasy is inextricably linked to the fetishism of the commodity and the absolute control over private property as it is registered in the copyrighted image.

As I see it, the individual's right to imagine and to give expression to unique ways of seeing is at stake in struggles against private property. Mickey Mouse, notwithstanding his corporate copyright, exists in our common culture. He is the site for the enactment of childhood wishes and fantasies, for early conceptualizations and renderings of the body, a being who can be imagined as both self and other. If culture is held as private property, then there can be only one correct version of Mickey Mouse, whose logo-like image is the cancellation of creativity. But the multiplicity of quirky versions of Mickey Mouse that children draw can stand as a graphic question to us as adults: Who, indeed, owns Mickey Mouse?

What most distinguishes Disney World from any other amusement park is the way its spatial organization, defined by autonomous "worlds" and wholly themed environments, combines with the homogeneity of its visitors (predominantly white, middle-class families) to produce a sense of community. While Disney World includes an underlying utopian impulse, this is articulated with nostalgia for a small-town, small-business America (Main Street, U.S.A.), and the fantasy of a controllable corporatist world (EPCOT). The illusion of community is enhanced by the longing for community that many visitors bring to the park, which they may feel is unavailable to them in their own careers, daily lives, and neighborhoods, thanks in large part to the systematic erosion of the public sector throughout the Reagan and Bush administrations. In the last decade the inroads of private, for-profit enterprise in areas previously defined by public control, and the hostile aggression of tax backlash coupled with "me first" attitudes have largely defeated the possibility of community in our homes and cities.

Whenever I visit Disney World, I invariably overhear other visitors making comparisons between Disney World and their home towns. They stare out over EPCOT's lake and wonder why developers back home don't produce similar aesthetic spectacles. They talk about botched, abandoned, and misconceived development projects that have wrecked their local landscapes. Others see Disney World as an oasis of social tranquility and security in comparison to their patrolled, but nonetheless deteriorating, maybe even perilous neighborhoods. A recent essay in *Time* captured some of these sentiments: "Do you see anybody [at Disney World] lying on the street or begging for money? Do you see anyone jumping on your car and wanting to clean your windshield—and when you say no, they get abusive?"[6]

Comments such as these do more than betray the class anxiety of the middle strata. They poignantly express the inability of this group to make distinctions between what necessarily constitutes the public and the private sectors. Do visitors forget that they pay a daily use fee (upwards of $150 for a four-day stay) just to be a citizen of Disney World (not to mention the $100 per night hotel bill)? Maybe so—and maybe it's precisely *forgetting* that visitors pay for.

If there is any distinction to be made between Disney World and our local shopping malls, it would have to do with Disney's successful exclusion of all factors that might put the lie to its uniform social fabric. The occasional Hispanic mother who arrives with extended family and illegal bologna sandwiches is an anomaly. So too is the first-generation Cubana who buys a year-round pass to Disney's nightspot, Pleasure Island, in hopes of meeting a rich and marriageable British tourist. These women testify to the presence of Orlando, Disney World's marginalized "Sister City," whose overflowing cheap labor force and overcrowded and underfunded public institutions are the unseen real world upon which Disney's world depends.

MONUMENTS

TO WALT

• • •

If all architecture is finite, if it therefore carries within itself the traces of its future destruction, the future perfect of its ruin, according to modes that are original each time, it is haunted, indeed signed, by the spectral silhouette of this ruin, at work even in the pedestal of its stone, in its metal and glass, what would bring the architecture of "this time" . . . back to the ruin, to the experience of "its own" ruin?—Jacques Derrida

Death is the sanction of everything that the storyteller can tell. He has borrowed his authority from death.—Walter Benjamin

Walt Disney's ability as a storyteller is legendary. He once acted out the entire story of *The Three Little Pigs* for his animation team, playing all of the parts, and leaving many who were present moved to tears.[1] Walt's concern with and successful presentation of narrative in his films is reproduced in Disneyland, and later Disney World, in the form of theming. In a description of "Pirates of the Caribbean," Susan Willis defines theming as the "stringing together [of a] sequence of events as you move through space, thus constituting a narrative." The creation and manipulation of narrative is central to the effect of theming, which is "most successful when the narratives are highly controlled and tightly organized."[2] Indeed, it seems to me* quite possible to read the narrative aspects of theming as one might stories created by a combination of technical and artistic effects working in tandem. The extent to which one

*Shelton Waldrep

is able to enter into the illusion created by the theming—or to enjoy self-consciously the effects that make the illusion possible—is paramount to an understanding of how theme parks function, especially Disney's.

Walt Disney World in Orlando was built after Walt died. It was, however, planned before his death. In many ways it seems to incorporate a notion of theming that goes beyond what he attempted in California. The vast size of the Orlando property allowed him to spread out and attempt to fashion not only another multithemed amusement park like Disney-land, here called the Magic Kingdom, but an entire "vacation kingdom." The lakes, hotels, golf courses, even kennels are all themed, so that they interconnect and function together in much the same way that the various "lands" do in the Magic Kingdom. Walking through any of the parks at the resort, or almost anywhere else "on property," is similar to going on the rides.

The architect Philip Johnson has said that architecture exists in time, not space.[3] He means that it is only by walking through architecture that one is able to experience the intersecting planes, spaces, and forms of which architecture is made. An interesting implication of Johnson's definition, however, is that architecture as spatial form requires a temporal element: one experiences it as space only as one moves through it in time. The architectural and spatial theming at Disney World seems to be a heightened, almost self-conscious version of this tenet. Whether you shop your way through the various plazas of Adventureland, stroll through the lobby of the Polynesian hotel, or loiter by the lagoon at MGM, the architecture situates you in a theme, a narrative that is dependent upon procession, upon your ability to move through it.

Because of changes in the American cultural matrix since Walt's death—and in the Disney Company's approach to entertainment during the 1980s—Disney's Florida resort has become a different place in terms of the approach to theming and architecture from the one embodied in Disney World when the resort first opened. During the 1970s, except for the addition of a few new rides, Disney World changed little. With the opening of EPCOT in 1982, however, Disney World began a pattern of rapid expansion that still continues. Two years after EPCOT, Disney produced its first non-Disney film, *Splash,* which created for Disney the possibility of a more adult market. EPCOT, similarly, seems to target adults at least as much as it does children and marks a profound change in Disney's approach to theme park design.

In fact, around the time that EPCOT opened, the market for Disney's brand of family entertainment had begun to dry up—fewer families fit the definition of family as portrayed in Disney's older conceptions of itself. In addition, the real creative talent in children's films was coming from Stephen Spielberg and George Lucas, who were weaned on Disney's products, but who understood the new market better than Disney did. Though Disney continued to market its classic films by recycling them every seven years, the film arm of the Company was unable to develop successful new products until it finally tapped into the adult market with a film division called Touchstone Pictures, which made a profit with R-rated movies. The Disney Company's executives suddenly seemed to realize that its obedience to Walt's wishes (always target the straight, white family) had to be ignored for the sake of making profits.

Problems with its film division in the late 1970s and early 1980s created a difficult financial situation for the Disney Company that resulted in its becoming increasingly the target of a hostile takeover. The chance to expand into other types of entertainment—in theme parks as well as film—was an inevitable temptation. The Disney film and theme park divisions were forced, in other words, to change to fit the realities of a new era.[4] When the Disney Company finally had to fight off a serious takeover bid, one result was that the Disney family, for the first time in the Company's history, was deposed. The new chairman, CEO, and later president was Michael Eisner, who moved quickly to accelerate the expansion of Disney's interests into as many market niches as possible. Eisner has turned out to be adept at creating new synergistic combinations of marketing—just as *The Wonderful World of Disney* on NBC both advertised Disney products and acted as a TV series—but he has been short on innovation. That is, he has never been able to invent new ways to entertain, the way Walt did, or to do much more than rehash ideas that were created by Walt and his staff prior to the 1970s. Although Walt's motives were certainly propelled by the desire for profit, it is also clear that he took personal and financial risks in order to create at least two new pop cultural forms: the feature-length animated film and the technologically advanced theme park. Eisner, by contrast, has focused more on elaborating new markets than imagining new paradigms.

From one angle it may seen that Eisner is simply doing his job well, in that business experts argue that the future of marketing is understanding and identifying market segmentation. Anyone who has ever been asked their zip code at the check-out line of the grocery or hardware store is participating in creating a profile that matches the types of products you buy within your geographic location: what's established, among other things, is a pattern of your buying habits and those of your neighbors. Some companies exist only to sell this type of information. Many of the changes at Disney World that have been brought about by Eisner can be said to be the result of this approach: add as much to the property as possible in the hopes that you will have something for everyone—or at least everyone you want to attract according to your market research. Although certainly profitable, the effects of this strategy on the park itself are complex. One way to read the effects on Disney World since the 1980s is to analyze the changes in the design of its buildings and rides that have been added with dizzying efficiency since Eisner's arrival.

In his comments on Disney World in 1975, Umberto Eco notes that "Disneyland's precision and coherence are to some extent disturbed by the ambitions of Disney World in Florida. Built later, Disney World is a hundred fifty times larger than Disneyland, and proudly presents itself not as a toy city but as the model of an urban agglomerate of the future. The structures that make up California's Disneyland form here only a marginal part of an immense complex of construction."[5] A thorough analysis of the construction at the resort that lies outside of its theme parks has not yet been done. However, it is there—in the hotels, service buildings, etc.—that clues to much of the resort's changing story can be found.

The hotels at Disney World function to some extent as their own separate resorts. In addition to their own themes, they each contain their own attractions: hula dancers at dinner, nature trails, or an especially elaborate swimming pool.[6] Although Disney World has always had hotels that weren't themed in a particularly acute way—the Disney Inn, for example—the less expensive hotels built away from the theme parks during the 1980s and 1990s (the Caribbean Beach Resort, Dixie Landings, and Port Orleans Resorts, for instance) are major examples of recent large-scale Disney theming and construction. These hotels are not like those clustered around the Disney Village Marketplace (Buena Vista Palace, Howard Johnson, Hilton, which look like typical Orlando hotels)— but they do represent a sort of zero degree of theming or, simply, minimalistic theming in which the sparest of narrative effects are employed, with the result that their architecture is less clearly distinct from what one might find in most non-Disney resort areas.

With the advent not only of each new hotel, but of each new building, Disney has developed a new theme, since every new structure is expected to have a story of its own to tell. The inevitable effect of this pressure is not only that the themes become more and more high concept—a problem with theming on a large scale—but that theming itself becomes a commodity. That is, the more important the structure to the company, the more carefully developed the theming, the narrative, that goes with it. If EPCOT, the Magic Kingdom, and MGM are at the heart of the Disney empire, it is perhaps not surprising that the structures placed farther from the center will have a more diluted theme. Little is done to disguise the fact that these hotels have the same basic layout as a Holiday Inn: a covered drive-up area that opens into a lobby; blocks of one- or two-level rooms; a swimming pool and recreation area; a self-service restaurant; and transportation to the Disney parks via "motorcoach," a fancy word for bus. In other words, these resort hotels should more accurately be termed motor hotels; the only outstanding differences between them and motels outside of the resort is that there is some theming apparent in the overall design of the outsides of the rooms, the lobby, and the swimming area. But the interiors of the rooms are motel generic, and, indeed, each resort is themed only enough to make it seem vaguely in sync with its place and time.

The architecture of the new Disney-designed hotels seems to owe much to that of EPCOT's World Showcase—a themed version of real places made up of a pastiche of carefully chosen details from the architectural heritage of a country or geographic region. However, much of the design of the pavilions in World Showcase represents a mistake that should have been learned at the original Disneyland; namely, that in order for theming of actual (past or present) places to seem real or succeed in the manipulation of memory, the theming must lack specific referentiality. That is, "Canada" ellicits more interest than "France" because it doesn't reference architectural or spatial structures that are specific to most people's memories: it is authentic, but not the same old thing. Although the design of the Canadian pavilion is based upon actual structures—a chateau in Ottawa, for example—these structures are not nearly as recognizable as the Eiffel Tower in the French pavilion. One is free, therefore, to imagine Disney's "Canada" as somehow the "essence" of the country without being reminded of an actual place. As with Adventureland in the Magic Kingdom, the aura of a country, place, or time—or at least a fictionalized mystique of the same—is tapped into most successfully by theming that doesn't remind you of something that actually exists, something you may have seen in the original. When this recognition occurs, the effect is to dissipate the illusion that the Imagineers strive to achieve. This does not mean that "Canada" is any less carefully detailed than "Italy" or "England," but simply that the references are to a combination of places and times that are difficult to pin down, rather than to easily recognizable tourist attractions in the foreign countries' capital cities.

Although Orlando is located in the South, the South as a theme was not represented in Disney World until the building of Port Orleans and Dixie Landings and the subsequent opening of the new ride in the Magic Kingdom called "Splash Mountain." The latter, themed after Disney's controversial movie *Song of the South,* is arguably not based on life in the South, but on a film whose series of tales were written by a white person posing as an African American. The resorts, in contrast, to some extent duplicate actual places. Port Orleans is a Disney reproduction of the French Quarter during Mardi Gras. Dixie Landings is based not on a specific place in the South, but on the South in general, or rather, the South as a region or "land." The two hotels, connected by the man-made Sassagoula River, divide the South into the specific urban experience of New Orleans with its Catholic flavor and emphasis on revelry, and the non-Catholic, non-urban South, where the aura is not of partying but of mellowness and an escape into a generalized mythological past.

Dixie Landings's theming further divides the rural South into two subareas or subthemes suggested by the resort's two areas of accommodation: Alligator Bayou and Magnolia Bend. The suggested dichotomy recalls the popular myth that most of the South is made up of a poor, rural, backwards region—symbolized by the Bayou area, themed for fishing—and an aristocratic landed gentry. That this division is allowed to stand both for geography and social class is not called into question by anything at the resort. In fact, one publicity shot of Magnolia Bend shows Minnie Mouse in a yellow taffeta-like Southern belle gown—the cliché image given a Disney twist. But it is not surprising that Disney would open a hotel themed on the South and provide no more sensitivity to the history and reality of this region than they do for any other time or place. Although New Orleans Square has been open in Disneyland since 1966, it is something else to open a representation of a region within the region itself. Perhaps Disney thought that, since many Southerners come to Walt Disney World, many of them would also like the idea of staying in a place that in some way represents their own region and identity. Although it is nothing new for guests from other countries to experience their own culture in the same clichéd manner with which Disney presents the Deep South, the inability of recent Disney theming to go beyond reproducing the most obvious versions of regional or national history is disappointing. As with the countries of World Showcase, "Dixie" simply becomes plantations and cane poles, just as "France" is wine, women, song.[7]

One explanation for Disney's turn toward this type of high-concept theming is that in order to charge less for the rooms at its moderately priced hotels, the hotels must have less to offer: no monorail, no bold architectural features, like those at the Swan or the Contemporary. If one wants successful theming, then one must pay for it. When Disney World first opened, its hotels and accommodations were less marked by class—or at least distinctions within the middle class—than they are now. The recently built Grand Floridian and Yacht Club share references to upper class pretension that the earlier Polynesian and Contemporary resorts avoided. The strategy behind these earlier hotels was to make available to guests fantasy-inspired accommodations that were equal in their intrigue and desirability. This egalitarian desire seems to have disappeared with the building of both distinctly "cheap" hotels, like the Caribbean Resort, and upper crust ones, like the Dolphin, with its "concierge levels" above floors of regular-priced rooms. Although Disney World has always provided some rooms that were more expensive than others, the appeal to class biases and stereotypes that is in evidence now seems to have arisen since the opening of EPCOT and the development of the resort as real estate—a sensibility that may always have been latent, but which has come to the fore during the resort's last fifteen years. The guiding principle behind most of the major changes to Disney World is, of course, strictly monetary; the point is to encourage visitors to stay within the park and spend their money on Disney's hotel rooms, which are considerably more expensive than those in the Orlando market. In fact, as Frommer's guide to Orlando has noted for years, the competition in the Orlando hotel market has kept room rates low. Since almost every hotel and motel provides free transportation to the Dis-

ney complex, the only reason to stay within Disney is to be able to say that you stayed there, that your entire experience was themed, that you treated the whole resort as a "ride." This type of thinking is exactly what Disney wants its visitors to give in to. In order to attract even more of them as overnight guests, it has devised a plan whereby an emphasis on class difference allows vacationers to choose—according to their budgets—from a range of hotels that includes both the four-star Grand Floridian and the "moderate" Dixie Landings. The logic seems to be that, with all this from which to choose, why would anyone want to stay in Orlando?

In other parts of the resort—the hotels and offices built by outside architects, for instance—theming has taken on a direction different from either the educational one in World Showcase or the merely serviceable one in the new budget motels.[8] In these commissioned buildings, Disney has succeeded in creating hotels and corporate offices that have been refreshingly effective at commenting on the best aspects of Disney theming and architecture, as well as functioning as important examples of postmodern architecture. Most significantly, however, the hiring of postmodern architects begun by Eisner represents his own version of the knack Walt had of bringing together talented people to create his theme parks and films. But whereas Walt had artisans fashion parks to fit his desires, Eisner, devoid of his own ideas, depends upon famous architects to provide the imagination and innovation for him.

On an episode of the television talk show *Charlie Rose* that aired in the summer of 1993, Rose asked his guest, Philip Johnson, what he thought about the other prominent postmodern architects in the United States. Johnson refused to speak unkindly—or too kindly—about them, but at one point he mentioned Robert A. M. Stern, "the builder of the Queen's Navy by being on the board of Disney."[9] This characterization is significant coming from Johnson, who has defined the patronage of the rich as essential if architects are to be able to express themselves through the building of actual buildings. Indeed, he has argued that it is only during the reign of tyrants that architects are in an ideal situation in which to build; that is, they don't have to worry about money as long as they are taken on by the official court. The resonance that Johnson's comment has for his own career is ambiguous at best. Schooled by Mies van der Rohe— a product of the German crafts tradition—Johnson is infamous for his possible connection with Nazi Germany and the monumental architectural tradition that it represents. Meanwhile, his partnership with fellow architect John Burgee produced some of the most famous versions of corporate postmodernist architecture in the AT&T (Sony) building, IDS Center in Minneapolis, and Pennzoil Place in Houston. In other words, Johnson knows a thing or two about support for architecture, and his comment—tinged with at least a hint of envy—can perhaps be read as to mean that the perfect model for his fantasy of architectural patronage resides in the example of the Disney corporation.

After the arrival of Eisner, Disney decided to build a system of hotels and office buildings deemed necessary for its continued growth. Disney gave this business to a group of postmodern architects—Stern, Michael Graves, Charles Moore, Helmut Jahn, Arata Isozaki, and the iconoclast Frank Gehry—who found themselves involved in a gigantic building project for a company that has ready cash. After years of obedience to one man's conservative, if prescient, personal taste, Eisner seems to have granted these designers a great deal of freedom to create works that express their own architectural styles. The results of their designs have been unusual, not only because each architect has a strong personal style, but because that style has inevitably come into contact with the theme-drenched landscapes of the parks.

The self-consciousness of these buildings reflects each architect's thoughts about and experiences with Disney's theming. In fact, many of the building projects completed so far seem to be essayistic or writerly meditations on the preexisting (and anonymous) architecture of the Disney parks, while at the same time acting as representative examples of postmodern architecture. Indeed, the Orlando and Paris Disney parks are becoming museums of postmodern architectural styles, as Eisner has attempted to include at least one building from almost every postmodern architect of note. Graves and Stern, probably the best known architects that Disney has employed, have each built more than one building at the resort and have had the opportunity, therefore, to comment fully through their designs on the merging of their own styles with that of Disney's.

Since at Disney World every hotel must have its own theme, it was suggested to Graves that he choose Disney characters for the two hotels he was to design for EPCOT. He decided upon the swan and the dolphin because he felt that Disney characters were "not sufficiently appealing to adults" and these hotels were meant primarily for conventions.[10] (His notion of a dolphin is a rather behemoth-like version from Greek antiquity.) Graves did make sure, however, that the complex emphasizes the amount of fun one can have with design, though from the point of view of an adult: the light-heartedness is cerebral and thus somewhat unlike the theming in the rest of the resort. The design of the Dolphin can be read as a loosening up of the homogeneity of the official Disney style to allow in influences from the outside.[11]

In fact, Graves calls the style of the hotels "entertainment architecture." He designed them in collaboration with the son of Morris Lapidus, the famous architect of Miami Beach hotel projects whose kitsch eclecticism looks as though it were created expressly for the proto-postmodernist theories of architect Robert Venturi. With the Dolphin, the result of this collaboration is a building whose interior design is refreshing in its sense of play—banana leaves, monkey lamps, visual puns—and self-effacing art-historical references. Throughout the hotel there are comments on the art of Matisse—from the elevators to various murals designed by Graves that echo Matisse-like forms and scenes. Graves's design lends a graphic quality to the interior that reminds one of Matisse's later work. Amid these references Graves has installed prints of paintings by Pop artists like Jasper Johns and Roy Lichtenstein, as if in an attempt to map his other artistic influences. Even someone who is not a fan of Graves's

earlier work can appreciate the boldness with which he attempts to strike a balance between postmodern architecture (which he, more than any-one, has helped to establish) and the general style of design in the rest of the park. Although enjoyable as pure form, the hotel's auto- and allo-referentiality is a major part of its charm.[12]

The use of procession throughout the Magic Kingdom is most evident in the rides, but it is also an important element in the park's architecture. A walk down Main Street, U.S.A., for instance, opens up vistas that are carefully planned and timed, with the view of Cinderella's Castle looming in the distance. The Castle appears at first to be far away—as if this symbol of childhood fantasy were at the heart of the collective memory of a small middle-American town, the dream we must, and now can, move toward, even enter. In his own subtle way, Graves seems to be comment-ing on his idea of movement toward a central dreamscape in his hotels. At the main entrance to the Dolphin one enters the Starlight Foyer, which leads to the Rotunda Lobby. Along the way, microphones pick up and amplify the sound of the waterfall on the hotel's exterior, but the sound dies down as one approaches the Lobby's large foundation so that the aural events will not be in competition. Above, in the ceiling of the foyer, fiber-optic stars twinkle. The various abstracted visual motifs—stars, squiggles, banana leaves—are first seen on the outside walls of the building only to be picked up in a variety of designs as one moves into the building's interior. The architecture reproduces the manner in which the deployment of theming in Disney rides depends upon the careful planning and spacing of visual and auditory effects placed in space but experienced in time—as one moves away from one room of the "Haunted Mansion" and into another, it is important that the sounds and visual effects merge but do not overlap. Graves's hotel combines a commentary on Disney's theming along with statements about postmodern architecture's dependence upon the legacy of contemporary painting and its relationship to the kitschy strain of U.S. architecture—a legacy of which Disney is a part.

The bold graphic and experimental designs of Graves's hotels suit the size of his complex, which is monumental; it contains the largest single convention space outside of Las Vegas. In sharp contrast in terms of size, yet nearby, is Stern's Yacht and Beach Resorts. Based upon New England waterfront recreational spaces and architecture, the design of the two resorts is supposed to recall maritime styles whose differences are mainly marked through class—middle-middle class (beach) and upper-middle class (yacht).[13] A commentary on market-driven style, the Beach Resort looks like a cheaper version of the Yacht Resort and, in fact, the room rates are less. In this sense, Stern's resorts echo the class stratification that now seems to be designed into all new hotel projects.[14] As the major player in Eisner's current building boom, the more modernist Stern has created much quieter works for Disney than have the other architects. His Casting Center, opened in 1989, is an especially striking contrast to Graves's reinterpretation of the Disney rides. Though built on a small scale, with obvious references to Fantasyland and not so obvious ones to the architecture of Tomorrowland, Stern's building is unabashed in its direct commentary on Disney's theming, and in its calling attention to the Disney employment ethos: this is not a personnel office, it is a *casting* center.

If Stern's building is mainly whimsical on the outside, the interior of the building plays with one's sense of scale. In order to reach the reception area, applicants must walk up an inside ramp—an idea borrowed from Frank Lloyd Wright.[15] Along the way they pass a series of murals that grow smaller as the ramp slowly inclines and seems to compress the height of the walls. The murals on the wall facing Interstate 4 depict Disney characters driving cars, while the murals on the wall facing the parks show characters visiting the Magic Kingdom, EPCOT, or Disneyland

in California. At the point where the murals are the smallest there is a trompe l'oeil: first one sees a banister, which looks as though it is part of the building's architecture, but then it also looks like a balcony opening out onto a jungle peopled with various Disney characters. At the upper right-hand corner there is yet another layer of illusion in the form of an image of cracked and peeling plaster. What one is witnessing is a multidimensional effect that comments on naturalistic representation in several ways, including the interaction between animation, architecture, and "reality." Trompe l'oeil is also used in the walkways that one passes under, which are suggestive of Venetian bridges but are constructed of two-dimensional stones among which are mixed more illusionary cracked plaster. Not simply paying homage to the Magic Kingdom, Stern playfully "exposes" its unrealistic elements: the forced perspectives, the carefully designed blending of various lands and building styles, the buildings themselves, the "stone walls" of Cinderella's Castle, which are made of fiberglass.

The primary element that connects Stern's and Graves's designs to the rest of the Disney resort is the sense of narrative that their buildings embody. Stern's Casting Center tells a story about what it means to work at Disney, or, as he says, "to clarify Disney's hiring process and give it an architectural dimension."[16] By channeling potential employees along a

ramp between carefully spaced murals that tell a story, Stern alludes to the effects of rides at Disney World; the procession through the building's architecture is itself a kind of ride, in which one learns the story of the park's secret: that all is illusion. The ramp suggests a stage, while the trompe l'oeil, by illustrating what is behind the Disney magic, metaphorizes the idea that the performance one gives as a Disney employee is simply that, and it is, as Jane Kuenz notes, a performance that is intended to create the illusion of natural happiness, sincerity, and joy. In a review of the Swan and Dolphin, Mark Alden Branch muses that "Graves has proved himself one of Disney's best storytellers."[17] Both Graves and Stern have tapped into the use of narrative, as promulgated by the theming in the Magic Kingdom, while at the same time injecting their own postmodern commentary and, by so doing, emphasizing that they are a part of the disruption of the tradition begun by Walt of having only faceless Imagineers do all of the planning and design.

   The most recent and successful example of a departure from this tradition is Isozaki's Team Disney building. Comprised of a number of different offices, but mainly used as a corporate headquarters, Isozaki's building is the most un-Disney of the recent complexes, yet also the most like the examples of corporate postmodern architecture that dot the suburban landscape of many North American cities.[18] The series of mouse-ear gates through which one passes in order to arrive at Team Disney and the bright primary colors on the building's exterior are the only overt references in Isozaki's design to the building's function and identity. The dominant feature is a massive sundial that takes up the building's central core. Although an actual working mechanism, the sundial is yet another theatrical element, a gimmick, or ride à la the Magic Kingdom not that different from the ramp and procession toward a central atrium in Stern's building (which is, in fact, the only part of either building where visitors are allowed). The contemplative nature of the sundial's interior is as evocative of Japanese Zen gardens as the building's name is of modern Japan. The emphasis on time is an interesting spatial twist on the usual Disney narrative, since the public procession into this building leads not to a climactic ending (the Casting Center's ramp leads to the original model for Cinderella's Castle), but to an interior monologue: the sundial court is furnished with only river rock and plaques inscribed with quotations on mutability. As one architectural critic notes, the sundial measures time spatially, not linearly. In place of a Western narrative with a dramatic arc of beginning, middle, and end, Isozaki has provided a device that seems either more primitive—time as measured by a crude instrument—or more sophisticated—space-time.[19] The sundial court is punctuated by several entrances at different levels so that one's relationship to the sun is made, in a sense, relative.[20] Isozaki's overall design manages to suggest both the quotidian and the extraordinary.

Isozaki is not a team player in the same way as the other architectural

stars that have been enlisted; he makes the most radical critique of the
Disney approach to architecture as narrative. Whereas Graves tries to
out-Disney Disney, by freezing time into space Isozaki creates an anti-
model that comments on the Disney approach to architectural design and
on the Disney parks' ability to thematize almost anything. In choosing as
the "theme" of his building the concept of—and literalization of—time
itself, Isozaki seems to be attempting to find a phenomenon that cannot
be co-opted.[21] Although there is movement within the sundial, his construction emphasizes stillness as a spatial experience that is the opposite
of the linear progression of a ride.[22]

Isozaki's building has been called "allegorical rather than symbolic,"
and it is possible to read it as resisting on several levels any incorporation
into the park on the usual Disney terms. One architect claims that Isozaki
has transformed Mickey's ears "into abstract form," in contrast to Graves's
"cynical game of utter superficiality."[23] If Isozaki is finally less an accom-
plice than in Graves, the difference may lie at least as much in Isozaki's
interest in the platonic concept of *chora*, of seeing space as an empty
vessel, as in an attempt to resist Disney.[24]

Since completing the Casting Center, Stern has gone on to design half
of Disney's new planned community, Celebration, in Osceola County,
Florida, as well as hotels at EuroDisney and an office building in Bur-

bank. His trademark architectural style is easily adaptable to a multitude of settings and is, at Disney World, fairly nondescript except for the use of ornament and self-reflexivity that imbues the Casting Center with a self-conscious playfulness that is wholly supportive of the Company's sense of itself. Graves and Isozaki are much bolder in their interpretations and indirect reflections on Disney themes and imagery. Isozaki, however, has created the only building that seriously questions the desirability of theming as an architectural principle.

Even as Disney has been courting various outside influences, it is also in the process of rediscovering its own origins. Stern's references to a palace in Venice recall the Venetian Hotel, a project planned during Walt Disney's lifetime but never built. Similarly, EPCOT's World Showcase echoes his plans for Cal-Arts, which was supposed to become his "City of the Seven Arts" complete with working artists and multifarious architectural references.[25] Even with Disney funding and oversight, the college developed into an avant-garde interdisciplinary school of the visual arts rather than into a showcase of "Imagineering."[26] In some ways the Disney-MGM Studios Theme Park may have completed Walt's dream. There one can see animation, special effects, stunt production: the sister arts as they are done at Disney. Even the landmark of the park, the Earffel Tower—a water tower with Mickey Mouse ears—is an idea an employee suggested in the 1960s for the Burbank studio. Walt Disney rejected it because, at least where the design of the studios was concerned, he wanted a generic corporate look that would not compete with his rides. The MGM park is not simply a simulacrum of Hollywood(land) but also Disney's own California studio, even if it represents a history that never quite was. The emphasis on pedagogy that seems to have come out not only in EPCOT and MGM but also in the plans for the new Disney's America park, fit the direction Walt was moving at the end of his life when he began to see his role as that of a teacher as opposed to entertainer. Although this dichotomy was present early in his career, Walt saw his EPCOT project and his interest in Cal-Arts as chances to better mankind. The current pride that is taken in creating themed environments that accurately reproduce details from the original inspirations may simply be another example of this pedantic desire. Even with the advent of outside creative talent, Disney's executives never seem to flee from their own corporate history. Like the postmodern style they are currently embracing, they ransack history for scraps wherever they can find them. The progression toward something new—a transformation of the Disney style—is paralleled with a gesture of remorse, a looking back to Walt for any ideas that have yet to be attempted or fulfilled.

As Graves's and Stern's buildings show, there is much nostalgia on the part of both Disney and the consumers of its products to celebrate or comment on the use of theming in the parks. But the future, as evidenced by the new hotels and planned parks, will bring types of theming different from those when the resort first opened. Although this result is partially brought about by Eisner's market strategies, the effect will be to make Disney World seem more like anywhere else, since Disney will be unable to keep up with the postmodernization going on outside of its resorts. With its new dependence on architects, performers, and experts from the outside—whether Robin Williams, Eric Foner, or Isozaki— Disney seems finally to have agreed to meet the world half-way. Just as the creation of Touchstone Pictures suggests a desire on the part of the company to become more like other movie companies, the resorts are becoming more like the postmodern suburbs, office complexes, and hotels that many people live and work in every day. Through the increased theming, the world beyond the Disney parks looks more and more like Disney architecture, which makes Disney World resemble the spaces and structures it once merely influenced. Disney seems to have had a contradictory response to this challenge. On the one hand, the architecture coming from the hands of postmodern architects continues to make structures on Disney property seem special or unique. On the other hand, Disney's new in-house designs, like those for its moderate resort hotels, look more like non-Disney vernacular architecture than anything Disney has built before.

The "Wonders of Life" at EPCOT—with its mall-like atmosphere—and the food court at Dixie Landings are literal examples of Disney's borrowing symbols of privatization from downtown and suburban architecture. That these symbols grew out of structures that were often themed along the lines of the Disney parks illustrates the architectural give-and-take between Disney and the public and private spheres. Disney has provided a heightened sense of atmosphere and theming for public and corporate architecture, but it is ultimately dependent upon the outside architectural world to provide it with new architectural forms for its own resorts.[27] In many ways Disney reflects the larger architectural world as much as it provides influences for it: hence the suburbanization going on in recently developed areas of the park, much of which is only or mainly accessible by car or bus.

When Disney World originally opened, part of the thrill of actually staying in the park was the idea that you could be in a semi-urban space and be completely rid of your dependence on a car. It is rare that people in developed countries ever have a vacation experience that is devoid of this dependence. But while motorized transportation is deployed everywhere for rides, cars are incompatible with architectural theming. As Johnson has recognized, the automobile's most troubling effect for architects is that one can't experience procession in a car.[28] The theming in the architecture of the new outlying hotels can only be experienced by the people who walk through it, not those driving by. The expanded road system does make some of Disney World's attractions more accessible to Orlando and surrounding communities—one can get to the Bonnet Creek golf courses, Typhoon Lagoon, etc., to spend money, which is one of the few ways in which the resort seems to take into consideration its surrounding metropolitan area. But the addition of roadways and overpasses makes this part of the resort look anything like an example of the progressive urbanism that Disney claims for the resort's design. In the past, the areas that one reached by car were in the minority—the Fort

Wilderness Camp grounds, for instance—but not anymore. A parking pass at Disney World used to allow one to park in only one lot for one day; a pass can now be used to park anywhere in the resort. It seems that even Disney has acknowledged that guests might want to drive from place to place. In the upcoming plans for Celebration and a new hotel/theme park area, the differences between Disney and non-Disney design is eroded still further. As the Disney property in Orlando expands its road system, Disney seems to be fashioning one more connection to the outside world. The theming that used to be a marker that signaled entry into a special vacation kingdom, rather than simply another resort, is beginning to disappear.[29]

Celebration represents Disney's literal attempt to reach beyond its borders. Incorporating rental housing with slightly advanced features like interactive fiber-optic cable and underground wiring, the planning for the project includes a school, a mall, and places to work. Disney's first adventure in full-scale residential property management should prove or disprove some of the theories about urban planning suggested by the Disney World resort. Whether or not the renters will feel more like vacationers, employees, or resort guests remains to be seen. In terms of architectural design, however, it will be important to watch the ways in which Stern and Disney integrate theming into an environment in which people will actually live.

A preview of Celebration may already be on view in Seaside, a residential resort town in the Florida panhandle that was designed by the architectural team of Andres Duany and Elizabeth Plater-Zyberk. Attacked by architects and critics interested in social issues, such as Peter Eisenman and Neil Smith, as a homogeneous version of faux-regional postmodern architecture, Seaside has been defended by its creators as an attempt to give people what they want in a town but don't often get: orderliness, human scale, and a sense of charm and nostalgia built into the architectural design. The homes built so far may be neo-Victorian in their abundance of gingerbread detailing, but there is the unsettling effect of knowing that everything in the resort is from the same design recipe. In other words, although the village is well laid out and the streets contain plenty of front porches with swings and interesting architectural details in an attempt to create the illusion of difference, there is still about the town the sense of sameness and stillness that one has in any planned community—whether a condominium complex in the suburbs or an upscale retirement "village" such as Fearrington, North Carolina. The potential problem with Celebration may be the problem with Seaside: the assumption that utopian planning can solve urban problems. If architects and urban planners have learned anything from creating utopian architecture—as opposed to a model for it like EPCOT—it is that architecture cannot by itself create social change. Social progress can come only from a community, not from its buildings.[30]

Seaside is further hampered by the fact that the representation of diversity that postmodern pastiche offers in the form of historical or regional effects is, as Smith claims, one in which "the future . . . is the past, only more so. Very strangely and paradoxically, the celebration of diversity actually misses the possibility of a *different* social world. The celebration of diversity actually flattens out history."[31] Antimodernist and utopian impulses are not only at cross purposes, but ultimately affirm the worst aspect of postmodern architecture: a desire to create a sense of community that is imposed by designers acting as social engineers; a simulacrum of regionalism posing as nostalgia while it is in fact a conservative reaction to modernist architecture; a dehistoricized pastiche of references to a past that is perfected and devoid of almost any real sense of the actual lived history in Florida—or anywhere else in the South other than, perhaps, Hilton Head, South Carolina. David Mahoney says that Seaside "has been reviled as a shameless appeal to nostalgic impulses; and, by being equated with the Disney parks, it has been criticized as a manufactured, controlled, ersatz public realm."[32] That this description will also apply to Celebration—only more so—seems almost certain.

In looking for a model for its design, the architects for Seaside apparently used Disney World, which can be surmised even in the brochure that advertises the community to future customers: "[Seaside provides] a theater for daily life"; "strolling is the preferred mode of transportation"; while "all streets lead to the beach, they also lead to downtown, where shopping takes on a sense of relaxed fun."[33] Seaside's designers have attempted to fashion an environment that is cinematic in intent and synergistic in its melding of procession, shopping, and atmospherics—much like Main Street, U.S.A. If Seaside's architects learned from Disney, they also beat Disney to the punch by creating a Disney-like environment that fetishizes the small town and the child's psychic landscape. Celebration's suburban design will follow suit: the theme for Celebration will be the mythic small town itself and, possibly, Disney's own parks. The most striking characteristic, however, may be how much Celebration will look like everywhere else.

The erosion of the conditions for theming at Disney World seems always to lead back to problems that emerge with EPCOT—specifically, EPCOT as a purported version of the future. If EPCOT represents a modernist fantasy of an urban environment—in contrast to the Magic Kingdom—then it is not what Corbusier and other modernist utopian architects had in mind; rather, it is a museum of a city that is completely separate from the world and stripped of any actual urban functions. Futurism at the Disney parks has often felt the pressure of this fate. The monorail system was the first to operate in the United States, but now it is not significantly different from BART on the West Coast or the Washington, D.C. Metro on the East. The nerdy costumes consisting of wide white belts and military-like shoulder decorations that the monorail operators wear seem oddly dated rather than a preview of a style from the future.[34]

The fate of the monorail is not too far from that of the Contemporary Resort Hotel, opened with the Magic Kingdom, whose supposedly avant-garde design was linked to the modular construction with which it was built. Modular design—in which parts of a building are constructed *in toto* off the building site, brought to the frame, and inserted—has become associated with cheap, dangerous construction. Hardly the best design of the future—although perhaps the one corporate capital intends for a replaceable population—the Contemporary's fate may also be Future World's: seen as somewhat radical when they were unveiled, Future World's buildings now remind one of the generic architecture of the exurb, whether Silicon Valley, California, or Research Triangle Park, North Carolina. That is, it seems to reference the architecture and social formations that have come into being as corporations have moved from city interiors to the outskirts, to landscapes that are dominated by a mixture of corporate (post)modernist architecture and total mall living.[35] Just as hotel chains, casinos, or research centers may have their own themes, monorails, and experimental "futuristic" technology, the Disney futurism can now only be an ideology from the past frozen in time—mainly, the 1960s and 1970s.[36]

Disney's futurism is a theme that doesn't work because it depends upon spatial as opposed to temporal metaphors. In choosing to comment upon the rides in the Magic Kingdom, as opposed to those in EPCOT, Graves and

Stern have correctly identified the location of Disney's successful theming. Modifications and changes that are now taking place at EPCOT, such as the installation of the new "Innoventions," suggest that Disney has realized that it must reconsider its current approach to theming.[37] In fact, the name of the park, "EPCOT Center," which suggests a spatial position, has been changed to "Epcot 94" (and one assumes, 95, 96, etc.) in what looks like an attempt to shift people's image of EPCOT away from the idea of a static or permanent world's fair and toward the idea that it is ever-changing and growing, like an actual world's fair.[38]

Indeed, although EPCOT may seem like the last place where Disney might reinvigorate its approach to theming, with the coming of interactive CD-ROM and virtual reality technology, EPCOT, and Disney World in general, could become important laboratories for the development of theming via the use of new computer technologies.[39] Ideas imagined in a fantastic way in Disney's *Tron*, a 1982 box-office failure, have to some extent become realities. The merging of flight simulator technology with George Lucas's work in "Star Tours," or the use of three-dimensional film technology, witty scripting, and Audio-Animatronics in "Jim Henson's Muppet-Vision 3-D," are examples of a marriage of technology with artistic talent to create extraordinary effects that are kin to theming, but also seem like a form of anti-architecture—the experience of a multimedia event that is close to a rock concert. As in a virtual environment, many of Disney's newer technology-dependent rides are not really rides at all in that one remains immobile throughout them: in "Body Wars," for example, a combination of film, sound effects, and simulator technology gives one the thrilling illusion of moving through an environment.

Although a virtual environment, unlike a Disney park attraction, might allow the illusion of some control over what one experiences, the set of effects are circumscribed by both the technological limitations and the creative choices available in it. Creativity, in fact, is what much of this type of experience lacks: one's own imagination can roam only as far as the technician's equipment will allow, and the effects that one experiences are still governed by aesthetic choices that are limited by the talent of the same. Just as Walt's multiplane camera allowed for a more realistic animated movie, but did not insure that cartoons would become aesthetically better because of it, virtual technology offers nothing other than a new instrument or medium to the artist or creative designer. Technology as an end in itself, therefore, is a danger to be avoided. The best themed or virtual environments depend upon design concepts that are focused on some type of merging of technology with familiar aesthetic forms to create an experience for the participant that is both recognizable and exceptional. Walt's breakthrough was in realizing that the use of stories taken from his culture could be reprocessed as three-dimensional experiences parallel to what went on in his films to create various forms of visual and aural synaesthesia. What the next breakthrough in theme park design might be is difficult to predict; it is probable that it will not be a technological breakthrough, but a conceptual one.

In its present form, Disney World needs something more from Eisner than contributions from outside architects if it is to stay in the vanguard of theming and design. Without a new form of creativity, Disney's parks risk becoming little more than monuments to Walt that enshrine all of his works, dreams, fears, and aspirations in a "palace of memory" where they can be read and remembered. In the period after his death, but before the coming of Eisner, the administrators of Disney World were known to ask, "What would Walt have done?" As John Taylor recounts, Disney employees would even joke, "This is necrophilia," or "We're working for a dead man."[40] Indeed, if Walt's corpse is frozen in California, his memory and influence are preserved in their most dramatic form in Florida. EPCOT may be the most expensive necropolis ever conceived; it was carried out despite enormous cost overruns because it was Walt's dying dream to see it built. The brainlike geodesic sphere that makes up Spaceship Earth looks like a postmodern tomb and resembles Boulee's 1784 project for a cenotaph for Newton: a design that incorporated a perfectly round sphere as a memorial to the principles of the Newtonian system.[41] Roy O. Disney and his company chose to make EPCOT function as a memorial for Walt when they decided to make it into a permanent world's fair rather than into an actual city of the future. The entire resort in Florida, however, can be seen to function in the same way: Walt's ideas cling to many of the design decisions even now, even when whatever is left of them seems anachronistic decades later.

Like theme parks, monuments rarely fit the definition of architecture in the usual sense of a structure made to dwell in. Monuments exist instead to preserve past ideas and assumptions by symbolizing or representing them in a permanent three-dimensional form. Both public and private, monuments exist somewhere between sculpture and architecture, space and time, as a form of collective memory, as something in and on which is encoded a way of reading the past. Though monuments exist in time, they are designed to withstand its effects. Like Isozaki's sundial, they call attention to time in order to establish meaning at a given point, if only to carry this meaning into the future. As James E. Young notes about monuments in general:

> The material of a conventional monument is normally chosen to withstand the physical ravages of time, the assumption being that its memory will remain as everlasting as its form. But . . . the actual consequence of a memorial's unyielding fixedness in space is also its death over time: a fixed image created in one time and carried over into a new time suddenly appears as archaic, strange, or irrelevant altogether. For in its linear progression, time drags old meaning into new contexts, estranging a monument's memory from both past and present, holding past truths up to ridicule in present moments. Time mocks the rigidity of monuments, the presumptuous claim that in its materiality, a monument can be regarded as eternally true, a fixed star in the constellation of collective memory.[42]

Despite the park's deft manipulation of time, it may—as Isozaki's building warns—be unable, ultimately, to escape it.[43]

It is not yet known whether the outcome of EuroDisney's restructured financial package will be successful or, if not, whether the Disney Company will continue to put funds into the resort in order to keep it going.[44] We do know that, in Europe and North America, Eisner may be suffering from his or his company's hubris, since theme park customers seem to be saying that Disney's attempts at marketing are finally going too far— becoming too global, too obviously greedy.[45] What can be discerned from the changes in Disney's approach to theming certainly does not bode well for a company that has been in the theme park business for over forty years. The failure of Disney's Mineral King ski resort suggests that expansion isn't always a sure thing. The very idea of a European Disney is a strange one given that for many Europeans the joy of coming to Disney World is at least in part because it means a trip to Florida—to someplace warm, with native attractions. Disney has already had to scrap plans for a water-themed park in Long Beach because of problems with zoning, and expansion plans for Disneyland and for EuroDisney are currently on hold. Eisner's decisions seem only to have been successful at Walt Disney World, where the amount of space and the continual success of the park as a magnate for tourists virtually guarantees that almost anything that is done there will be popular. Expanding beyond Orlando in order to create new theme park niches has been risky and, at least at this time, unsuccessful.[46] If EuroDisney closes, it may become an actual monument, but one that is unvisited and left to the effects of time.[47]

NOTES

. . .

The Problem with Pleasure

1 John Kasson, *Amusing the Millions: Coney Island at the Turn of the Century* (New York, 1978).
2 Pierre Bourdieu, *Distinction, A Social Critique of the Judgment of Taste* (Cambridge, Mass., 1984).
3 Derek Walcott, *Dream on Monkey Mountain and Other Plays* (New York, 1970).
4 Peter Stallybrass and Allon White, "Bourgeois Hysteria and the Carnivalesque," in *A Cultural Studies Reader*, ed. Simon During (New York, 1993). The authors chart the elimination of all the legendary fairs from Donnybrook (1855) to the transformation of the Nice carnival into a tourist attraction (1873).
5 Stephen Jay Gould, "A Biological Homage to Mickey Mouse," in *The Panda's Thumb* (New York, 1982).
6 Stallybrass and White, "Bourgeois Hysteria," 288.
7 Ibid., 291.
8 Carey McWilliams, *Southern California Country: An Island on the Land* (New York, 1946).
9 See Fredric Jameson, "Reification and Utopia in Mass Culture," *Social Text* I (1979).
10 Guy Debord, *Society of the Spectacle* (Detroit, 1983).

Reality Revisited

1 Stephen Birnbaum, *Walt Disney World: The Official Guide* (New York, 1991), 114.
2 Ibid., 27.

The Family Vacation

1 Walter Benjamin, *Illuminations,* ed. Hannah Arendt, trans. Harry Zohn (New York, 1969), 179.
2 See Dean MacCannell, *The Tourist: A New Theory of the Leisure Class* (New York, 1975).

3   Jean Baudrillard, *La Transparence du Mal, Essai Sur les Phenomenes Extrêmes* (Paris, 1990), 85. Translation mine.

4   Fredric Jameson, *Signatures of the Visible* (New York, 1990), 33.

It's a Small World After All

1   Guy Debord, *Society of the Spectacle* (Detroit, 1983), 192.

2   Louis Marin, "Disneyland: A Degenerate Utopia," *Glyph* 1 (1977): 61.

3   At the time, I worried that I was the only person who either could not appreciate the fun of these games or lacked the skill to play them. Alexander Wilson, though, seems to have had the same reaction both to these and to their more enjoyable counterparts in "Journey into Imagination." On this and other similar conclusions about EPCOT, see his "The Betrayal of the Future: Walt Disney's EPCOT Center," *Socialist Review* 84 (1985): 44–45.

4   John Kasson, *Amusing the Millions: Coney Island at the Turn of the Century* (New York, 1978), 50. EPCOT is, however, clearly modeled on earlier world's fairs and expositions. The 1964 fair in Detroit, for example, included General Electric's "Progress Land" and General Motor's "Futurama 2."

5   Ibid., 61.

6   Margaret King, "Disneyland and Walt Disney World: Traditional Values in Futuristic Form," *Journal of Popular Culture* 15 (1981): 120.

7   See Marin, "Disneyland."

8   It was this quotation from Lincoln that caught the attention of historian Eric Foner and resulted eventually in his hiring by Disney as a consultant for the updating of the "Hall of Presidents." In a letter to Disney, Foner pointed out that Lincoln's speech had been reproduced out of context to suggest Cold War hysteria about the communist menace living among us. Lincoln, however, was referring to racial violence, specifically lynchings, as the clear and present danger to domestic peace. See Jon Wiener, "Disney World Imagineers a President," *The Nation* (22 November 1993): 622.

9   Theodor Adorno, *Minima Moralia: Reflections from Damaged Life*, trans. E. F. N. Jephcott (London, 1989), 144.

10   Ibid., 145.

11   Judith Butler, *Gender Trouble: Feminism and the Subversion of Identity* (New York, 1990), 140.

12   Frigga Haug, et al., *Female Sexualization: A Collective Work of Memory*, trans. Erica Carter (London, 1987), 203.

13   Denise L. Almos, "Getting Married with Mickey and Minnie," *St. Petersburg Times*, 12 April 1992.

14   This story comes from Julie Tetel, whose son was disappointed with the film's end.

15   See John Fiske, *Understanding Popular Culture* (Boston, 1989); Michel de Certeau, *The Practice of Everyday Life* (Berkeley, 1984); Henri Lefebvre, *Everyday Life in the Modern World*, trans. Sacha Rabinovitch (London, 1984).

16   Stephen Birnbaum, *Walt Disney World: The Official Guide* (New York, 1990), 135.

17   Quoted in Stephen M. Fjellman, *Vinyl Leaves: Walt Disney World and America* (Boulder, Colo., 1992), 163.

18   Jean Baudrillard, *Simulations*, trans. Paul Foss, Paul Patton, and Philip Beitchman (New York, 1983), 139.

STORY TIME

1   Richard Schickel, *The Disney Version: The Life, Times, Art and Commerce of Walt Disney* (New York, 1968), 34, 173–74.

2   Scott Bukatman, "There's Always Tomorrowland: Disney and the Hypercinematic Experience," *October* 57 (Summer 1991): 60.

3   Hal Foster, *Decodings: Art, Spectacle, Cultural Politics* (Seattle, 1985), 121.

4   Schickel, *Disney Version*, 182–83.

5   Jean Baudrillard, *Simulations*, trans. Paul Foss, Paul Patton, and Philip Beitchman (New York, 1983), 142.

6   Ibid., 42.

7   *Walt Disney World*, ed. Steve Birnbaum (New York, 1989), 98.

8   Bob Thomas, *Walt Disney: An American Original* (New York, 1976), 290.

9   "Walt Disney World Resort Expansion Projects" (press release, January 1991).

10 See John Rajchman: "California, with its mix of Disney, Hollywood, and Silicon Valley, counts as an important site. . . . A universal reproducible *model*, good in itself, to be applied everywhere no longer matters, but rather a ubiquitous *condition* unavoidable in reach, from where there is not escape, allowing only various internal recombinations of its elements." "Anywhere and Nowhere," in Cynthia C. Davidson, ed., *Anywhere* (New York, 1992), 232.

11 Baudrillard, *Simulations*, 126–27.

12 Ibid., 127.

13 Ibid., 130.

14 Lester Faigley's comments: "Drawing on Guy Debord's *Society of the Spectacle,* Baudrillard maintains that we no longer live in an era of political participation but the simulation of the political. In making this claim Baudrillard denies that Politics any longer exists as the expression of the collective will of rational, freely choosing agents presumed by Enlightenment theorists of democracy. Rather people are now offered the stimulation of political participation through opinion polls and surveys." "The New Left Times," *Pre/Text* 13.1–2 (Spring–Summer 1992): 52–53.

15 Ibid., 136.

16 See Louis Marin, "Disneyland, a Degenerate Utopia," *Glyph* 1 (1977): 50–66.

17 Michel de Certeau, *The Practice of Everyday Life*, trans. Steven Rendall (Berkeley, 1984), 120.

18 Ibid., 127.

19 Ibid., 115.

20 Ibid., 129.

21 Ibid., 118.

22 Susan Buck-Morss, "Benjamin's *Passagen-Werk*: Redeeming Mass Culture for the Revolution," *New German Critique* 29 (1983): 222.

23 Walter Benjamin, *Illuminations*, ed. and intro. Hannah Arendt, trans. Harry Zohn (New York, 1969), 118.

24 For more on Benjamin on childhood, fairy tales, allegory, and myth, see Jeffrey Mehlman, *Walter Benjamin for Children*, especially the discussion on pp. 67–68 of Benjamin's radio show for children, in which he retold a fairy tale that deals with dangerous journeys. See also Benjamin's own discussion of the storyteller in *Illuminations,* especially "The Storyteller: Reflections on the Works of Nikolai Leskov" and "Franz Kafka: On the Tenth Anniversary of His Death," and Eagleton's and Jameson's

respective discussions of these themes in *Ideology of the Aesthetic,* 318 and 327, and "Benjamin's Readings," *Diacritics* 22.3 (Fall–Winter 1992), esp. 28, 31, and 33.

25 Ibid., 240.

26 Schickel, *Disney Version,* 323–24.

27 Buck-Morss, "Benjamin's *Passagen-Werk,*" 217.

28 See Ariel Dorfman and Armand Mattelart's discussion of the use of children and animals in the Disney comic books in *How to Read Donald Duck,* trans. and intro. David Kunzle (New York, 1984).

29 In addition to Benjamin's writing on childhood, we have Eisenstein's discussion of Disney and childhood in his writings—some never completed—on Disney animation. Eisenstein likens the Disney cartoons to a new art form—possibly even a new stage in artistic evolution—capable of harnessing a childhood "pre-memory" for the purposes of creating a pure form of entertainment.

30 Ibid., 217.

31 Richard V. Francaviglia, "Main Street, U.S.A.: A Comparison/Contrast of Street-scapes in Disneyland and Walt Disney World," *Journal of Popular Culture* 15 (1981): 147, 149.

32 Fredric Jameson, *Postmodernism, or, The Cultural Logic of Late Capitalism* (Durham, 1991), 118.

33 It is perhaps not by accident, then, that Walt Disney himself was delighted that the ratio of adult to children visitors to his Anaheim park was four to one. See David Kunzle, "Introduction to the English Edition," in *How to Read Donald Duck,* 20.

34 Unlike the Magic Kingdom or EPCOT, where most product logos are subservient to the park's major theme, here we have the logo "Walt Disney and Co." appearing anywhere a typical logo would. Disney itself becomes a theme.

35 Schickel, *Disney Version,* 335.

36 Thomas, *An American Original,* 265.

37 Margaret Morse, "An Ontology of Everyday Distraction: The Freeway, the Mall, and Television," in Patricia Mellencamp, ed., *Logics of Television: Essays in Cultural Criticism* (Bloomington, Ind., 1990), makes important connections among the freeway, the television, and the mall, many of which can be said to describe effects at Disney World, especially at EPCOT and MGM.

38 Animal Kingdom is the new theme park planned for the Orlando resort. The hotels for the park have already been described in some detail as Disney's All-Star Resorts. Themed as "pop-art icon elements ranging from sports to music," the hotels are references to broad cultural phenomena such as basketball (Hoops Hotel) and rock music (Rock Inn) and are described as "moderate" in cost.

Under the Influence

1 Michael Hoover and Lisa Stokes, *Welcome to Dislando: The Disneyfication of Fun and Leisure.* Videocassette (Sanford, Fl., 1993).

Working at the Rat

1 Unless otherwise noted, all quotations are from interview transcripts with current and former employees of Walt Disney World. These interviews were conducted over a two-year period in Orlando, Florida, and Durham, North Carolina, in person, over

the phone, via electronic networks, and in writing. With one exception, every person I spoke with requested anonymity and as much camouflage as I could manage. This was true even of the former employees, many of whom are either CTS or part of the more general amorphous service/entertainment labor force hovering in and around central Florida. Most of them expect to end up at Disney again, or, until the state's economy picks up, cannot count on avoiding it. As one worker put it, "people do their time at Disney." All of the workers' names have been changed, including that one exception who actually wanted to be known. Where necessary, I have slightly altered some of the identifying details of their jobs—specifically the particular attraction or area—but have kept as many of the important details as possible. If someone works in food service, I keep the food service designation but put him or her in a different resort or a different park. Elsewhere I identify workers just by the kind of work they do: sanitation, central reservations, attractions host, etc. Once their anonymity is assured, Disney employees are dying to talk about their work. About our interview, one woman said, "This is like the answer to a prayer that I'd been talking about for five years. Along with the mouse there is a God." Another told me that the brief ad I had placed in *The Orlando Sentinel* had been photocopied, enlarged, and posted throughout employee areas: in the tunnels, break rooms, cafeterias.

It should be emphasized that my interviews and the conclusions I've drawn from them are not part of a statistical study of Walt Disney World employees and do not pretend to offer that kind of representative overview. Though the ratio of current to former employees is roughly equal, the circumstances under which sources were secured may have resulted in a disproportionate representation of critical commentary. I have tried not to let strongly negative statements overshadow other voices in part by looking for patterns in the interviews as a group. If there is an imbalance, I would place much of the responsibility for it with Disney itself: the company's infamous secrecy has made it difficult to solicit honest appraisals—favorable or otherwise—and has led many of its employees to believe that what outsiders want are dirty secrets (see note 2 below). Consider, as illustration, the following statement by an Entertainment lead regarding the likelihood that he might be recognized from our interview even though he was highly positive throughout about his job and the company itself: "I'm behind the scenes but very visible. I can't really come out and say because it is because—see, you have to be careful because—if someone were to find out, they'd say, 'Oh, that's who it is.' And they'd tell someone else, then you wouldn't have this . . . they wouldn't be as careful not to tell someone."

My interest is less in the company than in the park and specifically the social practices of the people within it. Disney's workers are particularly significant in understanding the park's construction of its own reality, since they are both a cause and effect of it. In spite of their importance, Disney's workers have had few occasions to comment publicly on their work. The reasons for this vary: as a precondition of hiring, all employees must sign a statement to the effect that they will not disclose in writing anything related to their on-the-job experience. Disney's local reputation for winning lawsuits—85 percent in jury trials—has convinced most of them not to test the company's will (85 percent is cited in Stephen M. Fjellman, *Vinyl Leaves: Walt Disney World and America* [Boulder, Colo., 1992], 436 n.54). While studies of various Disney phenomena speculate about the park's employees—typically to the detriment of the workers—there has been no sustained attempt to analyze the park from a perspective that takes seriously their role within it and certainly not one that lets workers speak for themselves. As much as possible, I've let these people have their say; their comments reveal how much they are their own best spokespersons.

2 John Fiske's discussion of embarrassment in the context of women's enjoyment of *The Newlywed Game* has been helpful here. He defines embarrassment as a form of pleasure enjoyed when a dominant ideology's values "are experienced simultaneously with the everyday values of the subordinate that contradicts them." See *Understanding Popular Culture* (Boston, 1989), 64. His example is the woman in a traditional marriage who nevertheless enjoys watching a show that makes fun of just that kind of arrangement.

The embarrassment felt by guests and workers is complex and is complicated by my presence and representative status as an academic intellectual. Obvious as my insights are, I nevertheless command quite a bit of authority by virtue of how I express them and, literally, for the fact of my having expressed them at all. I've had fewer more stark demonstrations of Bourdieu's theses in *Distinction* than in my attempts to talk to people from all social and economic classes and groups about Disney World. They know what they like, what they're supposed to like, and the distance between the two. This was more the case with visitors I interviewed outside the park than with visitors I talked to inside or to employees I talked to anywhere, though the latter two are less embarrassed for different reasons. Many of the employees I interviewed could not conceive of any project involving their experience at Disney that was not, at base, an exposé for which their stories were convenient fodder. When told that my interest was in their feelings and ideas about the park, about visiting and working there, or growing up in the area, they were sometimes unclear about how to proceed. I am fortunate that most of my interviews were long enough (about two hours) to overcome some initial distrust and embarrassment.

3 As of October, 1993, Disney's job application packet listed the starting wage for most entry-level jobs as $5.95 an hour, $5.60 for Casual Seasonal. In 1985, it was still hovering around $4.55. Says one employee, "I'll never forget when we were all fighting for a twenty-five cent raise, it came over the papers that Eisner made a $43 million bonus. And we were fighting for a quarter." To be fair to Disney, hourly wages in Florida are typically low, and many are lower than those at the park. One former employee who started at Disney at $5.50 is now making $4.25 elsewhere. These figures should be taken as a measure of how hard Florida has been hit by the most recent recession. She was glad to have a job at all.

4 See Chapter 6, "The Habituation of the Worker to the Capitalist Mode of Production" in Harry Braverman, *Labor and Monopoly Capital: The Degradation of Work in the Twentieth Century* (New York, 1974).

5 For a detailed examination of Disney's legal status and a history of its entry to and take over of central Florida, see Fjellman, *Vinyl Leaves*.

6 De Certeau's examples are science and the military: "Thus military or scientific strategies have always been inaugurated through the constitution of their 'own' areas (autonomous cities, 'neutral' or 'independent' institutions, laboratories pursuing 'disinterested' research, etc.)." *The Practice of Everyday Life* (Berkeley, 1984), 36.

7 Along with the ubiquitous light bulb joke, this phrase, "fired on the spot," was the phrase most frequently recited in my interviews. Many people had stories of fellow workers who were "fired on the spot" for one infraction or another. The phrase is used to emphasize the black-and-white character of Disney rules and their enforcement. It is paralleled by the less frequent "hired on the spot," which suggests the ability of the casting department to know immediately if potential employees have that Disney

magic. Many interviewees, for example, assured me on first meeting that I, too, would be "hired on the spot." Some even continued confidently to specify what position in their area I would be designated for, generally an on-stage job working directly with the public at whatever constituted the middle to upper level of responsibility (e.g., among clerical workers, I was a sure bet for Executive Secretary; among hotel staff, I was likely to be some kind of guest liaison).

8 "Tickets they love. They can sell them for a fortune. They got forty something thousand tickets [from the Yacht Club]. Two months later they struck over at the Swan [for 20,000], both at gunpoint."

9 Annette, for example, regrets that the company's "bizarre" division of tasks prevents her from benefiting it even more than she already has:

> The worst thing about it is that it's such a big thing, the corporation's so big that we're losing the connections. . . . There's no way to breach that gap. I could be playing this other character. I could benefit the company in this way if I had these other costumes that are currently sitting here, but they say, "No, that's costuming, that's a costuming issue. That's not a performance issue. That's not an entertainment issue. You have a costume. Here's your costume." Each department is very involved within itself, and separate even though its under the Disney umbrella, and there are very few ways to get through that. It's bizarre at times. You ask yourself, "So, we're laying off people across property. . . . They've even cut one third of the cast across property." Yet, if you say "I could be even more valuable to you this way," they go, "No, that's costuming." Sometimes, I find it hard to get the answers.

10 Or keep them. In December 1993, a California GayNet user chronicled his attempts to secure from Disney health benefits for his partner living with AIDS. He also tried to recruit other net users to harangue Disney executives. He even supplied the fax numbers. Though his partner was an employee of Disneyland in Anaheim, most of his negotiations were with Walt Disney World in Orlando, which has been stonewalling.

11 Employees themselves can't always keep these labels straight; a number had to run down the whole list just to remind themselves which they were, and everyone transposed parts of one designation onto another.

12 For Disney, the virtues of CTs are self-evident: they're brought in when needed during peak seasons and let go when not, sometimes in time to avoid a review and possible upgrade with benefits. There's nothing particularly original about this: U.S. companies have been doing it for years, and it will surely increase, especially now, when such practices have been legitimized by the near institutionalization of temporary agencies, which often try to provide the benefits the companies will not. Consider in this context the case of Margaret, who worked six years as a CT:

> I'm a seasonal worker, a person that works in the high season. Those are maybe eight months during the year. I don't get any medical benefits. At times, if they need you and you're outstanding or you don't cause any problems or they don't think you'll be any problem, they will make you a permanent staff member. Other than that you are welcome to go back every year. In those eight months, I worked some twenty hours a day. I never came home. I slept in the park itself. The part-timers worked twenty-five to forty hours a week, but people like us, we worked sometimes twenty hours a day. There was seventy-six hours a week I worked once.

13 In the past, Disney's Central Reservations Office was on Republic Drive in Orlando outside of its official Lake Buena Vista boundaries. They have since moved back on property.

14 The exception here are the students in Disney's College Program who, because they live together in Disney-provided—though not paid for—housing, can get to know others outside their area, though these others are also, like them, in the College Program. For more on the College Program, see n. 17 below.

15 There are unions at Disney, primarily for crafts workers and entertainers. Because of the high volume of part-time and temporary workers, many people are not eligible for union membership. Many musicians, for example, come in seasonally from local colleges and high schools. Student and seasonal status automatically disqualify them as professionals. Costumed characters are not allowed to join the actors' union because, according to Disney, they don't have speaking parts (because no one could reproduce the voice of the real Mickey or Donald). Why this would disqualify someone as an actor is unclear.

16 In spite of the general consensus that most people do not have a shot at real promotion, one still hears stories among employees and Orlando residents about the boy who started out selling ice cream on Main Street, U.S.A. and who now occupies a corner office in Team Disney where he peddles finer wares. I'm sure enough of these stories are true or close enough to it to keep the PR people happy. They are certainly a major recruitment draw.

17 Among the most disillusioned are the young people recruited for Disney's College Program:

> Disney goes around and says what a great stepping stone it would be for a career even if it weren't a career at Disney, like this would be the most fantastic thing in your life. So all the kids come down from around the country. They live in Disney housing. They work at Disney for Disney hourly wage jobs. Usually they don't get the experience they're looking for unless they're in the hospitality industry. They can get some worthwhile experience, but it's usually not what they're expecting. Most people in the College Program leave disillusioned. One of the major points of disillusionment is that they barely get by because they come down here, and Disney puts them in Disney housing, and they have to have transportation. They can get bussed to work, but what kind of existence is that? Living in Disney owned and operated apartments, working only at Disney, having no car and being bussed to Disney. It's an exaggeration to call them a migrant labor force, but not too much of one. These people end up in hourly wage jobs: food, dishing out ice cream. They think, "Well, I'm a hospitality management major." "Well, good, you can work front desk at our hotel." Or "You can work baggage." Or, "I'm a PR/Advertising major." "O.K., you can work ticket sales." I'm sure that Disney exaggerates what can be gotten from each position they offer.

> When I first interviewed, I was hoping for a job on stage; however, because of my navy experience with warehouses, I was of course assigned to the warehouse. I was one of five people (out of five hundred) assigned there. I was disappointed. . . . The [College Program] jobs usually ranged from concessions, parking lot, attractions, custodial, tickets, or somewhere in the hotels. And the elite, friends of the Coordinator were given cake jobs like public relations, guest services, and office jobs. Certain people who were known kiss asses seemed to get great jobs with higher pay.

18 She was aware, by the way, of the macabre humor inherent in this description of metamorphoses from polyester to head. Disney workers frequently interrupt them-

selves to comment on their own stories, e.g., "It sounds crazy" or "We had a sign that said 'The Turtles will be out at this time.' It sounds so ridiculous when you talk about it."

19   Note the traditionally gendered "she." Though it may be that all of Disney's shoppers are female, the better guess is that they are simply assumed to be.

20   Fjellman, for example, quotes this tidbit from an EPCOT training manual called *Merchandise*: "Merchandise is an extension of the total guest experience. . . . Each of our guests will most likely want to take with them a momento, a representation of what EPCOT Center is. That's at the core of our merchandising philosophy. It expresses that the EPCOT Center experience will be a lasting one" (162).

21   I am not unaware that this and other kinds of electronic surveillance have become a ubiquitous presence in many large-scale operations, particularly those involving telephones and computer terminals, e.g., telemarketing and word processing.

22   This became something of a problem when taking messages and arranging appointments. No one gave a full name. Some didn't want to; it did not occur to others since they never use full names at work.

23   This was clear to people who felt as if they'd been burned by the system. One worker told me that a friend offered a drawing of "Mick Tracy" to Disney's Imagineering Department as a potential promotional item for *Dick Tracy*. After getting the runaround with them, he dropped the idea, "went home and at least had a picture for himself. Other people wanted it, so everybody had one in their office." Two weeks later he walked out of the Pleasure Island movie theater and saw his drawing on the front of a kid's T-shirt. Disney was sued by another worker who claimed to come up with the idea of selling pixie dust in the park—a commodity that eventually became hugely successful. The company won because, again, the man came up with the idea while he was working for Disney. As the friend of the uncredited creator of the original Mick Tracy put it, "literally, they're using everybody for everything."

24   Fjellman, *Vinyl Leaves*, 218.

25   Disney does drug testing, but only for selected positions. Personnel materials list these as Bus Operations, Over-the-Road Drivers, Mechanics who maintain buses, anyone transporting hazardous material, anyone working on pipelines containing gas or hazardous liquids. The thing to note here is the absence of drug tests for anyone working directly with the public in the park. The urine test screens for amphetamines, cocaine, marijuana, opiates, phencyclidine. Positive results or refusing to be tested require immediate dismissal, with the possibility for reconsideration in twelve months.

26   Originally, I tried to run an ad requesting interviews with "Disney World employees," but *The Sentinel* refused to run it without first clearing it with Disney officials. Confident that clearance would not be forthcoming, I changed the wording of the ad to read simply "theme park workers."

27   Quoted in Richard Schickel, *The Disney Version: The Life, Time, Art and Commerce of Walt Disney* (New York, 1968), 37 (ellipses in original).

28   Quoted in ibid., 33, and reproduced in Main Street's tribute to Walt Disney. Schickel says Disney had to be taught how to produce a makeshift Mickey and something that would pass for the themed Walt Disney signature (34).

29   Quoted in Fjellman, *Vinyl Leaves*, 117.

30   The ill-fitting Gummy Bears costumes were apparently the cause of some small uproar among the character department staff. Meetings were held to discuss the situa-

tion, with supervisors agreeing to look into the possibilities of modifying the costumes. The upshot of these discussions, however, was that at $2500 a pop it was more expensive and trouble to alter a head than to replace employees. Even with the heavy heads, workers have to monitor their movements and posture so as not to damage the costumes in some other way. A character lead discusses his task of monitoring the condition of the costumes: "You can tell if this person's not doing things right. He's kneeling down and wearing out the costumes. He's not allowed to kneel down and wear out the costume." This, by the way, was part of his daily roster of duties, the information gained from which is kept in an area log whose function he unabashedly announced: "We have a log. We put everything in it, who's working that day, anything that can be brought up in court, as much information as we need so we can look back. If someone needs to know what happened that day we can tell exactly where that person was."

31 Walt Disney was famous for controlling the look of his employees—and guests—when the first park opened in California. While the Walt Disney Co. no longer bars entrance for long-haired men, it continues to strictly enforce employee dress and behavior codes:

> You couldn't wear your dangling earrings, you had to wear the penny sized, no makeup, even behind the scenes. No necklaces, no bracelets, no wrist watches because then you're a time watcher. The only ring you can have is a wedding band and an engagement ring. Even fingernail polish because you may get it in the equipment. And your fingernails could only be a quarter of an inch. That kind of jazz.

> If you're in costume and you smoke a cigarette, you're fired. If you use profanity in front of a guest, you're fired. Even at night after work, I have to wait until I got to the car to have a cigarette.

There are limits, however, to what people will put up with though, as the following story indicates, not to what they expect being asked to do. When she returns to the zoo to change the T-shirt the characters wear under their costumes and which get soaked from the heat above, Pinocchio has the following conversation with her dresser:

> So I go in, this is four years I've worked with the same dresser. She takes a look at my chest—I took off my shirt and under your shirt is your T-shirt that says "Property of Disney World." She says, "Oh my God, what are those?"
> I looked down and said, "What do you mean, what are those?"
> She says, "Those breasts! Who put you in a Pinocchio costume?"
> I said, "Who cares. I've been playing this thing for four years."
> "You can't play with that chest."
> I said, "There's life after Disney. I'm not getting rid of the chest."

32 In order to measure the full worth of the opportunity this trip affords them, remember that at current rates ($38 per park), taking a family of eight to Disney World for a single day costs over $300; a more typical three-day stay—one day for each park—is over $900. This is just to walk through the gates. It is no accident that former employees seldom return to the park; without their ID passes, they simply can't afford it.

33 To wit: "You have to keep upbeat, and you can never call the *Empress Lilly* boat, 'the boat.' 'Do you want to reserve a place on the boat for breakfast?' No, you must call it the *Empress Lilly*. It was a very strange thing. You had to keep everything exact. You

had to make sure everything was perfect. If you abbreviated something wrong, you'd be written up."

34 She came back and continued to work for three years, during which time she tried to resume her old position, but found that she could not:

> I put the head on for the first time in about six months, and I couldn't breathe. I had an anxiety attack in the head. I kept trying to overcome it. I came back to work in the character department but I was now a lead—I was security for the characters. No one ever came near one of my characters. I was there. I understood what it was to be frightened. And those kids are frightened in those costumes. You're talking about 75,000 people, and they throw you out in a crowd.

35 A College Program employee who worked in the warehouses writes that "it depended on where you worked whether you were out or not. My friends worked Tomorrowland and seemed pretty open. However, they had a friend who worked "Big Thunder" and was scared to death one of his homophobic coworkers would find out. I guess Disney does stereotype people to the ride."

36 "Aren't you family?" winked one of my interviewees. Another recommended I go to "Family Night" at Mannequins on Pleasure Island. I did and it was.

37 I am indebted for this information on Lake Eola's history and future prospects to Michael Hoover and Lisa Stokes, "Dislando: The Disneyfication of Orlando," paper presented to the Modern Language Association, Toronto, Canada, 30 December 1993.

Public Use/Private State

1 John S. Friedman, "Big Business Goes to School," *The Nation,* 17 February 1992, 188–90.

2 Ibid., 190.

3 Hannah Finan Roditi, "Youth Apprenticeship: High Schools for Docile Workers," *The Nation,* 16 March 1992, 340–43.

4 Scott Bukatman, "There's Always Tomorrowland: Disney and the Hypercinematic Experience," *October* 57 (Summer 1991): 55–78.

5 Michael Sorkin, "See You in Disneyland," *Design Quarterly* (Winter 1992): 5–13.

6 "Fantasy's Reality," *Time,* 27 May 1991, 54.

Monuments to Walt

1 Marc Eliot, *Walt Disney: Hollywood's Dark Prince* (New York, 1993), 74.

2 Susan Willis, *A Primer for Daily Life* (New York, 1991), 58, 57.

3 Johnson discusses this idea in several published talks and essays. See especially his "Whence and Whither: The Processional Element in Architecture" in *Writings* (New York, 1979), 150–55. His own residence in New Canaan, Conn., is a literal experiment with the concepts developed here and elsewhere.

4 Just before the corporate shakeup of 1984 that put Michael Eisner in charge of the Walt Disney Co., one of the first major decisions acted upon by the new management was to establish Touchstone Pictures as an adult entertainment section of Disney films. In 1993 Disney purchased Miramax and its stock of movies—including such un-Disney-like pictures as *The Crying Game.* Tim Burton, director of *Batman,* had Disney produce his *The Nightmare Before Christmas* and was promised his own non-Disney film based upon schlock film king Ed Wood in exchange for a

much more Disney-like film to be made later. Disney is now also teaming up with Merchant-Ivory productions. In each of these instances the Disney Company is merging with the creative talents of "outsiders," though the tension between Disney in-house products and those that it—sometimes anonymously—supports is increasing.

5 Umberto Eco, *Travels in Hyperreality*, trans. William Weaver (New York, 1975), 47.

6 It is perhaps only at the hotels—around the swimming pools, when people from various countries and classes relax together away from the more overt crowd control in the parks—that differences among the tourists stand out.

7 It is only fair to say that what many people like about Disney culture is its very lack of distinctiveness or tradition, local color, or aesthetic subtleness. They prefer consistent, dependable homogenization. Disneyfication, in its easy accessibility and technological success, acts as a synecdoche for life as it is generally lived in North America and Western Europe.

8 From the standpoint of buildings and design, Disney has been much more successful with its water parks than it has with its modest-priced hotels. River Country, Typhoon Lagoon, and Pleasure Island are all examples of a highly successful merging of theme and function brought about, at least in part, by the imaginativeness of the themes and concomitant activities chosen for each park. Both River Country and the later Typhoon Lagoon incorporate popular recreations—rafting, tubing, sliding, body surfing—into narratives unique to each park. Pleasure Island, although not really "about" water, is literally separated from the rest of Disney World not just as a real island but as a place where adult desires and excesses are allowed to rule—in a controlled form, of course. Two of the island's clubs require that one be twenty-one to enter. On Thursday nights after ten, both of these clubs—Mannequins and 8Trax (formerly, Cave!)—become gay clubs, mainly attended by gay Disney employees who refer to each other as "family." Elsewhere on the island, the theme is nightclubbing itself: there is one country club, one golden oldies club, one comedy club, one jazz club. Compacting such choices into one geographic area is now a typical strategy of city planners; that is, Disney's model for the island paradise is an urban one. One can't help but note, however, that the name, Pleasure Island, comes from Disney's *Pinocchio*, where it refers to a nightmare island of young boys turned into donkeys. Disney seems to be making a wry joke worthy of Walt himself, who wanted his amusement parks to lack those features of county fairs that he most abhorred as a child and which he somehow mixed up in his own memory: dirt, sex, rude jokes and people: in other words, most of what we usually assume is a part—has always been a part—of the carnivalesque. Pleasure Island is theming of the ego's ultimate control over the id, the ultimate anality of an individual's—or a company's—desire to control everyone who enters its kingdom. The strict management of who gets to come onto the island and, once there, who gets to go into which club, and even by which door they enter and leave, is among the more chilling experiences one can have at Disney World. Pleasure Island is perhaps the one place where the Disney Company's famous quasi-invisible crowd control tactics become all too clearly visible, though overt screening of entrants into the parks was apparently not uncommon in the 1960s and 1970s at Disneyland and Disney World. Michael Real and others have commented on how this control was used to combat student activism. See his "The Disney Universe: Morality Play," *Mass-Mediated Culture* (Englewood Cliffs, N.J., 1977), 51.

9 Philip Johnson, *Charlie Rose*, transcript of broadcast (25 June 1993), 25.

10 "Graves's Swan and Dolphin Join Mickey, Minnie, and Donald," *Architectural Record* (March 1988): 59.

11 For more on Disney's new willingness to draw on outside creators, see "Story Time" in this volume.

12 Graves was commissioned by Disney to design not only the interior of the hotels, but the furniture and plates as well.

13 Overall, the design of the hotels is similar to residences Stern has designed for wealthy patrons in the New York/New Jersey area and to his Newport Hotel project in California.

14 Strangely, however, the two buildings are joined in the middle with no transition between the two designs, although there is a shallow beach area that runs behind both hotels and helps to connect them visually. Perhaps it is here, beside the man-made lagoon, that the two classes are supposed to mingle in a Jamesian mixing of social strata.

15 Paul M. Sachner, "Entertainment Architecture," *Architectural Record* (September 1989): 66.

16 Ibid., 66.

17 Mark Alden Branch, "Michael Graves, Architect: Growth and Diversity," *Progressive Architecture* 3 (March 1990): 82.

18 Isozaki's building is a better example of late modernist than postmodernist architecture. The interiors of the flanking wings of offices are nondescript and generically corporate. The exterior, although quite postmodern upon first impression, is a mixture of late modernist features (the syncopation and ordered repetition of some of the patterns and features) and even high modernist (the asymmetrical jutting sundial cannot help but evoke Corbusier's chapel at Ronchamp or even the stairwell of the Villa Savoye). The overall effect is one of an exceedingly clever manipulation of several different architectural codes, with the sundial as the wittiest feature.

19 See Thomas Fisher, "Architectural Timepiece," *Progressive Architecture* 4 (April 1991): 73.

20 Ibid., 73–74.

21 See Arata Isozaki, "Theme Park," *South Atlantic Quarterly: The World According to Disney* 92.1 (Winter 1993): 180.

22 Isozaki's central sculptural form relies not on ornament or interior decoration but on simple shapes that connote the eternal and the universal, and that connect the building to the larger realm of global postmodern design and debate. Both thematically, through the emphasis on time and space, and structurally, through the referencing of "classic" post- and late-modernist design vocabularies, his building invokes a decidedly un-Disney-like experience, while at the same time providing just enough Disney whimsy to satisfy the corporate executives.

23 Akira Asada, "Discussion A-1," Cynthia C. Davidson, ed., *Anyone* (New York, 1991), 91.

24 See Arata Isozaki, "A Fragmentary Portrait of Anyone," Cynthia C. Davidson, ed., *Anyone* (New York, 1991), 62–67, and "Demiourgos in Anywhere," *Anywhere* (New York, 1992), 238–45.

25 Richard Schickel, *The Disney Version: The Life, Times, Art and Commerce of Walt Disney* (New York, 1968), 359–60.

26 The university campus, with its separation of disciplines into buildings and quadrants, seems to be reflected in the design of the MGM park.

27 Stern and Eisner have brought Disney to midtown New York by revamping the New Amsterdam Theatre and staging a live version of Disney's film version of *Beauty and the Beast* at the Palace Theatre on Broadway.

28 See Johnson's "The Town and the Automobile, or The Pride of Elm Street" in *Writings* (New York, 1979), 80–83.

29 Disney architecture may ultimately look something like a rock concert. Architecture in Disney World is, at its best, an event rather than a structure or construction in space. For more on this definition of "event," see Peter Eisenman's *Unfolding Frankfurt* (Berlin, 1991), 10; "K Nowhere 2 Fold," Cynthia C. Davidson, ed., *Anywhere* (New York, 1992), 218–27; and "Unfolding Events," Jonathan Crary and Sanford Kwinter, eds., *Zone: Incorporations* 6 (New York, 1992), 422–27.

30 Neil Smith, "Reasserting Spatial Difference," *Any* 1 (July–August 1993): 21.

31 Neil Smith, "The Seaside Debate," *Any* 1 (July–August 1993): 31.

32 David Mahoney, "A Debate on American Urbanism," *Any* 1 (July–August 1993): 6.

33 *The Town of Seaside,* promotional brochure (Seaside, 1993).

34 What Disney calls its "prototype systems" and "innovative technologies" were developed and made possible not by capitalism, but through a lack of capitalism—by the fact that Disney World is the closest thing imaginable to an isolated and controlled municipal space. Disney's idea of an autonomous state is like the outmoded idea of a nation-state, which seems anachronistic in a free market global economy. One could say that Disney World does not represent a form of capitalism because it is in competition only with itself. However, in its elimination of democratic forms and economic competition, it might as easily represent a future capitalism—one which the global order seems to presage.

35 If EPCOT, the monorail system, and other technological symbols in the resort were truly available for the betterment of humankind, then they would not have been designed to exist in harmony with one of the largest collections of golf courses anywhere.

36 The architecture of EPCOT's Future World is a simulacrum of corporate architecture complete with urban accents like water and fountains, which are usually used in overbuilt city centers to soften the harshly impersonal architecture. Similarly, the detailing of the exteriors and interiors of the buildings looks—at best—like what one would find at an office complex in which one architectural firm (perhaps one that specializes in malls) is responsible for all of the designing. As with the architecture of John Portman, one can debate whether or not the architecture in Future World most represents late- or post-modern influences.

37 As I argue in "Story Time," it is the failure to tell convincing stories that marks EPCOT as different from the Magic Kingdom.

38 The growing business of expos, world fairs, and theme parks is evidenced by the success of a company like Iwerks, which provides films and attractions to expos; or the mere existence of the International Association of Amusement Parks and Attractions and their publication *World's Fair: The Quarterly Journal of International Events.* "Event" may well be the best word to describe the coming together to create theming on a mammoth scale of governmental and international corporate money, architecture and amusement parks, high-tech cinematography and sci-fi special effects. One can, as some do, travel the globe from one expo to another, some temporary, some, like EPCOT, not. A new type of business is in existence, and it is probable that not only will it not go away, but it will increasingly merge with our living environments—already themed and postmodern *avant la lettre*—via the electronic superhighway.

39 The technologies developed by Disney in the 1950s and 1960s were often attempts to perfect the hyperreal, in the form of Audio-Animatronic figures, or realistic effects in

rides that depended upon the careful coordination of movement, music, voice, and visual effects. Many of Disney's early technologies were displayed at world fairs; likewise, the use of dioramas and models as part of the mixture of pedagogy and showmanship at world fairs and museums has been borrowed by Disney for EPCOT and MGM. The Disney parks' creation of a seamless cinematic effect in its best rides, like "Pirates of the Caribbean," prefigured the effects of virtual environments.

40   John Taylor, *Storming the Magic Kingdom: Wall Street, the Raiders, and the Battle for Disney* (New York, 1987), 14.

41   See Marshall McLuhan and Quentin Fiore: "What remains of the configuration of former 'cities' [in the future] will be very much like World's Fairs—places in which to show off new technology, not places of work or residence. They will be preserved, museumlike, as living monuments to the railway era." *The Medium is the Message: An Inventory of Effects* (New York, 1967), n.p.

42   James E. Young, "The German Counter-Monument: Memory Against Itself in Germany Today," in W. J. T. Mitchell, ed., *Art and the Public Sphere* (Chicago, 1992), 76.

43   It is not by accident that the Vietnam Memorial in Washington is the most-visited monument in the U.S.: it uses procession to create a powerful visceral experience— you are entering into and then exiting a grave. The experience of this monument is not a static one (compare the Jefferson Memorial). This type of experience, such as one has in the nonfuturistic sections of the Disney parks, possesses a timeless quality.

44   Challenges to Disney have already been mounted by French intellectuals and will probably continue as the company deals with increasing cultural criticism both here and abroad. The Japanese have shown a not unexpected enthusiasm for Disney's world, but Western Europe has proven to be a different matter. As playwright Heiner Müller said of *Fantasia*, "[it is] good music and good orchestras and . . . stupid images. The children who see this movie will never be able to hear this music without seeing those images. That is for me the horror of the American experience, the colonization of fantasy by images and the production of clichés that zap your brains out." Laurence Shyer, *Robert Wilson and His Collaborators* (New York, 1989), 133. Existing prior to EuroDisney, *Parc de la Villette* in Paris is based upon deconstruction and designed, in part, by Eisenman and Jacques Derrida. It may never be any competition for Disney's park, but its existence indicates a cultural gap between French and U.S. versions of themed public spaces.

45   Tokyo Disneyland has been an unqualified success. However, the reasons for this have in part to do with the appeal of Disney products and the fact that the Tokyo park is a franchise owned by Asian investors. For more on the former, see both Mitsuhiro Yoshimoto, "Images of Empire: Tokyo Disneyland and Japanese Cultural Imperialism," forthcoming in Eric Smoodin, ed., *Disney Discourse: Producing the Magic Kingdom*; and Mary Yoko Brannen, " 'Bwana Mickey': Constructing Cultural Consumption at Tokyo Disneyland," in Amy Kaplan and Donald E. Pease, eds., *Cultures of United States Imperialism* (Durham, 1993), 617–34.

46   Although cartoons, unlike live-action films, don't seem to age, what Disney is now doing is creating a complex relationship between adult and child, parent and child, present and past—a past lived by us but, in part, scripted by Disney. Eisner's attempts to expand the venue for the Disney signature has been successful at harnessing a generation of pre- and full-fledged baby boomers' childhood memories of Disney in order to keep them interested in the company as something other than a marketer of products for children. The success of Anaheim's Mighty Ducks ice hockey team is but

one example of his slightly irreverent savvy. Eisner has added to the usual formula of the hockey game a dose of Disney entertainment during his team's appearances that has gone over well with fans. What is still unknown, however, even by him, is the border or limit to the use of Disney as a semipliable identity that is able to adjust to the interests and prejudices of new demographic groups.

47   To write about the creative demise of the Disney/Eisner empire in 1994 might seem odd to some who see this time as one in which the company appears to be rebounding with creative energy and nearly limitless potential not only to expand its control over global popular culture, but to encompass yet more markets and marketing strategies into its all-encompassing system. While this version of current events may be accurate in many ways—and is obviously the Disney strategy—it is also true that the Disney Company has not fully expunged the ghost of the decade after Walt's death when the company's film division could do little else but make embarrassing copies of ideas coming from either Spielberg or Lucas, as evidenced in their awful attempt at a version of *Star Wars* entitled *The Black Hole*. Similarly, a recent Disney release, *Blank Check*, is an execrable knockoff of the mega-hit *Home Alone*, but without even the small amount of charm contained in that sadistic, if novel, movie. Disney as a company, therefore, is still possessed on occasion with the desire to try anything in an effort not to be left behind in the film industry—however desperate some of the projects they attempt might be. Since the coming of Eisner, Disney's continued financial success may seem certain. However, the Walt Disney Company can always have another era of Roy Disney malaise—despite Eisner's seeming confidence and attempts to fill the shoes of Walt.

selected bibliography

• • •

Theme Parks in General and Disney World in Particular

Brannen, Mary Yoko. "'Bwana Mickey': Constructing Cultural Consumption at Tokyo Disneyland." *Cultures of United States Imperialism*. Ed. Amy Kaplan and Donald E. Pease. Durham: Duke UP, 1993. 617–34.

Bukatman, Scott. "There's Always Tomorrowland: Disney and the Hypercinematic Experience." *October* 57 (Summer 1991): 55–78.

Burton, Julianne. "Don (Juanito) Duck and the Imperial-Patriarchal Unconscious: Disney Studios, the Good Neighbor Policy, and the Packaging of Latin America." *Nationalisms and Sexualities*. Ed. Andrew Parker, Mary Russo, Doris Sommer, and Patricia Yaeger. New York: Routledge, 1992. 21–41.

Dorfman, Ariel, and Armand Mattelart. *How to Read Donald Duck: Imperialist Ideology in the Disney Comic*. Trans. David Kunzle. New York: International Generation, 1984.

Eco, Umberto. *Travels in Hyperreality: Essays*. New York: Harcourt, 1986.

Eisenstein, S. M. *Eisenstein on Disney*. Ed. Jay Leyda. Trans. Alan Upchurch. Introd. Naum Kleiman. Calcutta: Seagull Books, 1986.

Fjellman, Stephen M. *Vinyl Leaves: Walt Disney World and America*. Boulder: Westview P, 1992.

Francaviglia, Richard V. "Main Street USA: A Comparison/Contrast of Streetscapes in Disneyland and Walt Disney World." *Journal of Popular Culture* 15 (1981): 141–56.

Haden-Guest, Anthony. *The Paradise Program: Travels Through Muzak, Hilton, Coca-Cola, Texaco, Walt Disney, and Other World Empires*. New York: Morrow, 1973.

Johnson, David M. "Disney World as Structure and Symbol: Re-Creation of the American Experience." *Journal of Popular Culture* 15 (1981): 157–65.

Kasson, John F. *Amusing the Millions: Coney Island at the Turn of the Century*. New York: Hill and Wang, 1978.

King, Margaret J. "Disneyland and Walt Disney World: Traditional Values in Futuristic Form." *Journal of Popular Culture* 15 (1981): 116–40.

Marin, Louis. "Utopic Degeneration: Disneyland." *Utopics: Spatial Play*. Trans. Robert A.

Vollrath. Atlantic Highlands, N.J.: Humanities P, 1984. 239–57. Trans. of *Utopiques: Jeux d'Espaces*. Paris: Les Editions de Minuit, 1973.

Merritt, Russell and J. B. Kaufman. *Walt in Wonderland: The Silent Films of Walt Disney*. Baltimore: Johns Hopkins UP, 1994.

Real, Michael R. "The Disney Universe: Morality Play." *Mass-Mediated Culture*. Englewood Cliffs: Prentice-Hall, 1977. 44–89.

Schickel, Richard. *The Disney Version: The Life, Times, Art and Commerce of Walt Disney*. Rev. ed. London: Pavilion/Michael Joseph, 1986.

Smoodin, Eric. *Animating Culture: Hollywood Cartoons in the Sound Era*. New Brunswick: Rutgers UP, 1993.

———, Ed. *Disney Discourse: Producing the Magic Kingdom*. New York: Routledge, 1994.

Sorkin, Michael, Ed. *Variations on a Theme Park: The New American City and the End of Public Space*. New York: Hill and Wang, 1992.

Willis, Susan. "Fantasia: Walt Disney's Los Angeles Suite." *Diacritics* 17: 83–96.

———. "Learning from the Banana." *A Primer for Daily Life*. New York: Routledge, 1991. 41–61.

———, Ed. *South Atlantic Quarterly. The World According to Disney*. 92.1 (Winter 1993).

Wilson, Alexander. "The Betrayal of the Future: Walt Disney's EPCOT Center." *Socialist Review* 84 (1985): 41–53.

———. *The Culture of Nature: Popular Landscapes from Disney to Chernobyl*. Toronto: Between the Lines P, 1991. 156–90.

Zukin, Sharon. "Disney World: The Power of Facade/The Facade of Power." *Landscapes of Power: From Detroit to Disney World*. Berkeley: U of Calif. P, 1991. 216–75.

SElECTEd REAdiNgs iN CulTuRAl STudiEs

Adorno, Theodor. *Minima Moralia: Reflections from Damaged Life*. 1951. Trans. E. F. N. Jephcott. London: Verso, 1974.

———. *Prisms*. Rpt. Cambridge: MIT P, 1981.

——— and Max Horkheimer. *Aesthetic Theory*. 1970. New York: Routledge and Kegan Paul, 1984.

———. "The Culture Industry: Enlightenment as Mass Deception." *Dialectic of Enlightenment*. 1944. New York: Continuum, 1988. 120–67.

Althusser, Louis. "Contradiction and Overdetermination." *For Marx*. 1965. Trans. Ben Brewster. London: Verso, 1990. 87–128.

———. "Ideology and Ideological State Apparatuses." *Lenin and Philosophy*. Trans. Ben Brewster. New York: Monthly Review P, 1971. 127–86.

Barthes, Roland. *Mythologies*. Trans. Annette Lavers. New York: Hill and Wang, 1972.

Baudrillard, Jean. *America*. Trans. Chris Turner. New York: Verso, 1988.

———. *Simulations*. Trans. Paul Foss, Paul Patton, and Philip Beitchman. New York: Semiotext(e), 1983.

Benjamin, Walter. *Illuminations: Essays and Reflections*. New York: Schocken, 1969.

Bourdieu, Pierre. *Distinction: A Social Critique of the Judgement of Taste*. Cambridge: Harvard UP, 1984.

Brantlinger, Patrick. *Bread and Circuses: Theories of Mass Culture and Social Decay*. Ithaca: Cornell UP, 1992.

———. *Crusoe's Footprints: Cultural Studies in Britain and America*. New York: Routledge, 1990.

Buck-Morss, Susan. *The Dialectics of Seeing: Walter Benjamin and the Arcades Project.* Cambridge: MIT P, 1989.

Butler, Judith. *Gender Trouble: Feminism and the Subversion of Identity.* New York: Routledge, 1990.

de Certeau, Michel. *The Practice of Everyday Life.* Trans. Steven Rendall. Berkeley: U of Calif. P, 1984.

Clifford, James and George Marcus, eds. *Writing Culture: The Poetics and Politics of Ethnography.* Berkeley: U of Calif. P, 1985.

Debord, Guy. *Society of the Spectacle.* Detroit: Black and Red, 1983.

During, Simon, ed. *The Cultural Studies Reader.* London: Routledge, 1993.

Fiske, John. *Reading the Popular.* Boston: Unwin Hyman, 1989.

———. *Understanding Popular Culture.* Boston: 1989.

Foucault, Michel. *Discipline and Punish: The Birth of the Prison.* Trans. Alan Sheridan. New York: Vintage, 1979.

Gaines, Jane. *Contested Culture: The Image, The Voice, and The Law.* Chapel Hill: U of North Carolina P, 1991.

Geertz, Clifford. *The Interpretation of Cultures: Selected Essays.* New York: Basic Books, 1973.

Gramsci, Antonio. *Selections from the Prison Notebooks of Antonio Gramsci.* Ed. Quintin Hoare and Geoffrey Nowell-Smith. London: Lawrence and Wishart, 1971.

Grossberg, Lawrence, Ed. *Cultural Studies.* London: Routledge, 1992.

Hall, Stuart. "Cultural Studies: Two Paradigms." *Media, Culture, and Society* 2 (1980): 57–72.

———. "Encoding/Decoding." *Culture, Media, Language.* Hutchinson: Centre for Contemporary Cultural Studies, U of Birmingham, 1980. 128–39.

———. "Notes on Deconstructing 'The Popular.'" *People's History and Socialist Theory.* Ed. Raphael Samuel. Boston: Routledge, 1981. 227–40.

———. "On Postmodernism and Articulation: An Interview with Stuart Hall." Ed. Lawrence Grossberg. *Journal of Communication Inquiry* 10 (1986): 45–60.

Haug, Frigga and others. *Female Sexualization: A Collective Work of Memory.* Trans. Eric Carter (Material Word). London: Verso, 1987.

Haug, Wolfgang Fritz. *Critique of Commodity Aesthetics: Appearance, Sexuality and Advertising in Capitalist Society.* Trans. Robert Bock. Minneapolis: U of Minn. P, 1986.

Hebdige, Dick. *Subculture: The Meaning of Style.* New York: Methuen, 1979.

Jameson, Fredric. *Postmodernism, or, The Cultural Logic of Late Capitalism.* Durham: Duke UP, 1991.

———. "Reification and Utopia in Mass Culture." *Social Text* 1 (1979) 1: 129–48.

Kowinski, William Severini. *The Malling of America: An Inside Look At the Great Consumer Paradise,* New York: William Morrow & Co., 1985.

Kracauer, Siegfried. "The Cult of Distraction: Berlin's Picture Palaces." Trans. Thomas Y. Levin. *New German Critique* 40 (1987): 91–96.

———. "The Mass Ornament." *Critical Theory and Society: A Reader.* Ed. Stephen Bronner and Doublas MacKay Kellner. New York: Routledge, 1989. 145–54.

Lefebvre, Henri. *Everyday Life in the Modern World.* Trans. Sacha Rabinovitch. London: Transaction Books, 1984.

MacCannell, Dean. *The Tourist: A New Theory of the Leisure Class.* New York: Schocken, 1975.

McRobbie, Angela. "Settling Accounts with Subcultures." *Culture, Ideology, and Social Process: A Reader.* Ed. Tony Bennett et al. London: The Open University, 1981.

Marx, Karl. *Capital.* Vol. 1. *The Marx-Engels Reader.* Ed. Robert C. Tucker. 2nd ed. New York: Norton, 1978.

Morris, Meaghan. "Banality in Cultural Studies," *Discourse* 10 (1988): 3–29.

———. "Things to Do With Shopping Centres." *Grafts: Feminist Cultural Criticism.* Ed. Susan Sheridan. New York: Verso, 1988. 193–225.

Morse, Margaret. "An Ontology of Everyday Distraction: The Freeway, the Mall, and Television." *Logics of Television: Essays in Cultural Criticism.* Ed. Patricia Mellencamp. Bloomington: Indiana UP/BFI Books, 1990. 193–221.

Penley, Constance, and Andrew Ross, eds. *Technoculture.* Minneapolis: U of Minnesota P, 1991.

Ross, Andrew. *Strange Weather: Culture, Science, and Technology in the Age of Limits.* London: Verso, 1991.

Soja, Edward W. *Postmodern Geographies: The Reassertion of Space in Critical Social Theory.* New York: Verso, 1989.

Veblen, Thorstein. *The Theory of the Leisure Class: An Economic Study of Institutions.* 1899. Rpt. New York: Macmillan, 1912.

Wallace, Michelle. *Black Popular Culture.* Ed. Gina Dent. Seattle: Bay P, 1992.

Williams, Raymond. *The Long Revolution: An Analysis of the Democratic, Industrial, and Cultural Changes Transforming Our Society.* New York: Columbia UP, 1961.

———. *Problems in Materialism and Culture: Selected Essays.* London: Verso, 1980.

———. *The Sociology of Culture.* New York: Shocken, 1981.

Willis, Susan. *A Primer for Daily Life.* New York: Routledge, 1991.

Wolff, Janet. *The Social Production of Art.* New York: St. Martin's, 1981.

MEMBERS of THE PROJECT ON disney

· · ·

KAREN KLUGMAN is best known for her large-scale color photographs of beach culture—*Under the Influence of the Sun and Advertising*—which are represented in museum collections and have appeared in national exhibitions. She teaches and writes about the interaction of photography and social values from the perspective of living in a forest still populated with non-Audio-Animatronic deer along with her husband, three children, dogs, and cats.

JANE KUENZ writes about American literature and culture. Her work has appeared in *South Atlantic Quarterly* and *African American Review*. She is currently writing *Producing the New Negro: The Work of Art in the Harlem Renaissance* about African American cultural production in the teens and twenties.

SHELTON WALDREP writes on modernist and contemporary culture and theory. His work has appeared most recently in *South Atlantic Quarterly*, *Pre/Text*, and *Critical Essays: Gay and Lesbian Writers of Color* (Harrington Park). He is currently working on Oscar Wilde and his influence on twentieth-century writing and performance and editing a collection of essays on the cultural production of the 1970s.

SUSAN WILLIS teaches courses in minority writing and popular culture at Duke University. She is the author of *Specifying: Black Women Writing the American Experience* (Wisconsin) and *A Primer for Daily Life* (Routledge). Her work aims to apprehend the contradictions of capitalism in everyday situations, both intimate and trivial.

Library of Congress Cataloging-in-Publication Data
Inside the mouse : work and play at Disney World / the Project on Disney.
Includes bibliographical references (p.) and index.
ISBN 0-8223-1607-2. — ISBN 0-8223-1624-2 (pbk.)
1. Walt Disney World (Fla.) I. Project on Disney.
GV1853.3.F62W345 1995
791'.06'875924--dc20   94-40192CIP